PRAISE FOR TODD MILLER AND *BORDER PATROL NATION*

"Journalist Miller tells an alarming story of U.S. Border Patrol and Homeland Security's ever-widening reach into the lives of American citizens and legal immigrants as well as the undocumented. He describes the militarization of the Border Patrol and concurrent dehumanizing of 'unauthorized' persons; American citizens routinely harassed and arrested in Constitution-free zones that extend 100 miles from all borders; the expulsion of an exemplary Border Patrol agent for expressing his Mexican identity in casual conversation; and the Border Patrol's Explorer Academy for children, which, with its lock-step marching, black boots, law-enforcement training, and indoctrination is eerily evocative of fascism and Hitler Youth. Miller reveals the 'complex and industrial world' looming behind the border patrol, spanning 'robotics, engineers, salespeople and detention centers' and the new generation of Explorers. 'It is the world in which we now live,' he states, 'where eradicating border violations is given higher priority than eradicating malnutrition, poverty, homelessness, illiteracy, [and] unemployment.' In addition to readers interested in immigration issues, those concerned about the NSA's privacy violations will likely be even more shocked by the actions of Homeland Security."

—*Publisher's Weekly*, starred review

"What Jeremy Scahill was to Blackwater, Todd Miller is to the U.S. Border Patrol!"

—Tom Miller, author, *On the Border: Portraits of America's Southwestern Frontier*

"Todd Miller has entered a secret world, and he has gone deep. If you want to learn about the Border Patrol's world, you will find this book informative and startling. I'm not sure the Border Patrol will like all that he has to say. But his is a moral work that wrestles with a huge story. Powerful."

—Luis Alberto Urrea, author of *The Devil's Highway: A True Story*, among other books

"Todd Miller's book *Border Patrol Nation* has some eye opening reporting, especially for those of us who live along the border and think we know the facts of the expanding police state. Well, I didn't know the Border Patrol provided security for the Superbowl. And I was ignorant of their youth groups and the scale of such propaganda work. I don't think anyone can read this book without being alarmed by the growing presence of surveillance, the expense and the apparent acceptance by our fellow citizens of this new national police force. He illustrates how the border increasingly is running right through our living rooms regardless of where we live as the claims of the security state crush any ideas of personal freedom. And like any good book, the reader will argue with some pages and think about others. Miller also captures how the universities are become satanic mills for the growing industry of spying on us for our own good. Who knows, maybe the academy will stop accepting grants from the people who want to build more cages and instead become centers of critical thinking."

—Charles Bowden, author of *Murder City: Ciudad Juarez and the Global Economy's New Killing Fields*

"In *Border Patrol Nation*, Todd Miller takes us on a terrifying journey crisscrossing the borders of our nation to find decaying carcasses, loving families ripped apart by deportations and whole swaths of territory now militarized. Miller exposes the underpinnings of this ever-expanding surveillance state--military contractors that rake in fat profits and bloated government agencies that keep extending their tentacles while the core of our neighborhoods wither from neglect. Miller reveals the humanity of both the victims and the victimizers, and the inhumanity of the system. A fantastic book."

—Medea Benjamin, co-founder of Code Pink and author of *Drone Warfare: Killing by Remote Control*

"The U.S. needs a reality check about its border with Mexico, and none need it more than the Congress. I wish every member could get a copy of *Border Patrol Nation*, and see up close the impact of a quarter century of increasing enforcement and militarization. Todd Miller has done an important service for those who make our laws, and the rest of us too."

—David Bacon, author of *The Right to Stay Home*

"If you want to know what's really going on behind the Border Patrol code names and billion dollar budgets, read this book. Through lively narratives drawn from dozens of personal interviews with agents and the people they pepper spray or worse, Todd Miller connects the dots. From conventions marketing micro-robots and urine bags to the University of Arizona's curriculum based on Homeland Security funding, to the recruiting campaigns inducing people from retail jobs to 70k entry-level positions as border agents, *Border Patrol Nation* is a relentless, fast-paced, and sophisticated analysis that takes you from the tribal lands of Arizona to Goat Island, Niagara Falls, exposing embarrassing evidence of our government's meanness and stupidity."

—Jacqueline Stevens, Professor, Political Science Department, Director, Deportation Research Clinic, Northwestern University, and author of *States Without Nations: Citizenship for Mortals*

"Todd Miller provides a tour de force of the ever-growing, metastasizing border enforcement apparatus focused on immigrants, drugs, and nearly non-existent terrorists, from the U.S.-Mexico divide and the U.S.-Canada boundary and many interior areas between, to the Caribbean and the border separating the Dominican Republic and Haiti reinforced against Haitians with assistance from U.S. Border Patrol. He highlights the problem of the fetishistic over-use of coercive technology and human resources cum militarization to address what are essentially underlying social problems. Miller renders it all with the vivid human experiences and agency of residents, citizens, armed authorities, technocrats, contractors / profiteers, and immigrants and their families. This book deserves a very wide audience from concerned citizens to policy-makers, to students and scholars in a wide array of fields."

—Timothy Dunn, Professor, Dept. of Sociology, Salisbury University, Salisbury, MD, and author of *The Militarization of the U.S.-Mexico Border, 1978-1992: Low Intensity Conflict Doctrine Comes Home* and *Blockading the Border and Human Rights: The El Paso Operation that Remade Immigration Enforcement*

"*Border Patrol Nation* takes the reader on a voyage like no other book. From El Paso to Detroit, from reality television to corporate trade shows, from South Carolina to the Dominican Republic, Todd Miller paints a highly original and illuminating picture of the breadth and depth of the U.S. government's boundary and immigrant policing apparatus, and surveillance and social control in the era of 'Homeland Security.' It is a book that frightens and inspires, and one that demands a wide audience. Miller's message is one we ignore at our peril."

—Joseph Nevins, author of *Operation Gatekeeper and Beyond: The War On "Illegals" and the Remaking of the U.S.-Mexico Boundary*

"I encourage everyone to read this book and to recommend it to colleagues, friends and family who live far from the border and perhaps don't know yet that they live in Border Patrol Nation . . . They will soon enough."

—Molly Molloy, editor of Frontera List

"*Border Patrol Nation* dissects the 2,000-mile illusion—2,000 miles of greed and corruption, deception and death-that threatens to swallow our rights, our hope and our entire country. Todd Miller investigates the bloated bureaucracies, the corporate interests, the ruthless politicians and policies invested in this dangerous illusion. *Border Patrol Nation* documents the need to end the illusion."

—Roberto Lovato, writer, cofounder and strategist at Presente.org

"[Miller] offers a vision of what the military-industrial complex looks like once it's transported, jobs and all, to the U.S.-Mexican border and turned into a consumer mall for the post-9/11 era . . . [it's] a striking and original picture."

—Tom Engelhardt, editor of *TomDispatch*

BORDER PATROL NATION

Dispatches from the Front Lines
of Homeland Security

TODD MILLER

Open Media Series | City Lights Books

Open Media Series Editor: Greg Ruggiero

Some of the names of people interviewed in this book have been
changed at their request.

Cover design by John Gates at Stealworks

This book is also available in an e-edition: 978-0-87286-632-4

Library of Congress Data
Miller, Todd.
Border patrol nation : dispatches from the front lines of homeland
security / Todd Miller.
    p. cm. — (City lights open media)
ISBN 978-0-87286-631-7 (pbk.)
1. Mexican-American Border Region—Economic conditions. 2.
United States. Immigration Border Patrol—History. I. Title.
HC137.M58M55 2014
363.28'509721—dc23

                              2013043754

City Lights Books are published at the City Lights Bookstore,
261 Columbus Avenue, San Francisco, CA 94133.
www.citylights.com

For Lauren —
I love you and could not have written this without you.

In 2008, Vermont senator Patrick Leahy was traveling in a car 125 miles south of the U.S.-Canada border in the state of New York.

They came to a U.S. Border Patrol checkpoint, which stopped the U.S. senior senator, and an agent ordered him to get out of the car.

"What authority are you acting under?" Leahy asked.

The agent pointed to his gun and said: "That's all the authority I need."

CONTENTS

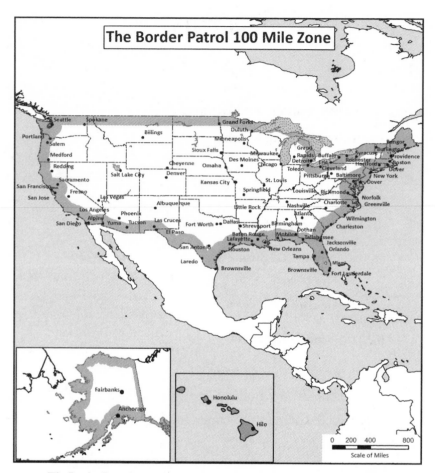

The Border Patrol's jurisdiction—100 miles into the interior from the U.S. international border and coasts—covers two thirds of the population in the country. Cartography by Louise Misztal. Data provided by ESRI, The National Map, and the ACLU.

chapter one

THE SUPER PATROL

It is a cool February day when the U.S. Border Patrol agent in a dark green uniform points up to a surveillance tower. The tower looks like one of the many such towers that are seen in the U.S. Southwest, either in the middle of the desert or at any one of the hundreds of roadside checkpoints in the region. The towers are always controversial to locals and always urgently needed, the Department of Homeland Security (DHS) tells us, for national security reasons. It is one of those same types of towers that the New York City Police Department has used to monitor Zuccotti Park in Manhattan since the Occupy movement erupted in September 2011, and which, as of the time of this writing in November 2013, remain there today. Like many of the new surveillance machines of the Homeland Security era, there is an insect-like quality to the tower. When dormant, the structure looks almost sad or as though it is sleeping. But when active, the cabin is mounted on a structure that looks like scaffolding and stretches upward like the craning neck of someone trying to see over their neighbor's fence. The cabin is packed with so many surveillance gizmos and night-vision capabilities that authorities can spy on the public below whether it's day or night.

But this particular surveillance tower is not located at a rugged outpost in the U.S. Southwest, part of the enforcement apparatus of "Protecting America," as the U.S. Border Patrol motto goes. This surveillance tower is located in front of a football stadium, Sun Life Stadium in Miami, Florida. Behind it is a large parking lot and the buzzing activity of the NFL's most affluent fans, corporate sponsors, and media who have gathered for the annual Super Bowl. ESPN has a team of writers who scour the nightly football-related parties that take place during the preceding week to see what celebrity figures they can spot. After all, as one announcer put it: "The Super Bowl is much more than sixty minutes of football, it's a super party that celebrates the competitive spirit that is America." This is the "America" that the Border Patrol has come to protect.

It might be strange to see the green-uniformed men (mostly men, but some women too) protecting a football game, but they have been doing this since 2002. A year later, the priority mission of the U.S. Border Patrol changed to that of its newly formed parent agency, Customs and Border Protection (CBP): it became to protect the United States from "terrorists" and "their weapons of mass destruction." Since then, the Border Patrol, along with a host of other federal and local law enforcement agencies, has had the task of "securing" the Super Bowl.

This change in scope of mission is the result of what journalist Roberto Lovato calls "the largest, most important restructuring of the federal government since the end of World War II,"[1] the formation of the Department of Homeland Security. The Border Patrol transferred into DHS from the Department of Justice as part of the creation of the third-largest cabinet-level department in terms of the number of people it employs. With this move, Border Patrol gained new national security powers on top of its traditional tasks of immigration enforcement and drug interdiction.

"Our mission statement says that we will defend the American public against terrorism," says CBP agent Jason Harrell while he flies a Blackhawk helicopter to guard the thirty-mile no-fly zone that will be in force around the stadium during the day of the game. His voice sounds metallic and official coming through the microphone that is attached to his headgear, which has the look of an old-fashioned football helmet. Around him there is the droning of white noise, the grumbling engines, and rhythmic beating of the Blackhawk's propellers chopping air. "The Super Bowl is a high-priority target," he says. "The U.S. government has come to us because we are a law-enforcement entity. And we have assets that other folks don't have."[2]

Super Sunday

At 4:30 p.m., a mere hour and a half before kickoff, U.S. Border Patrol agents gather in the muster room of the Dania Beach station. There is adrenaline in the room. Their Super Bowl mission, according to supervisor Lazaro Guzman, is to carry out a "trans-check."

Guzman stands in front of a dozen green-uniformed agents sitting behind a long, smooth, brown table. Behind him, both a U.S. flag and a dark green Border Patrol flag are hanging, just as they are in every muster room in the more than 150 stations the agency has across the country. Guzman's clean-shaven head reflects the overhead lights as he explains exactly what a "trans-check" is. They will be patrolling the Amtrak and Greyhound bus stations to check passengers.

This particular Border Patrol operation is one of many South Florida CBP missions leading up to the Super Bowl. For a week, mock scenarios have lit up Miami's skies as CBP pilots try to chase off aircraft that enter the no-fly zone. Other agents scour Miami's coastline, looking for suspicious boats. One that they spot is a large vessel crammed with old mattresses bound for Haiti. Just the combination of unruly-looking mattresses and impoverished Haiti as a destination provides enough reasonable suspicion for the CBP team to rip apart the entire vessel in search of contraband.

Another special operations CBP team wearing tactical bulletproof vests, helmets, and brown uniforms trains in a nearby warehouse to get ready for a worst-case scenario situation in which they would have to respond quickly. The training includes rappelling out of helicopters, just as the Border Patrol perennially shows in its adrenaline-pumping recruitment videos. The team, like the Border Patrol as a whole, is a paramilitary unit, and it acts like one.

Other CBP officers engage the parking lot around the stadium as if it were an honest-to-God international point of entry. Their mobile x-ray machine clears all vehicles and trucks entering the larger Super Bowl site. Long before the game begins, a team of forty dogs, all part of the K-9 unit, are unleashed to sniff out any contraband that may be hidden in the empty stadium. A nearby command center, straight from a Hollywood thriller, coordinates all the operations in progress and incoming surveillance feeds. At the same time, 3,000 miles away, the CBP's Air and Marine Center in Riverside, California, has the clear distinction as the "first line of defense." The agents there analyze dozens of monitors and digital maps tracking vessels flying over and around Miami, and do everything in their might not to become bleary-eyed.

On the ground near Miami, Border Patrol supervisor Guzman describes the scene with a no-nonsense tone. He has a job to do, and that job is to uphold the law. As he explains while driving to the Fort Lauderdale Amtrak station, what the law says is simple, and he and his fellow agents are there to enforce it. He's driving a Border Patrol truck with its quintessential green stripe painted diagonally on the back door.

"After 9/11, everyone at the airports are being looked at, so they tend to use the Amtrak," he says, gesturing with his hand, "or the Greyhound as a tool." This makes Amtrak and Greyhound an "all-threats environment." As he says this, he is pulling up to a stoplight. He takes his hands from the steering wheel and cradles the air: "We don't know what's going to happen."[3] Guzman's eyes are earnest.

Here in Miami, the Super Bowl site perimeter has turned into a de facto international border zone, but you don't even have to cross it to invite suspicion. Your simple proximity to it, and the fact that you are traveling, is enough. It has the same effect as the hundred-mile rule, which stipulates that Border Patrol can do a warrantless search on anyone who is within one hundred miles of U.S. coastlines and land borders. These Homeland Security officers have federal, extra-constitutional powers that are well above and beyond those of local law enforcement.

"The rule—which now operates to roll back Fourth Amendment protections from roughly two-thirds of the citizenry," says James Duff Lyall, a staff attorney from the American Civil Liberties Union of Arizona, referring to the 100-mile jurisdiction—"appears to have been adopted without any public debate or scrutiny."

The ACLU created a map called the "Constitution-Free Zone of the United States," which shows a thick band around the contours of the country, devouring the entire states of Florida, Maine, and even Michigan, and covering a population base of 190 million people. Sure, the Border Patrol isn't present in every place in this 100-mile zone, but the blueprint of the jurisdiction of the Homeland Security police is in place. Now it is common to see the Border Patrol in places—such as Erie, Pennsylvania; Rochester, New York; or Forks, Washington—where only fifteen years ago it would have seemed far-fetched, if not unfathomable.

"Again," Guzman explains, "our job is to go out there. Find out who that person is. Bring them into our station. Bottom line is what document do they have to stay in the United States. That's it," he says slicing his hand through the air with a sense of finality.

Guzman parks the truck underneath a couple of bushy palm trees at the Fort Lauderdale train station. A train rolls in, ringing its bell, and slowly comes to a stop alongside the cement platform. Dressed in a blue vest and red tie, an African American Amtrak employee steps down from the train. Guzman says something to him, but it doesn't matter; even if the employee were to object, Border Patrol overrules everything. Like an energizing shout to a nervous football team hitting the field, Guzman jumps on with a "Let's go" to the rest of the group.

"How you doin'?" Guzman asks a white woman sitting alone in a seat. His badge looks shiny even in the dim light in the interior of the train. His gun belt is loaded with a portable arsenal of tools for the "all-threats environment," including handcuffs in a plastic pouch, a holster and handgun, and a taser. "U.S. Border Patrol," he says, "state your citizenship please." The woman is a U.S. citizen but leans forward to look for her documents, something she doesn't have to do. She just has to reply appropriately. But she is right to think that the Border Patrol is powerful. If she does anything to raise their suspicion, they can and will pull her off the train and detain her.

The other passengers peer at the agents with a sense of astonishment, maybe some even seeing the Department of Homeland Security's soldiers for the first time. One woman looks at them as if this idea of a domestic security checkpoint was something that she had only seen in some movie about World War II but had suddenly become real.

The U.S. Border Patrol is the most visible of DHS's agencies and is now touching a lot more people's lives than ever before. It has increased its ranks to more than 21,000 agents, up from 8,500 in 2001 and 4,000 in 1994. And there is a constant push for more, a constant push to grow. One "immigration reform" bill passed by the U.S. Senate in June 2013 is typical: it envisions 40,000 "men in green," with agents stationed every 1,000 feet along the almost 2,000-mile U.S.-Mexico divide, and reaching farther and farther into the country's ever-expanding notion of borderlands. The 60,000-strong CBP—which includes not only Border Patrol but also customs, air and marine, and field operations officers—is by far the largest federal law enforcement agency in the United States and more than double the size of Ecuador's army. If you add Immigration and Customs Enforcement (ICE) to that number, then you are talking around 80,000 of DHS's more than 200,000 employees. Add to that the pool of 650,000 police officers deputized, trained, or working under a border security or immigration enforcement mandate for ICE and CBP, and Homeland Security's force of boots on the ground is the equivalent of a large army. National security analyst Tom Engelhardt has dubbed DHS the "second "defense" department,"[4] with its eyes and ears and guns increasingly in more places.

Another agent with a close-cropped military haircut and the type of sunglasses police officers use in movies (or professional baseball players during day games) walks alongside the off-loaded luggage with the K-9 unit. A dog jumps up and sniffs around the pile of suitcases, searching for hidden drugs and explosives. Several other agents walk up and down the train, asking every passenger to document their citizenship. The justification is the safety of the Super Bowl, but this is also business as usual.

They are an hour away from kickoff. Thousands of fans are converging on Miami, and the security apparatus is pumping full steam. CBP overflights are in progress; the security perimeter is operational. There are layers of CBP like the defensive alignment (front line, linebackers, defensive backs) on a football field. Millions of dollars and thousands of law enforcement authorities are at the ready, some doing surveillance sweeps on the faces of fans, with special thermal cameras called Forward Looking Infrared Radiometers. For more than ten years, the company that manufactures these devices, FLIR, has had a multimillion-dollar contract to provide cameras for CBP. In FLIR's career recruitment it captures the rhetorical spirit of CBP and its operations: "Do you ever wonder if what you do at work really makes a difference? Here it does! Our products are used to save lives, capture criminals, provide safety and security around the globe, and protect our natural resources."[5]

in the human race has a tremendous amount of meaning." He enunciates every word. "You symbolize many years of pride." Aguilar is one of the only people in the auditorium not dressed in a uniform—though he would be more than comfortable, one imagines, in a Border Patrol uniform after being a foot soldier for so many years in the agency. He is dressed in a dark suit with a red tie, his D.C. outfit. The CBP chief pauses, so that his next words will have deep, resonating significance.

"You symbolize the future," he says.[9]

His voice raises with strong, yet controlled emotion. He is talking as if he were looking into a crystal ball, able to articulate the mission of the growing weaponized bureaucracy with foresight and grace.

Along the U.S. border with Mexico there are communities that have been so altered by the Border Patrol's advancing mission that they have been rendered almost unrecognizable, a deranged version of what they once were. The border enforcement apparatus is much more than the sixteen-foot walls, stadium lights, cameras, sensors, and the overall concentration of its agents in every urban—and many rural—areas along the 2,000-mile U.S.-Mexico boundary. From the actual boundary line, it has expanded into the interior, creating an intensely controlled border zone buzzing with armed authorities openly patrolling strip malls, flea markets, residential areas, train stations, and bus depots—to the degree that many in the borderlands, from federal magistrates to grassroots activists, have compared what they experience to a military occupation. There aren't many towns on the border where you can transit without passing through a fully armed federal checkpoint, a secondary layer of enforcement by the Border Patrol.

Variations of this model are now increasingly ubiquitous. If you arrive in Erie, Pennsylvania, on a Greyhound bus, odds are you'll run into Border Patrol authorities eyeing passengers getting off the bus. If you live in Southwest Detroit, the Mexican part of town, you'll probably see the cruising green-striped vehicles every day. In the north, Border Patrol operations are conducted from Maine to the state of Washington, covering New England, the Rust Belt, and the Pacific Northwest in numbers that take many by surprise. Indeed, in the last ten years the policing apparatus has expanded at a higher rate along the northern border than on the southern one.

According to Aguilar, the Border Patrol's mandate goes beyond this domestic expansion: "You are part of a team that will protect our hemisphere, and the way of life of our people."[10] He uses the word "hemisphere" instead of "country," as if U.S. national domain extends well beyond the country's international boundaries, as if the homeland were much larger than originally suspected. Maybe that's why, when I meet with a colonel of the Dominican Republic's border guard, who patrols the border with Haiti, he talks about attending a U.S. Border Patrol training seminar in Santo Domingo the very week that I am in his country. And when I ask him if they have a lot of contact with the U.S. Border Patrol, he kind of laughs and says that CBP has an office in the U.S. embassy, as it does in many other countries.

Even the word "hemisphere" unduly confines the U.S. Border Patrol. Iraq is only one of the more than 100 overseas countries where CBP has gone on training missions. There the border and immigration enforcement agency has used its expertise to get the country on the "right track" to nation building with its border-support team program. Jay Mayfield of CBP's *Frontline* magazine explains that "for the past six years, U.S. Customs and Border Protection personnel have been on the ground in Iraq for every twist and turn in the country's rebirth and recovery, and in America's role in that process."[11] CBP Agent Adrian Long says that in Iraq they train them "in Border Patrol techniques like cutting sign, doing drags, setting up checkpoints and patrols."[12]

In an article titled "Forget Arizona, Obama Sends Border Patrol to Afghanistan," Fox News describes U.S. CBP agents training Afghani forces to police that country's border with Pakistan.[13] Throughout southern Afghanistan there are hundreds of border checkpoints with stacks of sandbags and green metal guard shacks.

Aguilar reaches the punch line of his inspired speech in Artesia by saying: "It is the heart in these uniforms that distinguishes us. That holds us up to the responsibilities we have. The responsibilities you now bear to protect the borders of the United States. To protect a way of life."[14]

This book is about the vision of Aguilar's promised future, a future that is already here.

The Complex

Before President Dwight D. Eisenhower's 1961 farewell speech, when the retired five-star general famously warned against the military-industrial complex, he said at another public event: "The jet plane that roars overhead costs three quarters of a million dollars. That's more than a man will make in his lifetime. What world can afford this kind of thing for long?"[15] At the time, according to National Public Radio, Eisenhower was growing more and more concerned about the cost of the arms race with the Soviet Union. He was concerned that it was going to get expensive, take away resources from the nation's health and education and other core needs.

Eisenhower said that the United States didn't even have an armaments industry until World War II. But now, he said, on the precipice of a bloody conflict in Vietnam, the industry was of "vast proportions."

"This conjunction of an immense military establishment and a large arms industry is new in the American experience."[16]

In much the same way, the ever-more expensive border enforcement apparatus is also new to the American experience. When Eisenhower stood up at the podium before John F. Kennedy took the presidency, the U.S. Border Patrol only had 2,000 agents, a mere 10 percent of the current level. This was decades before the roughly 700 miles of barricades, and a national surveillance grid coordinating and analyzing incoming data and intelligence against that acquired through satellite and international sources. This was long before the unmanned drones were buzzing over the borderlands in the South, the North, and the Caribbean. This was before DHS awarded lavish contracts to private prisons, detention centers, and even county jails. Today's sophisticated border apparatus was simply unimaginable at the time of Eisenhower's visionary speech.

The existence of lines of division that control and criminalize the movements of certain people is a "recent development in human history,"[17] according to geographer Joseph Nevins. Worldwide, a very small percentage of people today can travel. A much larger percentage are prohibited from crossing borders. This, according to Nevins, is "highly significant" and "speaks to the extraordinary power of these lines of division and control—and the agents and institutions behind them—in shaping the very ways in which we view the world and our fellow human beings."

The modern notion of "border security" has gone from a non-issue, to a non-debated issue. In 1971, after a member of her security group cut the barbed-wire fence, first lady Pat Nixon crossed from California into the Mexican city of Tijuana and told the people gathered, "I hope there won't be a fence here too long."[18]

It is impossible to imagine the same thing happening more than forty years later. This new world of border security was explained to me most succinctly by Glenn Spencer, the founder of the group called the American Border Patrol—a tech-savvy, anti-immigrant organization that the Southern Poverty Law Center considers a hate group.

"Everybody wants the border secure," Spencer told me at his compound in Hereford, Arizona, a rural area located right on the international border. As he talked I was captivated by the massive, blue 200-foot-long wall that his group had built, with the words SECURE THE BORDER written on its surface in giant red letters. Behind this was the real metal border wall, built as a result of the Secure Fence Act of 2006. The real wall demarcated the line between Sonora and Arizona, and continued a quarter mile to the east into the San Pedro River Valley, a riparian, environmentally sensitive area that was constantly defended by environmentalists against further encroachment by the border-security apparatus. To the west, the border wall extended as far as the eye can see. Set amid this dramatic landscape was Spencer's SECURE THE BORDER sub-wall, which seemed almost like a monument to the anti-immigrant forces in United States.

But no, Spencer insisted, this was for everybody, because everybody agreed with this. Each letter was composed of hundreds of U.S. flags, each with a small tag and a message from what Spencer said were more than 10,000 American Border Patrol supporters. On the other side of that wall was the state of Sonora, extending into the horizon under a vast, cloudy sky.

"There's a consensus that we need the border secure," Spencer said with emotion. "The president said, 'I have made securing the Southwest border a top priority since I came to office.' The president!" He said this as if it was beyond credibility that the Democratic president Barack Obama could be for border security.

Spencer continued his quotations, which he had written down in a notebook. This time he read something from Republican senator Kay Hutchison (Texas), who once said: "Border Security is paramount."

"Even Harry Reid says this," said Spencer, referring to the powerful Nevada Democrat who has been the Senate majority leader since 2007.

He paused, then exclaimed, "Even the human rights activists!" He searched for another quote "from Colorado human rights." And he found the phrase: "First of all we all want a secure border," he said, quoting Julien Ross, director of the Colorado Immigrant Rights Coalition.

"Everyone agrees. Left, Right, center, top, bottom, we've got to secure the border. There's no dispute. It's a given. Stipulated."

Spencer was right: any "serious" immigration reform packages need a border-security stipulation to be taken seriously. It's not a point to be contended, rather a normal part of the landscape that needs attention, cultivation, and—always—growth. According to the Associated Press, the U.S. government spent $90 billion on border security during the first ten years following 9/11 alone. Now the

$18 billion spent on border and immigration enforcement in 2012 outguns the budget of all other federal law enforcement bodies *combined*. That is 24 percent more than the $14.4 billion combined budgets in the last fiscal year for the FBI, the Secret Service, the Drug Enforcement Agency, the Marshals Service, and the Bureau of Alcohol, Tobacco, Firearms and Explosives. Add the billions more anticipated in any of the various immigration reform bills, and you have what the trade publication *Homeland Security Today* calls a "treasure trove" for contractors in the border-security industry.

Border-security analyst Tom Barry says, "The term [Border Security Industrial Complex] may at first seem overheated, a facile take-off on the concern that President Dwight Eisenhower expressed about the 'military-industrial complex.'" But Barry concludes that "as it turns out, the Border Security Industrial Complex, while not a term that slips off the tongue, has much in common with its older brother and is equally deserving of attention, concern and perhaps alarm."[19]

In his speech, Eisenhower talks about the the "total influence" of the military-industrial complex. He warns that its "economic, political, even spiritual" impact "is felt in every city, every State house, every office of the Federal government." This book offers glimpses into this complex's rapid advance into the U.S. experience, installing bright lines of division between people, places, and communities across the hemisphere, a brave new world unfathomable in the days of Eisenhower.

It was Vermont Senator Patrick Leahy—eyeing the $46 billion price tag of the U.S. Senate 2013 immigration reform package and its call for 19,000 more Border Patrol agents; 700 miles of fencing, barriers and walls; and billions of dollars toward more technology—who saw things in a strikingly similar way to Eisenhower, when the president in 1961 looked up to the sky aghast and saw an incredibly expensive military attack plane.

If Senator Leahy were to look into the sky today, he might see not only fixed-wing military aircraft but also, possibly, one of the ten $4.5 million Predator B CBP drones buzzing above. Immigration reform bills pushed in the U.S. Congress have called for 24/7 drone flights with "persistent surveillance," regardless of the fact that up to twenty Border Patrol agents are needed to operate one drone, with a per-hour cost of $3,234. *Homeland Security Today*'s Mickey McCarter writes that "based on that figure, keeping one UAV in the air every hour of the year would cost about $28.5 million."[20] CBP's plan is to have eighteen drones in flight by 2016, and up it to twenty-four after that; the private, San Diego-based company General Atomics signed a contract for the work in 2012.

Joe Wolverton II writes, "Think state and local law enforcement aren't watching you with high-tech federally-owned drones? Think again."[21] CBP has lent its drones more than 500 times to domestic law enforcement agencies, other federal agencies, and the military. And these are also the drones that the Border Patrol wishes to weaponize non-lethally—with what "could feasibly include rubber bullets, tear gas, or a Taser-like shock"—to be able to "immobilize" supposed "targets of interest," according to documents obtained in 2013 by Electronic Frontier Foundation.[22]

All of this would have been a shock in the times of Eisenhower when only flimsy chain-link fences, if that, separated the United States and Mexico. But there's more. In June 2013, for just one proposed immigration reform bill Senator Marco Rubio laid out a list of border-security technologies that could read as something Star Trekian: "86 integrated fixed towers, 286 fixed camera systems, 232 mobile surveillance systems, 4,595 unattended ground sensors, 820 handheld equipment devices, 416 personal radiation detectors, 104 radiation isotope identification devices, 62 mobile automated targeting systems, 53 fiber-optic tank inspection scopes, 37 portable contraband detectors, 28 license plate readers, 26 mobile inspection scopes and sensors for checkpoints, nine land automated targeting systems, and eight nonintrusive inspection systems."

In addition, Rubio said, the immigration bill would include "four unmanned aircraft systems, six VADER radar systems, 17 UH-1N helicopters, eight C-206H aircraft upgrades, eight AS-350 light enforcement helicopters, 10 Blackhawk helicopter 10 A-L conversions, five new Blackhawk M Model, 30 marine vessels, 93 sensor repeaters, 90 communications repeaters, two card-reader systems, five camera refresh, three backscatters, one radiation portal monitor, one littoral detection, one real-time radioscopy, and improved surveillance capabilities for existing aerostat."[23]

After eyeing this extensive list that was part of the Hoeven-Corker Amendment, Senator Leahy, a Democrat, said the Border Security, Economic Opportunity, and Immigration Modernization Act read like "a Christmas wish list for Halliburton."[24] He then voted for its approval. "This is not the amendment I would have drafted," Leahy said, but "because their amendment will increase Republican support for this historic, comprehensive legislation, I will support it."[25]

Border Patrolization

Lazaro Guzman and his group of Border Patrol agents defending the Super Bowl in Miami are part and parcel of this new world.

After Amtrak, they go to the bus station in Fort Lauderdale. When they board the bus, it is half an hour from kickoff. Guzman is all business. It is highly unlikely that any passenger will be going to the game on the regional bus, a traditional mode of transportation for the poor. On a Sunday they might be on the way to visit family, or maybe to a job. Little did they know that a virtual international border was approaching *them*, indeed, arriving at their seats.

One of the agents wears a tactical green flak jacket over his uniform, as if they were getting into a little more dangerous territory with the Greyhound than the Amtrak. The words CBP Border Patrol Federal Agent are emblazoned on the back of the flak jacket in yellow letters. The bus says LOCAL above the windshield, underneath which the iconic Greyhound dog runs as if the symbol could outrun the Border Patrol itself.

Looking at the picture of the bus, all you can hear is audio on this episode of National Geographic's *Border Wars*.

"Can you tell me what country you are a citizen of, sir?" goes Guzman's voice, all business.

"Chicago. I'm from Chicago," says an accented voice.

"Where are you from? Jamaica? Do you have a passport with you?"

"No."

In the next shot, the camera pans onto a pair of hands, with handcuffs around the wrists. Seven days in, minutes before kickoff, the Super Bowl operation has caught its first person, a Jamaican man who does not have documents.

An agent with a radio snapped on his shoulder leads his suspect to a green-striped SUV.

Next comes a handcuffed Nicaraguan woman who wears a purple blouse and dark jeans. Her face is blurred to protect her identity, but the technique also disfigures the second Super Bowl arrestee, making her seem non-human. The narrator says nothing about this woman. Does she live in Fort Lauderdale? Does she have family? Children? A job? The woman agent who escorts her to the back of the SUV also wears a bulletproof vest.

A man who appears to be East Asian comes out last. His lack of command of the English language and the extraordinary amount of cash he has on hand make him the most suspicious of all. All three of those arrested face a probable fate of incarceration, expulsion, and banishment from the United States. After the game, CBP issues a press release lauding its operations as "instrumental for the overall success"[26] of the Super Bowl. Every football fan left the game unscathed.

The booth of FLIR Systems at the Border Security Expo in Phoenix, Arizona. Photo by Todd Miller.

PART I

HEARTS, MINDS, AND BODIES

Since 9/11, the war on terror and the campaign for homeland security have increasingly mimicked the tactics of the enemies they sought to crush. Violence and punishment as both a media spectacle and a bone-crushing reality have become prominent and influential forces shaping American society. As the boundaries between 'the realms of war and civil life have collapsed,' social relations and the public services needed to make them viable have been increasingly privatized and militarized. The logic of profitability works its magic in channeling the public funding of warfare and organized violence into universities, market-based service providers and deregulated contractors. The metaphysics of war and associated forms of violence now creep into every aspect of American society.[1]

—*Henry Giroux*

The most obvious manifestation of the growth of the U.S. Border Patrol is its massive physical presence in the U.S. borderlands with Mexico and Canada. Imposing sixteen-foot walls snaking through the rugged hills, ogling cameras eyeing you everywhere you look, and the ever-increasing number of armed agents making their rounds via mud-crusted trucks, bikes, ATVs, and even horses. The most common media narrative is that this most necessary federal police force and surveillance cloud represent the will and resolve of the United States to protect its people, property, and homeland by keeping out enemies, criminals, and evildoers of all kinds.

However, there is also a rarely acknowledged world behind this vast, growing, and militant federal force that impacts U.S. society well beyond its borders, and often in not-so-obvious ways. There are serious questions as to how big and how far this Border Patrol world should reach, and how many people—and whom—it may touch, impact, employ, exclude, or violate. How is this well-armed, well-funded culture sustained, and to what extent does it impact or deter the very freedoms and democracy that it claims to defend and protect?

The following three chapters are portals into this behind-the-scenes Border Patrol world of trade fairs, tech parks, classrooms, and community service projects with youth. They offer a poignant view into the construction and maintenance of the Border Patrol worldview via a seemingly innocuous conversation between bored Border Patrol agents during an ordinary work shift.

For an armed forces–related industry to grow and expand it needs a profit incentive, a robust marketplace, and the threat of enemies to drive sales. As we are seeing today, such enemies—real and potential—seem to be everywhere, and nothing less than a Border Patrol Nation, the logic goes, will suffice to keep the country totally safe.

in camouflage and helmets with surveillance gizmos hanging off them seem as if they might walk right out of the
exhibition hall and take over the sprawling city of Phoenix
with brute force. Little imaginable for your futuristic for-
tressed border is missing from the hall. There are Brief
Relief plastic urine bags. There are ready-to-eat pocket
sandwiches—with a three-year shelf life!—maybe for Border Patrol agents on detail in one of the many Forward
Operating Bases, rudimentary military-style outposts that
are on the rise throughout remote stretches of the U.S.
borderlands. Checking out all these products, a stream
of uniformed Border Patrol, military, and police officials
move from booth to booth alongside men in suits in what
the sole protester outside the convention center called a
"mall of death."

If there is anything that catches the control-mania at
the heart of this expo, it is a sign behind the DRS Technologies booth proclaiming this promise: YOU DRAW THE LINE
AND WE'LL HELP YOU SECURE IT, as if the lines in question
could be placed anywhere by whomever has the buying
power to do so. And an ideal place to express such a sentiment is Phoenix, Arizona, the seat of Maricopa County,
where "America's toughest sheriff," Joe Arpaio, regularly
sweeps through neighborhoods on the hunt for people of
color who look like they may have just slipped across the
line dividing the United States from Mexico. Also it is the
place where Arizona's infamous SB-1070 obligates police
to play the role of de facto border guards and use their
"reasonable suspicion" skills to identify people who have
entered the United States without the proper paperwork.
Unlike Arpaio or SB-1070, however, the Border Security
Expo causes no controversy at all. Border enforcement has
become business as usual.

It has been fashionable to treat the state of Arizona as a phenomenon of the U.S. fringe, a population of lunatics hell-bent on passing bluntly racist anti-immigration laws. However, as the expo indicates, something far more profound, widespread, and systematic is at work. There's nothing fringe about the companies in the convention hall that are eager to build up the Homeland Security state, and are doing so with a flood of taxpayer dollars. Arizona is not only the hot spot, but also the testing ground, laboratory, and model.

"We first increased the pressure in Texas and in California, and as we succeeded in driving down illegal activity there, it steadily moved toward the middle—toward Arizona," said former U.S. Customs and Border Protection Commissioner Alan D. Bersin in the Spring 2011 edition of *Frontlines*, a CBP publication. "As we adopt our operations there, we do so knowing that it's time to clamp down on this corridor. It's time to finish the job." Over the past ten years, more than half of the U.S. Border Patrol's arrests have taken place in the Arizona corridor.

With rumors of this clampdown in effect, all eyes at this Border Security Expo seem to be drawn to the Arizona-Mexico frontier, though Texas, specifically the Rio Grande Valley sector, shows a significant increase in border crossings. From the perspective of the border-control business, Mexico might as well be seething with enemies, an "Axis of Evil" country that urgently needs to be contained by towering walls and the armed forces of the U.S. Border Patrol.

The technology already in place in the Arizona borderlands (much of it since the late 1990s with Operation Safeguard) seems to confirm this national security perception of imminent threat. An array of cameras, many of them mounted on gigantic posts, peers over these walls into Mexico, sending a constant flow of images to dark monitoring rooms in Border Patrol stations along the 2,000-mile southern border, where bored agents watch mostly pedestrian traffic on glowing screens. Every once in a while a motion sensor will go off, but is there a violation in progress? Often there is not. Every border-security company worth its salt is trying to develop the smartest sensors, ones that detect not rain or wind but "illegals," terrorists, and smugglers.

"In terms of technology," said Border Patrol agent Felix Chavez, "the capability of what we have acquired since 2004 is phenomenal." At an October 2012 conference in El Paso, Chavez vividly described "unprecedented deployment of resources" along the entire U.S.-Mexico border: 377 remote video surveillance systems, 195 local video surveillance systems, 305 large-scale nonintrusive inspections systems, 75 Z Backscatter vans, 261 Recon FLIRs, more than 12,000 sensors, and 41 mobile surveillance system trucks.

"We have over 651 miles of border fencing [of which] 352 is pedestrian, 299 is vehicle. We have sixty-nine miles of border lighting. One hundred and twenty-five miles of wall with a road and [we are] providing maintenance to an additional 734 miles of road. In addition to that we have several forward operating bases employed all along the Southwest border . . . clustered in Arizona and New Mexico primarily."[1]

The difference in technology, Chavez said, is "like night and day over the last few years."

Predator drones and mini-surveillance balloons regularly patrol the skies, overlooking some of the world's most dramatic landscapes of inequality. In 1993, there were only flimsy fences separating communities on either side of the international divide. Now heavily populated Mexican border towns brimming with "cheap labor" for hundreds of foreign factories crowd right up to the borderline. These cross-border communities that share so many political, economic, social, and familial ties look disfigured, as if they had been under the knife of some sort of botched experiment.

Bersin's proclaimed clampdown means an intensified expansion of this surveillance apparatus into the interior of Arizona. For example, StrongWatch's Dodds tells me that his company is hoping for a fat contract for its border technology, and it is pumping up Freedom On-the-Move with all its might. After all, everyone knows that DHS is on the lookout for proposals to build its latest version of a "virtual wall"—not actual fencing, but a barrier made up of the latest in surveillance technology, including towers, cameras, sensors, and radar. And much of this virtual wall will not be on the actual borderline. This complex array of surveillance hardware will be installed miles into the interior. It will complement the already established, but ever-increasing policing apparatus of Border Patrol's fixed interior checkpoints. As anthropologist Josiah Heyman says, "The whole border zone virtually becomes a wall." [2]

In January 2011, Homeland Security cancelled its previous attempt at a virtual wall, known as SBInet, and the multibillion-dollar contract to the Boeing Company that went with it. Complaints were that the costly and often delayed technological barrier was not properly tailored to the rugged terrain of the borderlands, and that it had difficulties distinguishing animals from humans, though DHS still uses its tall surveillance towers, especially in the high desert lands near the border town of Sasabe.

Now Homeland Security has altered its strategy to focus on Arizona as a testing site and pilot program for this new virtual wall. It's called the Arizona Technology Deployment Plan, and it will focus on the 387 miles of border that Arizona has with Mexico, particularly in the area around Tucson. With the projected funding, CBP should finish initial technology deployment in Arizona by 2014 or 2015, according to *Homeland Security Today*. It is looking for both mobile, fixed, and remote surveillance systems, and integrated fixed towers. Mark Borkowski, CBP's assistant commissioner for the Office of Technology Innovation and Acquisition, says that the "current plan is to finish the Arizona plan first and then we will go wherever is next on the priority list."[3] However, Borkowski also said, at the Border Security Expo in March 2013, that some of the technology might shift to Texas, if there continued to be an increase of people crossing the border there.

Regardless of geographic location, for this new world of boundary builders like Dodds and others, these are serious opportunities with the potential for billions of dollars to be budgeted for border policing and immigration control. A white-collar Border Patrol regime has come to life in the United States and across the world. While the international boundary is indeed a line, the militarized apparatus evolving out of policing it is something much larger and more complex. For this apparatus to work, an infrastructure similar to that of a city or a town is needed to support it. Construction workers, electricians, plumbers, architects, engineers, and visionaries are needed. Expertise to service surveillance towers, drones, communication systems, computer networks, and surveillance feeds is needed. Nerds are needed as much as are Border Patrol agents.

The most important thing for all the companies at the

expo—and the larger marketplace of boundary-building of which it is a part—is making profit. According to Visiongain, an independent information-provider for businesses, border security is a sure-shot growth industry that has expanded at a 5 percent clip right through the recession. Visiongain projected that the final 2013 global border-security market earnings would be close to a $20 billion industry for the private sector.[4]

Add in contracts for U.S. Customs infrastructure and the Coast Guard and border security is one of the strongest branches of the homeland security industry, which will grow from $74.5 billion in 2012 to $107.3 billion in 2020 in the U.S. domestic market alone, according to estimates by Homeland Security Research, a Washington, D.C.-based consulting firm.[5] Worldwide, the potential for profit becomes outlandish. By 2018, another marketing research firm, known as MarketsandMarkets, estimates that the global market for homeland security and emergency management will reach $544.02 billion. "The threat of cross-border terrorism, cyber crime, piracy, drug trade, human trafficking, internal dissent, separatist movements has been a driving factor for the homeland security market," MarketsandMarkets says after studying high-profit markets in North America, Europe, and Asia. The U.S. market for drones alone, it says, will create 70,000 jobs by 2016.[6]

The global video surveillance market, which totaled $13.5 billion in industry revenues in 2012, projects to be almost $40 billion by 2020, in what Homeland Security Research, a marketing specialist, projects will be a "booming market."[7] In 2013, 200 million video surveillance cameras worldwide captured more than 1.7 trillion video hours, an amount that is expected to double by 2020. Other border-related submarkets such as those for "non-lethal weapons"[8] and "people-screening technologies"[9] are only growing. In Arizona, there was once a time when copper mining drove the state's fiscal prosperity. In many ways, that economic force has been replaced by the business of border control.

Arizona's Laboratory

In that vast, brightly lit cathedral of science fiction in Phoenix, it isn't the guns, drones, robots, or fixed surveillance towers and militarized mannequins that startle me most. It is the staggering energy and enthusiasm, so thick in the convention's air that it envelops you.

This day, I have no doubt that I'm in the presence of a burgeoning new multibillion-dollar industry that has every intention of making not just the border but this entire world of ours its own. I can feel that sense of excitement and possibility from the moment Drew Dodds begins explaining to me just how his company's Freedom On-the-Move system actually works. He grabs two water bottles close at hand and begins painting a vivid picture of one as a "hill" obstructing "the line of sight to the target," and the other as that "target"—in fact, an exhausted person migrating "the last mile" after three days in the desert, who might give anything for just such a bottle.

I have met many people in Dodds's "last mile"—hurt, dehydrated, exhausted in the Arizona "killing field," a term coined by journalist Margaret Regan in her book *The Death of Josseline: Immigration Stories from the Arizona Borderlands*. One man's feet had swelled up so much, thanks to the unrelenting heat and the cactus spines he had stepped on, that he could no longer jam them in his shoes. He had, he told me, continued on anyway in excruciating pain, mile after mile, barefoot on the oven-hot desert floor. Considering that the remains of more than 6,000 people have been recovered from the borderlands since the process of militarization began in the mid-1990s, he was lucky to have made it through alive. And this was the man Dodds was so pumped about nabbing with Freedom On-the-Move's "spot and stalk" technology; this was his football game.

In the end, though, he abandoned football for reality, summing up his experience this way: "We are bringing the battlefield to the border." Dodds is echoing the words of Dennis L. Hoffman—an economics professor from Arizona State University who studies future markets for the defense industry—who told the *New York Times*, "There are only so many missile systems and Apache attack helicopters you can sell. This push toward border security fits very well with the need to create an ongoing stream of revenue."[10]

However, Dan Millis of the Sierra Club's Borderlands Campaign sees this in an entirely different light. As he told me: "It's as if the United States is pulling out of Afghanistan and invading Arizona."

Underscoring Millis's point is the Border Patrol's use of the Vehicle and Dismount Exploitation Radar (VADER) system (manufactured by the company Northrup Grumman) on one of its Predator B drones. The U.S. military has used this "man-hunting" radar system in Afghanistan to locate potential roadside bombers. From October 1, 2012, to January 17, 2013, CBP did its preliminary border-testing phase of the VADER. The surveillance system was incorporated into a drone that made overflights of the Arizona Sonoran desert. As with enemy combatants in Afghanistan, it looked to detect border-crossers in the desert.

According to Border Patrol's "internal reports,"[11] with VA-DER's help the agency arrested 1,874 people. The expensive, loud, and buzzing drones over the Sonoran desert in the United States have begun to resemble more and more the ones over the Dashti Margo desert region in Afghanistan, and from the halls of U.S. Congress they are asking for more.

The Border Security Expo was the first of many visions of what the military-industrial complex looks like once it's transported, jobs and all, to the U.S.-Mexico border and turned into a consumer mall for the emerging national surveillance state. You can sense it in the young woman from RoboteX, who looks like she has walked directly out of her college graduation and onto the floor of the expo. She loans me her remote control for a few minutes and lets me play with the micro-robot she is hawking. It looks like a tiny tank. The Oakland police and their SWAT team are already using it, she tells me.

It is the breathless excitement of another young man, the University of Arizona graduate student who describes to me the "deception detection" technology the university is developing, along with a "communication web" that would allow drones to communicate without human mediation. His nerdish command of intricate technological vocabulary, his ability to pour out these words in massive quantities, rising and falling in tones of utter and complete excitement, reminds me of the talk of a video-game buff or a sports fan. It gets to a point that I just want to stand there and listen to him talk, even though I can only pick up fragments of what he is saying. It is as if I were desperately trying to understand a foreign language. He has blond curly hair and a boyish face and is dressed in a pressed white button-down shirt and black pants. He is a believer, almost in the religious sense. Everything is possible. The sky is the limit.

And why wouldn't he be so enthusiastic? He is a part of the DHS Center for Border Security and Immigration, known as BORDERS. He is supported by powerful institutions, and there is a future, and possibly employment, in what he is doing. The University of Arizona is the lead school of the R&D component of this homeland security endeavor. In 2008, the university received a $17 million, six-year grant to develop such enthusiasm for border security with its students. BORDERS leads a consortium of fourteen "premier institutions" consisting of not only universities spanning the country but also the RAND Corporation and the Migration Policy Institute, a Washington, D.C., think tank. BORDERS, according to its mission statement, is meant to develop "innovative technologies, proficient processes, and effective policies that will help protect our nation's borders from terrorists and criminal activity, facilitate international trade and travel, and provide deeper understanding of immigration dynamics and determinants."[12] It is one of the places where the technologies seen at that Phoenix convention center are born.

The BORDERS research at the University of Arizona covers a wide range of technologies from surveillance to "deception detection," according to Elyse Golob, the program's executive director. For example, UA Aerospace Mechanical Engineering students are studying locust wings in order to develop miniature surveillance drones that they call Micro Air Vehicles. "The flight of birds and insects is still not well understood," an unnamed researcher tells the reporter for KVOA, Tucson's NBC affiliate.

Another graduate student explains further, while

holding a micro-drone that has wings. "You can have one Border Patrol agent execute a program launching twenty of these, and you can fly twenty trails at once and he can be watching a video display and basically be doing the job that otherwise would take far more Border Patrol agents."

The reporter is impressed. He gushes that these "toys," which can make pinpoint stops and move through thin crevices, could someday "help secure the U.S.-Mexico border" by going after "terrorists, drug smugglers, and other intruders."[13] But the reporter ignores the bigger story: the University of Arizona has become a laboratory for the Department of Homeland Security.

Manufacturing the Complex

Bruce Wright doesn't look like a Border Patrol agent. He wears a suit coat and tie. He speaks the language of a technocrat, with military jargon sprinkled in only if necessary. He has short graying hair, parted on the side. He seems to be constantly in motion, constantly talking, often with enthusiastic gestures if the subject is border security and management. Wright talks about it with such passion that you would think that even during his off hours he is consumed with devising endless ways to rework, maintain, and further fortify the U.S.-Mexico border's enforcement and trade model. He is a boundary builder. His dream is to sell the gadgets and systems made at his workplace to the rest of the country and the world.

Wright is the CEO of the University of Arizona's Science and Technology Park and has many ideas for this sprawling 1,345-acre campus, which is tailoring itself to accommodate the up-and-coming border-security industry as it seeks to develop, test, and eventually commercialize its products—including sensors, fencing, perimeter surveillance, drones, and other instruments of social control. Although the UA Science and Technology Park is separate from BORDERS, they work together in many ways to advance and strengthen the capacities of the national surveillance state.

Even though less than one hundred miles away from the international divide, the tech park actually seems much farther away from the border. Once you get cleared to pass through the security gates, you find a modern office complex and something of a future world. Its vast solar farm has 18,000 linear feet of fencing, Wright explains to me, which could be used as a mock wall where they could test detectors or sensors. The tech park's green technologies give the impression that this place is ushering in a sustainable, Earth-friendly way of life. It has a sophisticated and artistic infrastructure system that includes its own water treatment, central utility plant, and on-site EMT and Fire and Rescue Unit. It has a full-service cafeteria and catering center, a Starbucks, and an outdoor recreational center for its 7,000 employees. The UA Tech Park is one of the top employers in an otherwise economically depressed Tucson.

In 2008, when Arizona was reeling, the park boasted a 98 percent occupancy rate and contributed $3 billion to the state's economy. Indeed, with its parking lot full, the gigantic fourteen-structure park seems to be booming. Certainly there is more to the park than its border control component, but Wright quickly makes it known that it is a prominent focus of the institution and an industry that will be growing.

Inside were the young professionals of this apparatus, dressed business casual, some with shaggy hair, some with floppy haircuts like Justin Bieber in his tween phase. Almost none had the brawny build of a Border Patrol agent, few had military-style flattops, but many were serving equally important roles in border security and enforcement, even if they were studying laser technology or robotics in a laboratory.

Bruce Wright fits into this world completely. He has the air of both a modern man and an innovator. He has an articulate and passionate way of talking. When he gets going, like the BORDERS student, his words exude unbridled enthusiasm.

For instance, he talks about rapid-response teams that can be quickly mobilized in the tech park. These are not the rapid response teams from BORTAC, the Border Patrol Tactical Unit, who, in the recruiting videos, always seem to be heroically rappelling from a helicopter on some undefined national security mission. Rather, they are a combination of faculty and masters students from the University of Arizona's College of Engineering, who can be mobilized to evaluate border-security technology when a company presents it to the tech park, who have a need to present "their technology in 90 to 120 days"[14] to the Department of Homeland Security.

Wright is no anti-immigrant warrior, not even close. He is personable and earnest, and it seems as though he would never say anything bad about someone from Mexico. While we are talking he quotes the governor of Sonora, who said that he thinks 15 percent of people living in Tucson have family living in the Mexican states of Sonora or Sinaloa. He stresses how intertwined Sonora and Arizona are as states. He says that "20 percent of the retail trade in Tucson is generated by Mexicans crossing over the border and shopping at Costco" or any one of Tucson's local malls.

It is *Arizona Republic* columnist Linda Valdez who tries

to define this entirely new category for people like Wright. Gushing, she says that there are "academics, innovators, entrepreneurs and industry executives," as opposed to those who sling "sound bites" at each other from opposing sides of the immigration and border debate. Wright and his ever-enlarging group of white-collar boundary builders are those "who look south and see possibilities. They see the reality of the border. . . . The border has the potential for commercial opportunities that are largely untapped."[15]

And this idea that the border itself is now being tapped for economic development, like any other natural resource, is fully present in Wright's tone.

"Here we are living on the border, turning lemons into lemonade. If we are to deal with the problem, what is the economic benefit from dealing with it?" Wright asks me in the tech park's conference room. He sits across from me at a long brown table. The lights are dim because Wright is showing me a PowerPoint presentation that vividly illustrates the tech park's evolving roles in connecting the Department of Homeland Security with the private industry—both start-up companies and old military powerhouses.

"Well, we can build an industry around this problem that creates employment, wages, and wealth for this region. . . . And this technology can be sold all over the world." In fact, according to the *Homeland Security News Wire*, "the border security crisis" is already boosting Tucson's economy, welcome words for an area afflicted with a poverty rate of nearly 23 percent.[16]

The tech park's director of community engagement, Molly Gilbert, continues this train of thought: "It's really about development, and we want to create technology jobs in our border towns."

For Wright, it's all about supply and demand. If there is money available for something, then the technology can be produced to meet the demand. This growing industry is where the North American Free Trade Agreement (NAFTA) meets border militarization and its tripartite wars against terror, drugs, and immigration, playing out so ferociously in our borderlands.

This is where the seemingly contradictory notions of a border opened wide for merchandise and cash flows, and a border that restricts the movements of people, gets ironed out.

Indeed, all that Wright is explaining started with NAFTA in 1994, at the University of Arizona's Economic Development Center, a forerunner to the tech park. In 1992, the state of Arizona mandated that the center lead "a statewide effort to position Arizona in NAFTA and show we can exploit commercial opportunities with Mexico, the border, and Latin America," Wright says. He explains that in 1992 there was going to be this new free-trade area, and the "Arizona-Sonora border was right in the middle of it. This cross-border trade and development program led the center to focus on infrastructure development, border ports of entry, and trade corridors."

Since the early 1990s, calls for enhanced border security had been on the rise, but the UA Tech Park didn't focus on border policing technology until after 9/11. Under the new free-trade regime, border security fast became a competitive industry with products and services to produce, package, and pitch.

And, as with any other industry, it needs to be coddled, cultivated, and grown. This is the role of the tech park, along with its tenants. Many companies present at the park are at work on border technology, such as DILAS, Pillar

Innovations, Raytheon, IBM, Oracle, Canon, NP Photonics, and DRS Technologies. The lines between academics, private industry, and border enforcement are becoming increasingly blurred.

These are examples of some of the companies, Wright says, that could make the virtual wall in Arizona happen.

"We're working with companies that have forty- to eighty-foot towers. Companies that are working with motion detectors. Companies that have look-down cameras. Companies that can integrate communications. A company that we're working with has a web-based technology platform that could display all this information and piece it together, so that the general public as well as the agents in the field could use it."

The tech park has been in conversation with several small Tucson companies such as Zonge International, which is helping develop an underground fiber-optic line that will supposedly distinguish between cattle and humans. There are also much larger companies, including Boeing, IBM, Honeywell, Motorola, and Raytheon, that could possibly acquire some of the small companies or use their technology to supplement and complement their own border-related products and services.

And there is the "bring the battlefield to the border" dynamic. The UA Tech Park will be able to take some of these traditional military hardware companies, explains Wright, and make border-security subsidiaries that could then be housed in the park. In order to test the U.S. border-security market, they have a global initiative that can help international companies create a subsidiary in the United States, and they are working with several Israeli companies to make that happen. They have the lawyers, the accountants, and all the technical know-how as well as the connections with the big federal government players who are shopping around, ready to give contracts. They are in the perfect position to help manufacture the entire border-security industrial complex.

In addition to the solar-farm fencing, a railroad spur, and roads on the tech park's property, there is an immensity of space for offices and labs. Due to its proximity to the border, Wright says, companies can also field-test their products on-site in the actual theater of operations where the war to secure the border is being waged. And if this technology delivers as pitched and can be effectively deployed on the southern border, there are other surveillance markets to move on to next. This starts with the Canadian border, given the significantly increased attention it has been receiving in the halls of power. And it also includes the coasts—since there is more and more talk in Congress about maritime security—especially the "third border" around Puerto Rico.

Also, Wright stresses, emerging surveillance technology and services can be deployed by airports, power plants, gated communities, and all varieties of police. And beyond the U.S. market is the global market.

"There is a worldwide market for border technology. I mean, there's a border between Ukraine and Russia, between Poland and Russia, between the Palestinians and the Israelis . . . all around the world there are border issues," he says enthusiastically.

As I talk with Wright, his colleagues from the University of Arizona, and people at the Border Security Expo, it occurs to me that I have never met so many people who were so pumped up about the U.S.-Mexico border. I have talked with Border Patrol agents who lay out the situation using militaristic terminology—rigid, cold language to make sense and strategize around their mission. I have talked with activists and rights advocates who describe the border situation as a humanitarian crisis and are outraged by the number of lives lost trying to cross the desert each year. And I have talked with people right before they make the high-risk journey from Mexico into the United States in search of work, many of whom are apprehensive and say they never wanted to leave their homes. But this is the first time I have met with people who speak with such enthusiasm about the border and the immensity of money to be made from its protection.

The Border Patrol Salesperson

In the Phoenix Convention Hall, after he gave me the demonstration with the water bottles, Drew Dodds says that he will be bringing out his product to an "operation" later that day. He points to a Ford Raptor truck (purposely bought to mimic the Border Patrol trucks) that actually has the words FREEDOM ON-THE-MOVE written across its front. I say "what?" when he uses the word "operation." Though he's an ex-marine, he is still only a salesperson for a company; he can't really be part of an operation, can he? Before Dodds joined their crew he was a door-to-door salesperson in the mortgage business.

"It's going to be in southern Pinal County," he says. Paul Babeu, the sheriff of central Arizona's Pinal County, is a well-known, and rather controversial, border hawk, and he treats his county as if it were indeed on the Mexican border, even though it is not.

"You mean Casa Grande?" I ask, because a large Border Patrol station is located there. "With who? Border Patrol? The Pinal County Sheriff's Office?"

"Yes, but with others," he tells me, "DPS. CBP. A joint task force." I look up at the word FREEDOM again, and think about the Xbox controller.

"It helps me get out the marine in me," he confides. He tells me he will be bringing his assault rifle, motioning to the empty passenger seat as if that is where it will be during the ride. He doesn't explain to me what they will be doing, but Babeu claims that several smuggling corridors run through the south side of his county. I try to imagine Dodds out there, rumbling along the dirt road with the stiff mast upright behind him with its camera, as he explained earlier, getting the panorama of this stretch of southern Arizona's Sonoran Desert. Then I think Dodds is exaggerating his role. He is a salesperson, not a Border Patrol agent.

But even so, Dodds is describing the audacity of this brave new world of border control where the lines of separation between private industry and the U.S government are increasingly blurred.

chapter three

DOING NICE THINGS FOR CHILDREN

It is hot and sunny in El Paso, Texas, on this late-March morning. The moderator of the Poppies Festival, an annual celebration of the Mexican poppy bloom, is a stout woman wearing a straw hat. Using a screechy microphone, she gushes about the local Democratic congressperson, Silvestre Reyes. Before them the canyon in the Franklin Mountains is full of red-golden poppies, blooming well this year because of the winter rains. The moderator makes sure everyone knows that Reyes is much more than a politician. She makes sure we know that we are in the presence of a national hero. No one else has done as much to advance border security as the El Paso native, the moderator says. The country is a safer place because of this silver-haired man who walks up slowly to the microphone to a brief but intense round of applause.

In the crowd before him is a wide array of El Pasoans—there are young couples pushing strollers, there are families, artists selling jewelry and paintings, naturalists guiding nature walks, and agents of the U.S. Border Patrol. The sunglasses-masked agents are not in uniform, except for their dark green pants. These federal agents, in fact, look more like camp counselors, doing their best to organize and corral a group of approximately thirty teenagers who are part of U.S. Border Patrol Explorer Post 910. This relationship between Border Patrol agents and the children of El Paso is precisely the sort of thing that Reyes strove to cultivate during his stint as El Paso sector chief. This is in no small part what brings him local fame, although in the 2012 Democratic primary he lost his seat to Beto O'Rourke, partly because of accusations of corruption and nepotism regarding border-security contracts.

Reyes is a Border Patrol pioneer, a far cry from his activity as a little kid in the 1950s blowing the horn to warn the field hands if agents from the "migra" were in the vicinity of his farm, which was to the west of El Paso. "When I was young," he told sociologist Timothy Dunn in a 1996 interview for Dunn's book about the border blockade, *Blockading the Border and Human Rights: The El Paso Operation that Remade Immigration Enforcement*, "I would act as a lookout. . . . So it was kind of ironic that as an adult I'd go to work for the very agency I had served as a lookout against. But that's life on the border."[1] Indeed, after his time as a soldier in the Vietnam War, in 1969 this grandson of a Mexican immigrant joined the Border Patrol. Overcoming racist hostility within the agency, after fifteen years of service Reyes was promoted to lead the McAllen sector and became the first Latino sector chief in the history of the U.S. Border Patrol.

But his true rise to fame came after his appointment to the El Paso sector in 1993. On September 19, 1993, he lined up 400 agents, each in a green-striped patrol vehicle, side by side on the international boundary between El Paso and Ciudad Juárez to block unauthorized entries into the United States. Placed from fifty yards to one-half mile apart, Border Patrol formed an impenetrable human wall along a twenty-mile stretch of border, supported by low-flying surveillance helicopters. In doing so, he was not only transforming the way the international border would be policed and publicly perceived, he was also responding to a crisis between El Paso's Mexican-American population and the Border Patrol.

In 1994, El Paso's Bowie High School settled its historic civil rights case after accusing the Border Patrol of systematically harassing students both on school grounds and in surrounding neighborhoods. At the time, the Border Patrol's strategy was to roam El Paso's Mexican-American neighborhoods where, they claimed, they were on the lookout for people entering the country without authorization. Testimonies from students, teachers, and administration from Bowie—almost all of Mexican origin—painted a portrait of an aggressive authoritarian climate in which Border Patrol ran roughshod on campus, just 500 feet north of the border. They constantly ordered students to prove their citizenship. They regularly assaulted students, throwing them against walls or vans to search them. During the case, Bowie High School insisted that the Border Patrol was mistaking U.S. citizens for "illegal aliens" and that the agency needed to be on the actual boundary line, not on their campus.

And that's exactly where the Border Patrol went with Operation Blockade (later renamed Hold-the-Line). It moved the bulk of its forces out of El Paso's neighborhoods and took up positions directly on the border. On Mexico's side, Operation Blockade cut off an institutionalized, yet undocumented, workforce from its source of employment in the United States. The operation cut the flow of people who provided services for hundreds if not thousands of homes and businesses, including child care.

When hundreds of people from the Mexican side protested by taking over the main international bridge and shutting down traffic, little did they know they were witnessing the advent of a new U.S. border policy, a blueprint that Border Patrol would use from San Diego to Brownsville, with El Paso-inspired operations named Gatekeeper (in the San Diego area), Safeguard (in Arizona), and Rio Grande (in South Texas).

According to geographer Joseph Nevins, the intense hold of these operations has brought about a significant shift in the very language we use: "The division between Mexico and the United States has shifted from a border, a zone of gradual transition, to a boundary, a stark line of demarcation—one that divides law and order from chaos and lawlessness, and thus civilization from something less than fully civilized."[2]

The perception was that deployments like Operation Blockade vividly slammed the door on these "uncivilized" undocumented border crossings in densely populated areas. But the operations simply redirected the flow of determined work seekers to newly developed ways to get to the U.S. job market. More people began crossing through places such as the Arizona desert. These are places so dangerous, desolate, and deadly that the hostile terrain itself, according to Border Patrol's "prevention by deterrence" strategy, is supposed to stop prospective migrants in their tracks. This did not jibe with Mexico's post-NAFTA exodus, in which historic numbers of people began journeying to the United States—often through terrain where it was impossible to carry enough clean water necessary for the three-day trek. The region is literally littered with bones.

At the time, Reyes was not concerned with the far-reaching impacts of Operation Blockade. He was trying both to smother a public-relations nightmare and to respond to a local call for change from teenagers at a local El Paso High school. In a significant way, Operation Blockade—and its sweeping social, political, and economic impacts on the border region—began as public relations offensive. Instead of enemies, those high school students were future Explorers.

The Poppies Festival moderator's gushing about Border Patrol operations' effectiveness is part of Reyes's masterful public relations savvy, developed over a span of many years. When in December 1993 El Paso's Border Rights Coalition held a press conference to criticize Operation Blockade, Reyes dispatched a Santa Claus, not with a sled and reindeer, but in a noisy helicopter. The military-style entrance of "Operation Santa Claus" stunned the small audience, who could barely hear the findings of the human rights group through the roar of the low-flying federal aircraft. The helicopter landed across the street at a community center where the Border Patrol Santa gave presents to throngs of assembled children, getting all the media thunder. This was just one of Reyes's many efforts during his two stints as chief of both the McAllen and El Paso sectors when he was always attempting to establish a "good rapport with the community." This included volunteer work in schools and feeding the poor around Christmastime. As Reyes told Dunn: "I learned very early that people respond very favorably to you if you're doing nice things for their children."[3]

Reyes wasn't just selling a product, he was selling a worldview that he had to package like a product. He had to sell the idea of a world in stark black-and-white terms—the citizen vs. the criminal, the good vs. the bad, the legal vs. illegal, the "innocent us" vs. the "terrorist them,"—the notion that there was a clearly defined line between the two that had to be rigorously defended. Reyes's vision was the blueprint for today's expanded "American front lines" with their massive infrastructure of walls, surveillance technology, and weaponry that would feed into the Border Patrol's post-9/11 brand motto: "Protecting America." Reyes's vision also included the blueprint for today's Explorer, for today's Border Patrol youth.

The Key to the Community

Before the festival starts, approximately thirty youths, between the ages of fourteen and twenty-one—every one of them brown-skinned and Latino—are hoisting up white canvas tents in the denuded landscape, giving shade to the vendors and organizations setting booths for the day. The Border Patrol Explorers are eager volunteers with a lot of morning pep. Kids crowd around their two adult leaders, advisors to their post, from the El Paso sector of the U.S. Border Patrol, who talk strategy and tasks for the day with help from the festival's organizers. Later the kids help out with parking for the hundreds of El Paso residents who are making their way up to the Franklin Mountains for the festival. All day the kids patrol the trash areas and check for full garbage bags that need to be replaced with empty ones. This is how, as CBP Public Affairs Officer Stephanie Malin explains it to me in an email, "the youth of America" are connecting with "the largest federal law enforcement agency in the country." What's more, she says, the "Explorer program is a great opportunity to instill the same values and commitment CBP employees bring to the job every day."

The advisors are Border Patrol agents Raul Cadena and Gio Cisneros, who balance each other in important ways. Cadena is even-keeled and soft-spoken and is more inclined to say, "Ah, they're just kids." When, earlier that morning, the advisors made the Explorers march in lockstep around the Border Patrol Training Center near sector headquarters on Montana Boulevard, Cadena told me that "they're just giving them a little exercise," as if playing down the normal associations that come with marching and militaristic subordination. Cisneros is tall and built like he'd be a high-scoring power forward on the University of Texas El Paso's basketball team. But when he talks and gestures, he seems more like a head coach laying down strategy during a heated game. The kids seem to like both of these guys, who play a role that is part career advisor, part guidance counselor.

The trophy that many of the thirty Explorers aspire to win is the gray polo shirt that says U.S. BORDER PATROL EXPLORERS on the back in black letters, which only a dozen of the youth are wearing. If you don't have the shirt, it means that you haven't to made it through the months-long Explorer Academy, which, in the case of Post 910, is run not only by Border Patrol agents but also a military drill instructor. One sixteen-year-old Explorer who has on his gray polo complains about the whole ordeal. When they recruit, he tells me, "they only tell you the good things, they only tell you about the field trips and the fun stuff; they don't tell you that they yell at you." Those who haven't gone through the academy wear the dark green Border Patrol pants and black boots, but stand out awkwardly, manifesting their lower hierarchal status by wearing white T-shirts. The newest Explorers don't have the green pants, but even they have to make sure that their T-shirts are perfectly tucked in to their jeans during the uniform inspection such as the one that took place at the

Border Patrol Training Center that morning, before we went to the festival.

Before Reyes steps up to speak, a small group of Explorers participates in a ritual circle dance whose sacred purpose is to reunite the "spirits of the native peoples in the region." Indigenous men pound drums in the middle of the circle as the small group of girl Explorers joins a larger group of people and slowly dances to Earth's powerful heartbeat, quite a sight considering that Border Patrol regularly rides roughshod over Native American communities. One of the dancing Explorers who wears a gray polo shirt tells me later that the Explorers experience "helps me present myself better, it helps me talk to people better." Other Explorers are chatting with the kids in the El Paso Youth Orchestra, also teenagers but whose wild flashy clothing, big hair, and love for performing 1980s covers of Van Halen and Journey contrasts with the mission-focused Border Patrol in ways that are difficult to reconcile, except that they are all kids, just in different uniforms.

There is an environmental focus to many of the booths. There is an arctic wolf, its caretaker a man with long, straight, blond hair who never smiles. The man constantly tosses Tupperware containers full of ice at the blank-faced snow-white wolf. He tells agent Cisneros, with a bit of attitude, that the wolf "can never be tamed." Of course, Cisneros's question was typical Border Patrol: "How long does it take to tame the wolf?" When he comes back to the spot where Cadena and I are standing, he tells us that the "long-haired" wolf guy is an "asshole."

Many of the Explorers tell me that Post 910 is working on a handcuffing technique right now. This is what they would be doing on a normal Saturday if it weren't community service week. They are learning how to handcuff a person who is resisting arrest. In the scenario, three Explorers play the roles of smugglers, "illegals," or terrorists. They dive to the ground, face first. Even though they dive, the idea is that the Border Patrol agents—played by three other Explorers—are forcing them to the ground. First these "agents" cuff the left wrist. They kneel into the subject's lower back while cuffing his right hand. Then they lock the mock criminal's wrists together. They've got to be quick if they want to do well when they compete against other posts. The competitions are like a law enforcement Olympics. It isn't easy, because you're doing a lot of things at once. Only a few can do it really quickly, like a real agent.

In May 2009, the *New York Times* ran a story on the post-9/11 changes to law enforcement youth programs, focusing on the youngsters participating in various national security drills. The article, "Scouts Train to Fight Terrorists, and More," quotes a youth trainer who instructs the kids what to do if a person they are arresting resists or puts up a fight: "Put a knee in their back; that will shut them up."[4]

According to the CBP website, Explorers are "trained in numerous law enforcement scenarios that are based on actual training received by CBP officers and agents."[5] To bolster endurance, they train by doing push-ups and sit-ups. They are expected to be able to run 1.5 miles in less than fifteen minutes. There are a number of role-play scenarios in which they use their "red guns," fake red handguns and assault rifles. Cadena tells me that the guns are for trainings that prepare Border Patrol Explorers for pursuing "intruders" in the desert, raiding marijuana fields, and responding to hostage-taking situations.

The Explorers learn about borders, citizenship, CBP history, and even a little bit of immigration law. They learn not only the values of an ideal Border Patrol agent, but also the agency's language and vernacular. "Intruders," they learn, could be smugglers or traffickers, but most likely they are "undocumented aliens" (UDAs) or "bodies"—as if people who cross the border were commodities, lumps of flesh to be stacked and stored until they can be shipped off. Then there is the "Other Than Mexican" (OTM). An OTM could be from a "special-interest country," so designated because of the presence of "terrorists" there. In one Explorer role-play scenario in California, Imperial County Deputy A. J. Lowenthal told the *New York Times*, one of the kids wore traditional Arab dress. "If we're looking at 9/11 and what a Middle-Eastern terrorist would be like," he told the *Times*, "then maybe your role-player would look like that. I don't know, would you call that politically incorrect?"[6]

Cadena tells me that as a reward for all the kids' hard work the agents "bring them out to show them some of the stuff we do." They bring the kids to the desert where they get to search for real "signs"—any indication that people have passed through. Often the Border Patrol will do "drags" with several tires connected to the back of their vehicle to smooth out the dirt so they can see fresh footprints better. The Explorers also get to go to the Interstate 10 checkpoint between Las Cruces and Deming in New Mexico for a tour and to play with some of the equipment used by Border Patrol. This checkpoint stops all westbound traffic in order for agents to verify whether or not each and every person is a U.S. citizen or has the proper paperwork to be in the country as a visiting foreign national. There are dogs and plenty of surveillance equipment for the Explorers to check out.

CBP Post 910 in El Paso is not the only CBP Explorer post. There are more in San Diego, Nogales, Miami, and San Juan, Puerto Rico. They are also in Tampa, Chicago, and Anchorage. They are in Maine and Montana and New Jersey. John Anthony, the national director for the Boy Scouts of America's Learning for Life, the parent organization of the Explorers Program, told the *New York Times* in 2009 that there were 2,000 law enforcement posts across the country hosting roughly 35,000 of the group's 145,000 students, with an increasing number of CBP-focused groups. The stated purpose of the program is for teenagers to explore potential career opportunities in law enforcement. Many sheriff and police departments, taking on increasing border, immigration, and national security responsibilities, have incorporated CBP and DHS missions into their Explorer programs. "Before it was more about basics," said Border Patrol agent Johnny Longoria to the *New York Times*, "but now our emphasis is on terrorism, illegal entry, drugs and human smuggling."[7]

Sheriff Paul Babeu of Arizona's Pinal County, a gay border hawk who had a romantic relationship with an undocumented Mexican man and then threatened to deport him when it went sour, claims to have the largest Explorer program in the state. Kids not only learn about "paramilitary and law enforcement tactics," Babeu explained at a recruitment meeting in a Phoenix suburb, but are also training for a "leadership role" involving lessons "of discipline and respect that we want to teach youth in our area." Babeu wants to see a double barrier on the Arizona-Sonora border, and to deploy 6,000 soldiers during its construction. He asks: "If more than 400,000 illegals made it into Arizona last year undetected, and Mexican cartels have hundreds of lookouts on Arizona mountain tops to safely escort their drug loads, what do we think is the likelihood of those with military training or a possible terrorist sleeper cell sneaking across?"[8]

There is also a similar type of Explorer program in the Modi'in region of Israel known as the "No'ar Magav," "Border Police Youth." The program, while much smaller than its U.S. counterpart, has thirty-six teenagers (between the ages of sixteen and eighteen) who can, according to *Haaretz*, "in their spare time . . . help catch 'illegal residents,' " generally Palestinians, "or stand at checkpoints and help guard the neighboring settlements." One member of the group, by the name of Eran, explained its activities to the newspaper: "It's a fun feeling—you are filled with adrenaline and energy during such operations. We also feel pride for protecting our home."[9]

While there is great power in teaching youth about this terrifying world of border-related national security threats and organized crime, Cisneros tells me the true power of the youth program comes with things like the Thanksgiving parade.

What? I ask.

The El Paso Thanksgiving parade, he says.

For years, the Border Patrol has been a part of the parade. They come out with their horses. They come out with their ATVs. They march in their fancy uniforms. When Cisneros talks, it always seems as though he has a sneaking suspicion that many people aren't too keen on the Border Patrol. He tells me they get only a "mixed reaction, at best" in the parade.

But with the kids, it is a completely different story. In 2011 they added Explorer Post 910 for the first time. The teenagers march with their red guns right alongside the U.S. Border Patrol contingent. Every 200 feet or so the kids act out a "takedown move." While the ATVs and horses get little response from the crowd, the kids' move is wildly applauded. If it's not the Explorer's immediate family, it's their cousins, their aunts and uncles, their friends.

"The kids are *key*," Cisneros explains, "to our relationship with the community." As Reyes says, it's harder for people to harshly criticize you if they know you.

The Dog and Pony Show

Just a hop, skip, and a jump down the hill from where Reyes speaks is the U.S. Border Patrol Museum. Filled with so many strangely organized items—posters, vehicles, and artifacts collected since the Border Patrol's creation in 1924—it seems almost like a shrine or Mexican altar to the agency, rather than an actual museum. I walk through it like someone walking through an attic, having an idea of what one will find, but at the same time surprised at every turn. There is a human-size replica of the Statue of Liberty in front of a U.S. flag. There are posters of friendly K-9 Border Patrol dogs with names like Rocky, Barry, and Sylvia who tell kids to "say no to drugs." There are Border Patrol poetry and Border Patrol lyrics. There is Border Patrol art. One piece shows stoic agents traveling through rugged canyons on horseback; another is a still life of handcuffs and a handgun placed on a Border Patrol uniform. There are old photos of checkpoints and mannequins of a Border Patrol agent and the Royal Canadian Mounted Police on the northern border. A new exhibit focuses on the recruiting efforts on the NASCAR circuit between 2007 and 2009. A plaque admits that the Border Patrol NASCAR team never won "but made countless contacts and received lots of free radio and television time promoting Border Patrol."

One section tells the history of the agency since the 1920s. It holds a yellow newspaper clipping from the 1940s calling the Border Patrol "Uncle Sam's first line of home defense." The article goes on to say that "no average male is likely to be Border Patrol material. . . . Physical and I.Q. requirements almost demand a Joe Louis body and an Information Please mind." There is a sign on the wall about the Kooskia Internment Camp that was run by the INS and the Border Patrol in northern Idaho and detained men of Japanese descent. You can see the varieties of handguns and long rifles from Border Patrol's firearm history dating back to the 1920s. Taking in the history of the U.S. Border Patrol reveals not only the long-standing worldview of the agency, but also that of the nation and its borders.

In the area showcasing old vehicles—a car, a helicopter, an ATV, and a fast boat—there is also a robot. The robot is painted forest green, as if it were wearing a Border Patrol uniform. In a picture next to the robot, you can see it talking to a class of youngsters from what must be the first or second grade. The children looked mesmerized by the technological border agent before them. One child has risen to his feet and is pointing to the wide, friendly face of the robot as it explains the Border Patrol's mission to the kids. The circa-1980s robot is like a prophecy of the high-tech pizzazz the agency boasts today. This includes the modern robot: the Predator B surveillance drone that patrols our international borders and beyond from the skies.

Maybe the robots are different, but Border Patrol agents still go into classrooms with show-and-tell objects—almost like a mobile Border Patrol museum for kids. For example, if we go to El Centro, California, the dogs and ponies not only excite the young ones but also help them set their career goals. Take ten-year-old Jessica Acosta, who says that she really wants "to be a Border Patrol agent" when she grows up. "I like that [the agents] get to work with dogs to catch the bad guys."[10] And if it's not the dogs, it's the ponies. In one of the Border Patrol's youth programs, students at local schools get to name the agency's new horses. As reported in the *Imperial Valley Press*, eight-year-old Mino Chavez chose the name Storm for the Border Patrol's new mustang. Agent Fabian Morales said that these types of programs raise the "community's morale."

Other hands-on activities include the December holiday program, "Shop With a Cop." U.S. Border Patrol agents, along with other law-enforcement personnel, accompany young children who have been determined to be "in need." They usually bring youngsters to a local Walmart with $100 to buy clothing or shoes. Tara Mylett, chair of the Shop With a Cop program, said, "Within the last fourteen years, over 2,000 children have been helped."[11] Walmart, Target, and McDonald's are some of the donors to the program.

The Border Patrol's attempts to appeal to youth precede their 1980s robot by decades. In the mid-1950s, for example, Border Patrol proposed to General Mills that its agents be promoted on cereal boxes like other superheroes. These included Captain Midnight's Secret Squadron, Superman's Junior Defense League, the Lone Ranger's Victory Corps, and Little Orphan Annie's Commando Unit, which encouraged young readers to form their own junior commando club. The Border Patrol superhero also arose in the context of significant terminology shifts in the agency's vernacular in the 1950s. As explained by historian Kelly Lytle Hernandez in her book

Migra! A History of the U.S. Border Patrol, new terms such as "criminal alien" and "border violator,"[12] with their provocative tone, came to life and helped expedite the shift so that people without papers, predatory criminals, and terrorist suspects were increasingly perceived and treated with equal severity. Only a superhero would be able to grapple with such terrible and terrifying foes. "The patrol's mandate may have been migration control," Lytle-Hernandez writes, "but its mission was crime control in general by preventing the entry of criminal aliens and deporting border violators."[13]

The idea with the General Mills proposal was that kids would collect box tops and form junior Border Patrol groups. This follows a long line of "junior" or "boy" patrol groups that normally included instructions in "good citizenship" and offered recreational opportunities. These ideas came from a similar nineteenth-century initiative, the Children's Aid Society, whose purpose was to help the "moral development" of the "lower classes."[14]

When General Mills declined, the INS regional commissioner was undeterred. "The turn-down has not discouraged us in the least," he wrote. "There are many other ways and means of focusing attention on the objectives of the Border Patrol and its fine accomplishments." This was done by creating Junior Patrol Clubs with the missions to promote the Border Patrol's "crime-fighting" tactics and to create "goodwill" in the communities where Border Patrol was working.[15] The roots of the post-9/11 Explorer post were thus born.

"No doubt," writes Martin Greenberg in his essay "A Short History of the Junior Police," "the events of September 11, 2001, and the proliferation of popular television programs have contributed to the phenomenal growth in Exploring."[16] These include the National Geographic Channel's *Border Wars* and its imitators, which portray Border Patrol much they way their own recruiting videos do—full of adrenaline-arousing moments in a world defined by the clash between good guys and bad guys.

A Religious Experience

Andres Lozano, from the border town Nogales, Arizona, says that friends who are Explorers in high school might try to "pressure you, saying there's a group of us already in it, why don't you join?" Since Nogales is such a small town, everybody is aware of the different youth programs, Lozano tells me. It's true, Nogales only has a population of approximately 25,000 people—much less than the figure for Nogales, Sonora, across the line, where the population is close to 400,000, though it's hard to tell, given its highly mobile sector that works for low wages in U.S. factories. Between the two cities, the border wall snakes up and down through the hills in the high desert, now a permanent line of division in a border zone referred to as "Ambos Nogales" (Both Nogales), underscoring the fact that this was once, and still is, one community. Lozano grew up with the border wall as a permanent fixture in the landscape, although his father—when he was a kid—used to cross through a hole in the chain-link fence from Mexico to the United States to pay bills, play basketball, and occasionally raise havoc with his water gun (which once got him detained by the Border Patrol in the late 1970s).

There are a number of different youth groups, Lozano says, but two of them always seem to put pressure on everyone else. One is a group of kids who are "very religious, and they go to religious meetings over the weekend and they'd try to get you to go to the weekend meetings."

The other group that "sticks out to me," he says, is the group of kids "involved with the Explorers."

Lozano says that there are only two places where kids hang out in Nogales—City Hall and Peter Piper Pizza. City Hall has a park, but in the back is an area for events such as small carnivals and other functions where businesses and city agencies put up booths. Border Patrol is also almost always there. Lozano says that in the mid-2000s he and a group of his friends had an encounter with Border Patrol at City Hall when they walked bouncing a basketball past the Border Patrol booth. A uniformed Border Patrol agent rushed out, stood in their path, and said, "Hey! You guys seem young, you seem athletic. Why don't you sign up for the Explorers?" The agent pointed to the booth.

But Lozano, like many youths in many border towns, doesn't like the Border Patrol. He spent his youth playing "hide-and-seek" with agents. He and his friends would provoke the "men in green" to get them to chase them, a fairly easy endeavor. They would also chuck rocks at agents' vehicles and run when they pursued them in response. They ran fast with danger-pumped adrenaline. The danger is real: agents have shot and killed youths after they threw rocks.

A few weeks before agents tried to recruit Lozano and his friends at City Hall, another Border Patrol agent had pulled a gun on Lozano after he climbed a slow-moving train to get across the train tracks. There is no overpass in Nogales, so when the train rolls through, it cuts the town in half and there is no way to get to the other side until the whole thing chugs through. Lozano was on the way to his best friend's house, on the other side of the train tracks. After a Border Patrol agent saw Lozano climb down from the train, he peeled out from where he was stationed, jumped over the curb, came to a screeching stop, pulled out his gun, and yelled, "Freeze!"

Lozano stopped and tried to get his identification out of his pocket, and the agent yelled for him to get his hand out of his pocket. The agent came over, pulled Lozano's wallet out, looked at his ID, and then, according to Lozano, slammed it on his chest and told him that the train was federal property. Lozano was only fifteen years old at time.

The incident was still fresh in his mind a few weeks later when the Border Patrol recruiter tried to entice him over to the information booth

"I'm not interested," Lozano tells him. "Go away." The "go away" part is for effect, Lozano admits to me, to impress his friends.

"Fine, whatever. Blow me off. You think you're cool. Do whatever you want. See that Corvette?" responded the agent, according to Lozano. There was a nice yellow Corvette parked out in front of the park. He let the four boys' eyes settle on the sleek car.

"What about it?" Lozano asked.

"It belongs to my boss." Again the recruiter paused for effect. "My boss, who has only been in the Border Patrol for two years more than me, is driving around in that bad-ass car. Wouldn't you like to be driving around that car?"

The problem is, Lozano points out, little kids would think this was cool, as he himself did briefly, he admits. "[But] it just hits you weird," says Lozano. "It seems funny to wave the little toy in front of a little kid and say check out that Corvette, it could be yours if you chase around your own people." In a place like Nogales, where opportunities beyond minimum wage are difficult to come by, such words carry weight. Every kid anywhere near the border knows that in Border Patrol agents' first year they can earn more than double that of a secondary-school teacher—who makes $30,000 a year in Nogales, and that's a good job in the city's minimum-wage economy.

During a lunch break at the Poppies Festival back in El Paso, both Cisneros and Cadena tell me that there are often problems because some of the kids don't bring any money, "even though we tell them to bring money for lunch." A lot of them come from "tough backgrounds," and their families don't have much money. "But we can't just lend them money every week." They need to plan out to have money, they say; it's a part of the program to learn this sort of responsibility. They have to know that there will be consequences if they don't bring their money.

The fiscal discipline taught through the Explorer program, though, is multifaceted, as Cisneros explains while we, and most of the kids, eat Taco Bell fast food. Today, ten or so Explorers do not go to the Poppy Festival. Rather, they are hitting gas stations in El Paso with boxes of chocolates to fund-raise for a trip to Washington, D.C., for Law Enforcement Week later that year. Cisneros says that the fund-raising efforts can get a little sticky at times, especially when prospective money-givers dislike the Border Patrol.

"Sometimes they come up to the kids," he says and then pauses, remembering a specific incident. "*The kids*," he repeats, his voice rising with emotion and disbelief. "So they'll come up and say, 'the Border Patrol, are you kidding me? You locked up my sister and now you want to give me your money?'"

But then you also get the opposite, he says. You get the "Yeah, the Border Patrol! You guys need to lock up those Mexicans."

In moments like these, Cisneros says, "I want to hide

under something." Then he pauses and looks up at the blue sky and back again.

"You know what? There *is* a disparity. In the richer, whiter part of town," and he points off to the north, "they are all for us and want to buy the whole box of chocolates."

"But in the south," says Cisneros, and then he looks toward Cadena and stops talking. They are both thinking of the poorer, more Mexican part of town. "We don't even go there," they say in unison.

Yet these are the very neighborhoods, areas around Bowie High School, from which Border Patrol recruits many of their Explorer cadets. They go into classrooms with videos that show teenagers doing intense law enforcement exercises with their red guns. The videos are edited with the cutting-edge music of Vernon Reid, the founder of the band Living Colour, whose noisy cover of Radiohead's "The National Anthem" is part of the video's sound track. Throughout the presentation, words such as EXCELLENCE, DEVELOPMENT, SACRIFICE, TEAMWORK, and HONOR flash on the screen. If the prospective teenager gets motivated, they cannot immediately become an official Explorer. First, they have to go through a vetting process and face the dreaded Border Patrol oral board.

Cisneros says that in many ways, the Explorer application process mimics the Border Patrol's real-life hiring process, which is, his eyes tell me, not easy. The Border Patrol candidate goes off-site, to a hotel room where three or four senior agents yell out different scenarios to see how the candidate responds. The agents are rude, they scream, and they question the applicant's every move. They are also testing the candidates' ability to stand their ground.

Explorers have to go through a similar process. Three

Border Patrol advisors are sitting there, staring down the kid as if in an interview. Instead of barking out law-enforcement scenarios, however, they subject the applicant to something more like a moral interrogation. Cisneros recollects one such scenario with a seventeen-year-old:

"Have you ever drank?"

"No."

"Have you ever smoked?"

"No." The kid pauses. "Yes."

"Oh, how much?"

The kid winces.

"Tobacco?"

"No, marijuana," the kid says.

"Marijuana?" Cisneros says as if I'm the kid, "Don't you know that's against the law?"

"In order to become an Explorer," they tell the kid, "you will have to stop that." Cisneros doesn't tell me who the kid is, but that he is here today at the festival—a success story. The Border Patrol is not only an agency with a mission, but also a moral force. Its aim is to create the ideal U.S. citizen, the "true-blooded American guy and girl," in the words of A. J. Lowenthal.[17] As Lozano says, there is a religious resonance to the Border Patrol, a feeling of gospel to its mission.

I Want to Be a Border Patrol Agent

"I want to be a Border Patrol agent," fourteen-year-old Miguel Martinez tells me in his house in Nogales. He comes from the same place as Andres Lozano, where bored kids shuffle from Peter Piper Pizza to City Hall and back. Martinez comes to the door dressed in the camouflage uniform of the Civil Air Patrol. We first talk with his mother, in Spanish. He is in the CAP youth program, its equivalent of the Explorers. While not the Border Patrol, the Civil Air Patrol does run surveillance missions over the borderlands. Throughout the interview, Martinez insists that he doesn't want to work in an office, that he wants an "active" job. He loves to fly, he says. He likes the horses, the ATVs; that's why he wants to become a Border Patrol agent.

Martinez's athletically challenged brother also wants to be a Border Patrol agent. Problem is, he only lasted two weeks in the Explorer program. Lenny liked the exercise they did when they simulated breaking into a house to go after an intruder. They got to handcuff him and arrest him. But Lenny doesn't like the marching part of it so much.

Another Border Patrol prospect is Cory Roddey from the Explorer post in Naco, Arizona. He says, "Ten years from now, when I'm twenty-seven, I'll probably be in the Border Patrol stationed somewhere around here. . . . And if I could pick a post, it would be right here. Naco Station. Truth is, I have no desire to go to Mexico at all. I just don't find it very interesting. I like it here, and I can't find any reason to go over there."[18]

Luckily for Miguel, Lenny, and Cory, there will be plenty of opportunities to get involved, to make a career. According to the 2005 article "College's Hottest New Major: Terror" in the *Washington Post*, "at hundreds of post-secondary schools, Sept. 11 is influencing how many topics are taught—from medicine to firefighting to politics to computer networking."[19] There are multifaceted dynamics driving this new trend: "legislation and policy, interest from students and faculty, demands from employers, a sense of mission—and money." And now the University of Texas, El Paso, is developing "educational programs" to academically prepare "current and future practitioners and researchers in the relevant disciplines" relating to "border security and immigration in the global context."[20] Their curriculum development will be certificate concentrations for undergraduates and grad students, associate degrees, four-year bachelor's degrees, and master's degree programs in border security and homeland security education.

Now you can major in the Border Patrol as an undergrad, even though to be an actual agent all you need is your high school diploma.

The homeland security major, like the Explorers program, focuses on border security and counterterrorism but goes into further and deeper realms of law enforcement—biosecurity, cybersecurity, chemical security, disaster relief, and defense on every single level of the "homeland." Whole new academic, vocational, and corporate realms have come into existence due to the fear of the United States coming under attack.

When Steven R. David, who directed the Homeland Security Certificate Program at Johns Hopkins University told the *Washington Post*, "Homeland security is probably going to be the government's biggest employer in the next decade,"[21] you could almost hear him saying the same thing to his students. What the Explorers are doing is valuable career training for an expanding market that needs employees.

CriminalJusticePrograms.com identifies more than 113 community colleges in every state offering homeland security degrees. The website says, "Those with a degree in homeland security may go on to work as a border patrol officer, a police officer, or a hazardous material removal worker." They say it is a "promising career field," with employment "expected to grow faster than average over the next four years."[22]

And the kicker, as always, goes back to the yellow

Corvette. Such a degree can "boost your income, with the average border patrol officer earning more than $64,000 per year."

The Martinez brothers still do cross the border regularly to visit family and get haircuts. Even so, Lenny says that he thinks the large wall that slices through the community is good. He says it keeps out the *desmadre*—the total fucking mess—without going into what exactly that means.

When Nogales piano teacher Gustavo Lozano, who is trying to connect the border youth's unique experience with music, asks Lenny and Miguel, both of them his students, if they would like to work for an agency that harasses and arrests fellow Mexicans, sixteen-year-old Lenny pauses, looks for words, and says, "Of course I don't want to arrest my own people . . . but I still like what they do." He offers no further explanation. Miguel is more defiant: "I wouldn't let that happen." He pauses. "I would sue them." In his camouflage you could almost see the fourteen-year-old's muscles tense up.

Their allegiances will be just another *desmadre* to be ironed out. This is clear to me as I watch Cisneros and the two Explorers in charge do the uniform check in the parking lot of the Border Patrol Training Center, with the sun barely breaking over El Paso. They go from kid to kid and do a march-step in front of each and every one of them. They lean over to make sure that each shirt is tucked in adequately, and they lean down even farther to make sure that the pants are tucked into the polished black boots. Subordination to authority, chain of command, and agency policy are indoctrinated through submission to the exercise. The correct way to dress, present yourself, and think are embodied and reinforced by the ritual, which is then followed by a lock-step march around the Border Patrol

Training Center two times, just as they do at the Federal Law Enforcement Training Center in Artesia, New Mexico, each and every day during the sixty-nine-day training conducted there.

But there is something else too. There is Silvestre Reyes's vision of camaraderie between the Border Patrol and the community. For an entire day, Border Patrol agents hang out with the kids, laugh with them, talk with them, and at times advise them. Maybe some of the kids don't like the marching or the uniform inspection so much, but they all seem to like Cisneros and Cadena. They, like Reyes, are examples of Mexican Americans from the border region who have found a career in the Border Patrol. And they, like Reyes, are only helping the Border Patrol's mission by doing nice things for children.

Close to where they were lined up in rows of four is a Border Patrol recruiting bus. It is about the shape and size of the kind of tourism bus you might see at a beach resort, and probably based on a similar marketing tactic. On the side of the vehicle is a large, fun image of an agent standing next to his SUV, looking into the desert landscape through a pair of binoculars. An ocotillo, a desert plant with whip-like stems, stands next to the agent as a symbol of a suspicious landscape. The supposition is that it is crawling with Cadena's "intruders," that the desert is both a crime scene and a war zone. Above the back window of the van is a question printed in large letters: ARE YOU UP FOR THE CHALLENGE?

chapter four

"EXACTLY THE WAY WE THINK"

When Border Patrol agents Bryan Gonzalez and Shawn Montoya pull their vehicles side by side on April 13, 2009, Gonzalez doesn't realize how much the conversation that they are about to have will affect his career. Gonzalez and Montoya are in the same sub-unit of the Deming station, located in southern New Mexico. They are parked fifteen feet away from the border fence, and they can see the Mexican state of Chihuahua from where they sit. It looks a lot like the U.S. side, an empty and mountainous desert landscape dotted with the yucca plants' long, sword-shaped leaves and large stem, and other desert shrubs. They are about twenty miles to the east from where General Pancho Villa and hundreds of revolutionary fighters invaded the United States and attacked the small border town of Columbus, New Mexico, on March 9, 1916.

Montoya claims that it all starts when Gonzalez pulls out that day's edition of the *El Paso Times*. There is an article about a U.S. citizen who was deported by the Los Angeles sheriff's office. The hour-long conversation between Gonzalez and Montoya will get heated. They will discuss Mexico. They will discuss citizenship. They will discuss the drug war. Gonzalez doesn't realize that what he says

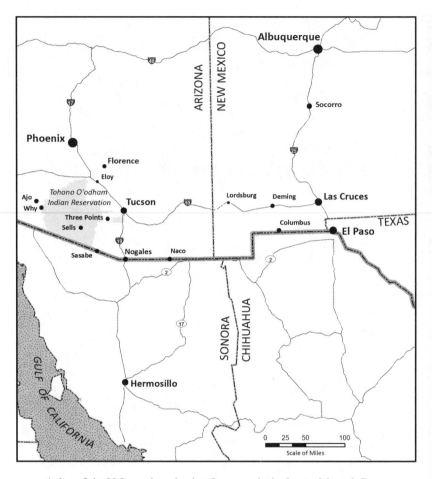

A slice of the U.S. southern border. Cartography by Louise Misztal. Data provided by ESRI and The National Map.

will bring into question his loyalty to the United States. He doesn't realize that there might be broader ramifications to what he says to another agent. His story is about what makes and unmakes a U.S. Border Patrol officer, and what happens when you articulate views inconsistent with those of the agency and the government of the United States of America.

Montoya and Gonzalez have been friends for a year. Today, they are assigned to a two-mile stretch along the borderline near a Border Patrol observation tower that the agents call the "Arenas sky box." As they look out into the high Chihuahua desert, the feeling in this economically depressed piece of country is that you can see into eternity. Sometimes dust storms rise out of complete stillness; the wind stirs up swaths of dust that blot out all.

Gonzalez is an agent known for his work ethic. Five months after he started working at the Deming station in January 2008, he won employee of the month, an almost unheard-of achievement for a rookie officer. He was born in El Paso, Texas, and he has a lot of family in Mexico, particularly on his mother's side, around Camargo, Chihuahua.

Montoya's nickname is "McLovin," after the nerdy kid from the movie *Superbad*. Montoya is tall and awkward, and wears glasses. He comes from the Santa Fe region of New Mexico, and, like Gonzalez, he wears his surname proudly. But to Montoya it is a testament to his Spanish, not Mexican, heritage. Gonzalez says that Montoya's father is a vet, and that he comes off as very "pro-American" in the "if you aren't with us, you're against us" sense. Montoya detests being called Mexican.

When Gonzalez and Montoya begin to talk, Gonzalez thinks it is just two agents burning time on another long shift. He thinks they are just shooting the shit. They always do it. Agents work ten-hour shifts, with mandatory and well-paid overtime. Much of that time, Gonzalez says, is spent doing nothing, sitting around. As an avid soccer player who likes to keep in shape, Gonzalez is pissed that he's gotten a little bulky, gone from 200 to 250 pounds.

Up to this point, Gonzalez has only caught five "undocumented aliens" since he started his career. He says there is so little activity where they are working that if someone calls in a "sign," meaning that they have seen footprints, everyone will show up because "everyone is starving for action." When he caught his first people without documentation, he was one of eighteen Border Patrol officers in hot pursuit of three Mexican males. It was at night and they could see by their footprints where the men were walking. A swarm of officers cut ahead onto the roads, and they had them on the cameras. The people they were pursuing were hiding in a bush.

Gonzalez is looking into the emptiness as he talks with Montoya. The first time Gonzalez feels the conversation getting heated is when Montoya asks him, according to Gonzalez's account, "Why are Mexicans coming to the United States to steal American jobs?"

Gonzalez looks across to Montoya. He has heard people in the Border Patrol say bad things about Mexicans plenty of times, but this time something in him breaks. He says, "You know I have ties to Mexico. You know that I am Mexican," by which he means that he is of Mexican ancestry. "All my family is still over there. My mom's family is still there. My mom has dual citizenship. I had dual citizenship until I was eighteen." He tells Montoya that there are no jobs in Mexico, that's why.

Montoya tells Gonzalez that when he joined the Border Patrol he needed to forget that he was Mexican. "You are either Mexican or American. You can't be both." Montoya will later write that he thought that Gonzalez was claiming allegiance to Mexico over the United States.

"I can't get away from the fact that I'm Mexican," Gonzalez says, "I mean, look at me, I'm brown-skinned. We're all Mexicans," he pauses. "Your last name is Montoya. Your last name is fucking Montoya. Go to fuckin' Chicago, and see how white you are there."

Even in his explanation to me, Gonzalez gets heated. "It doesn't matter what anybody tells me," Gonzalez tells me as if I'm Montoya, "nobody can take away the fact that I am proud to be a Mexican. It's part of who I am."

Montoya responds to this by calling Gonzalez a racist.

"I'm not racist," Gonzalez says, then corrects himself. "Yeah, I'm racist, that's the society we live in—I mean it's 'color-based.' I went to Illinois for six months, and I was a Mexican up there," Gonzalez tells him. "They were like, 'Hey, how are things in Mexico?' Good, I guess. I got asked, 'When did you get your citizenship?' I have to remind them that I was born in the United States."

Montoya looks at Gonzalez and is startled, and questions Gonzalez's loyalty to the Border Patrol. "Doesn't the oath of office mean anything to you?" Montoya asks Gonzalez.

Gonzalez tells Montoya that when he is on duty he gives 100 percent as a Border Patrol agent. When he is off duty, he tries to forget about it.

But Montoya, according to court documents, thinks that Gonzalez is telling him that he is a Mexican national and not a U.S. citizen. He thinks that Gonzalez is telling him that "he is only in the U.S. to work."

The conversation turns to the drug war. Gonzalez tells Montoya that he is from El Paso and that the drug issue is very close to anyone who lives in El Paso, "because we have the deadliest city, I mean I can see Juárez from my backyard. So that's something, I grew up going to Juárez every weekend and I'm of the belief that we can't go out and fix other people's problems, we have to fix the problems here domestically. We have to fix the drug-consumption problem."

Gonzalez mentions the organization Law Enforcement Against Prohibition. He tells Montoya that legalizing marijuana would make a big dent in the drug war, that it would reduce the violence.

It is a matter of debate exactly when a third Border Patrol agent, Richard Carrasquillo, pulled up in his green-striped government vehicle and entered the conversation between Gonzalez and Montoya. Gonzalez says that he didn't show up until after the conversation is well over. Montoya claims to have radioed Carrasquillo to come and join the conversation in progress. Carrasquillo claims that he was there during the heat of the debate. Carrasquillo is a military veteran who had just joined the Border Patrol. He is thirty-nine years old and of Puerto Rican descent. According to Gonzalez, he likes to smoke cheap cigars. Gonzalez got mad at him often because every time Carrasquillo drove Gonzalez's Border Patrol truck it would come back reeking of tobacco smoke. He would tell him, "You can't be smoking, it's against regulations to be smoking inside a vehicle. You can't be doing that shit."

Gonzalez often got on Carrasquillo's case too, while doing the paperwork for the people that they caught. This is Gonzalez's forte; he has a knack for it. He is one of the few agents who likes doing paperwork. Gonzalez likes to advise the people who get caught entering the country without authorization. He tells them to try to do it the right way. He tells them that their money is wasted coming up here. He tells them that they "could've at least tried to apply." But Gonzalez says they're mostly tired and don't pay attention. "They're like, let me go on my way. Let me try again."

Carrasquillo says that he saw Montoya and Gonzalez in their government vehicles, which were facing each other. He says he exited his vehicle, and he "heard Border Patrol Agent Gonzalez making the following statements: he did not consider himself an American, and he does not believe in or care for the U.S. Constitution, declared himself a socialist and stated that the United States should be a socialist country. He stated that he considered himself a Mexican. I considered this statement as a testimony of his allegiance to Mexico and not the United States." Then Carrasquillo said that he "witnessed BPA Montoya ask BPA Gonzalez, "Why don't you go back to Mexico?" BPA Gonzalez responded that "there are no jobs in Mexico."

Thirteen days later, Carrasquillo sent a Report of Unethical Behavior to Officer Daniel C. Serrato, who is in charge of the Border Patrol's Deming station. Serrato forwarded the report to the Washington, D.C.-based Joint Intake Center. On May 5, 2009, CBP Internal Affairs Special Agent Teena Gayle was assigned to work the case out of the Dallas Field Office for Investigation.

The Buckeye Blitz

In 2007, Bryan Gonzalez was just a dude working at Circuit City, sensing that the country was on the verge of an economic collapse and that Circuit City was going to go down with it. He was right on both counts. A history major, he was going to school when he found out that a friend of his had joined the U.S. Border Patrol. "What am I going to do with a history major?" he asked out loud.

The Border Patrol was in its massive hiring surge, trying to hire 6,000 agents in two years. The goal was to go from 12,000 to 18,000 agents. Although at the time of this writing, in November 2013, the figure is more than 21,000 and there are calls to double again the ranks of the Border Patrol, the 2007 spurt was going to be the agency's most accelerated growth in its history. In two years Border Patrol was going to add more agents than it did from its inception in 1924 to the early 1990s, when it grew to a little more than 4,000 agents.

Gonzalez had always been attracted to working in law enforcement—"the FBI, the CIA, all that stuff." But his first thought was economic. He wanted a stable job with benefits and a nice salary. With the obligatory overtime, even a rookie agent can earn close to $70,000 a year.

Like a multinational corporation trying to pitch product, the Border Patrol hired private companies Image Media Services and JWT INSIDE for the hiring binge. Image Media Services calls itself a team of "storytellers." According to its website, "all great brands are built around a compelling story. To shape a company, sell a product, or achieve a goal—an emotional connection needs to be made."[1] With this philosophy, the Border Patrol's message was revamped. The new brand would symbolize that the Border Patrol was going beyond its traditional mission of, as the CBP publication *Frontline* put it, "intercepting illegal aliens, smugglers, and drugs." The brand would signify that the Border Patrol would guard "our nation from a wider scope of threats than ever before."[2]

Recruiting brochures carried a new brand image, as if the Border Patrol were a fast food restaurant and needed its own golden arches to be identified by the public. The words PROTECTED BY U.S. BORDER PATROL were stamped over an outline of the United States, surrounded by a light green circle. The brochure warned that "facing threats to America at our border frontiers puts Border Patrol agents on the front line in the war on terror." But it continued to say that "despite the dangers, the vast majority of agents enjoy the work."

From this came a slick, nationally broadcast Border Patrol TV commercial. The ad begins by showing gorgeous mountainous landscapes and a lone Border Patrol jeep traveling on a dirt road at dusk, presumably on the U.S.-Mexico border. The image then changes to a small white child wearing a rabbit costume and riding a tricycle. We seem to be in a suburb in the U.S. Northeast. As the camera focuses on the innocent face of the child, rabbit ears cocked back, a narrator with a deep voice says, "Every day on the job, there is a child to protect." Border Patrol agents riding on horses replace this image for a moment, before the camera focuses on an African American woman and her daughter playing the piano in an affluent home. "Every mission, a family," the narrator continues. There is an image of a lone man rappelling from a helicopter. "Every day we defend our freedom. Our liberty. And our way of life." After "life" the camera pans to the image of a white couple, one of them swinging on a tire, a picture of complete rural happiness.

"Our calling is to protect the people of our country," the narrator says, "and this to us"—now a Border Patrol agent is shown returning to his two-story suburban home—"hits very close to home." The agent embraces his daughter and then walks into the house.[3]

Border Patrol's 2008 "Buckeye Blitz" conducted simultaneous recruiting events in seven different cities in Ohio to "make use of a statewide media campaign and to build on previous recruiting success in that state by capitalizing on the current unemployment and housing trends." The "Sunshine Blitz" followed this prototype into Florida. CBP officials say that it would take "200,000 recruits"[4]— presumably by which they meant aspirants—to increase the current ranks of the Border Patrol by 6,000. They went to the Indiana Black Expo and Job Fair. They reached out to local police, outdoor hunters and fishers, military videogamers, and even high school graduates who might be "extreme bikers, skaters, or skiers."[5] Their "Tiger Teams" had "take-down" events in Chicago, El Paso, Tucson, and Miami. They had targeted efforts with army, navy, Marine Corps, and air force installations. They expanded their efforts overseas to a military base in Germany in order to leave their "awareness footprint."[6]

From 2007 to 2009 there was the NASCAR sponsorship. Recruiters were on hand before, during, and after every race. A car was blazoned with the words BORDER PATROL and the number 28, because the federal agency was founded on May 28, 1924. The car had the dark green PROTECTING AMERICA motto on its hood, and forest green stripes that matched the uniform. The Border Patrol car was driven by NASCAR legend Kenny Wallace, who never won a race for Border Patrol but at times had actual green-uniformed agents in his pit crew. "I look forward to helping them continue to raise awareness," Wallace said, "to recruit men and women to protect our borders."[7] Wherever he went, the sponsorship showed up on commercials, television broadcasts, billboards, and on the sides of metropolitan buses. At an event in Richmond, Virginia, Border Patrol chief David Aguilar led the crowd in the Pledge of Allegiance with five other agents standing solemnly behind him with their hands behind their backs. The Border Patrol was truly becoming a brand.

This recruiting thrust swept up not only Gonzalez but Montoya and Carrasquillo as well. Before Gonzalez knew it, he no longer worked at Circuit City and was on his way to being hired by the U.S. Border Patrol. Like many agents, Gonzalez believed he was starting a career—a job with a good salary and benefits—a job that, as the commercial suggests, you could dream on: the house, the family, the American Dream.

Do You Consider Yourself a Socialist?

It is July 2009, and Gonzalez's field operations supervisor calls him into his office. He tells Gonzalez that he has to show up in El Paso on Monday. He tells him that there is an Office of Internal Affairs investigation.

Gonzalez is flabbergasted. He racks his brain trying to figure out what he's done. An internal investigation is huge. He doesn't remember anything. What did I do? Did I do something wrong? Did I see anyone do anything wrong? He is baffled. Gonzalez knows that he is one of the better ones at the station. He talks to a senior Border Patrol officer who puts him in touch with a union representative. Gonzalez and the union representative meet up before entering the building on Executive Drive in El Paso. Gonzalez has never met the man before, but he feels immediately comfortable with him. "He is a cool guy, really dedicated to helping the agents out."

They enter a little office, and behind the desk sits Teena Gayle, dressed in a business suit. Gonzalez is out of uniform, disarmed, and wearing a button-down shirt. Gayle is nice and straightforward, and Gonzalez says one of the first things she asks is if he recalls the conversation that he had with Shawn Montoya. Gonzalez's eyes go to the ceiling, "This is about *that*?"

Although he is telling me this years later, Gonzalez says the word "that" as if he is just as surprised about it now as he was when it happened. The following dialogue is taken verbatim from the court transcripts.

Gayle asks: "Where were you born?"

"El Paso, Texas," Gonzalez responds.

"Do you have dual citizenship?"

"I did until eighteen years of age."

"What countries?"

"U.S. and Mexico."

"Did you ever say: 'I don't consider myself an American?' " Gonzalez looks at her, sitting right across the desk, with disbelief on his face.

"Not that I remember," he tells her. "Some American ideas, like social, not political, I don't agree with" [*sic*].

"Did you ever say: "I do not believe or care for the United States Constitution"?" Now Gonzalez feels ashamed. He knows he is "under threat," and that if he doesn't answer he will lose his job. He has to answer, despite "the ridiculousness of it," he tells me.

"No."

"Did you ever say: 'The United States should be a socialist country'?"

Gonzalez looks at her long enough for her to admit that she is just joking. When she says nothing and continues to wait for a response, Gonzalez only says: "No."

At this point Special Agent Richard Lopez walks in. Gonzalez says that when he introduces himself, Lopez pronounces his last name like an Anglo. He is wearing cowboy getup—boots and a tie with the two little strings. Gonzalez says that while Gayle is just asking questions, Lopez is "kind of being an asshole." They start playing "good cop, bad cop." Lopez is aggressive. Gonzalez says that Lopez tries to intimidate him.

"Did you ever say that you keep your allegiance to Mexico?"

"As far as being Mexican heritage, yes, but not as government."

"Did you ever say that the drug problems in America are due to the American demand for drugs, therefore Mexico supplies it?"

"Yes."

"Are you a member of any organization or website that is for legalizing drugs?"

"Yes, I am not a member, but I read the website of LEAP."

The questions from Lopez get more and more aggressive. He is sitting off to the side of the desk, directly facing Gonzalez. He is poised, according to Gonzalez, so that "if I do anything he's ready." He's intimidating.

"Are you loyal to the U.S. government?"

"Yes."

"Are you loyal to Mexico? To the Mexican government?"

"No."

"Do you consider yourself an American?"

"Birthright, yes."

"Do you consider yourself a socialist?"

"I am partial to social beliefs," Gonzalez responds. Gonzalez again is thinking to himself: *Are you serious? Is this why I'm here?*

"Do you consider yourself to be trustworthy?"

"Yes."

Lopez sits up more, raises his voice and asks: "Have you ever planned to overthrow the U.S. government?"

This time Gonzalez almost says *c'mon*.

"No," he says.

"Do you remember the nature of the conversation [with Shawn Montoya]?"

"I was talking to Shawn Montoya about politics and my beliefs. I don't recall the specifics of the conversation."

"Did agent Carrasquillo join in the conversation?" This is the first time they mention Carrasquillo. At this point Gonzalez is not aware that Carrasquillo is the person who reported his conversation with Montoya. Gonzalez isn't aware that Gayle and Lopez met with Carrasquillo only a few days before, on July 13. Gonzalez is not aware that during the interrogation they are quoting Carrasquillo's accusations almost directly. Carrasquillo reported that Gonzalez "does not consider himself to be an American." Carrasquillo reported that Gonzalez "does not believe or care for the U.S. Constitution."

Gayle and Lopez record that Gonzalez answers: "No, he came after the conversation was over. I didn't discuss anything with BPA Carrasquillo that was discussed with BPA Montoya." And they continue.

"Did you take an oath when you were hired?"

"Yes."

"Do you recall the oath?"

"Not word by word. To protect the U.S. Constitution and the laws of the country."

"Do you believe in the U.S. immigration laws?"

"Yes."

"Did you ever say: 'I'm only here to work, because there are no jobs in Mexico?'"

"No."

"Are you loyal to the Mexican Government?"

"No."

"Do you believe that the U.S. Constitution is prejudiced towards minorities?"

"It is perfect on paper."

Gonzalez refuses to take a polygraph examination. He tells them that, based on the evidence available, it is unreliable. He also tells Gayle that he does not give his statement freely and voluntarily. He tells them he is compelled to give this statement "with fear of possible termination of my employment."

Gayle says, "Thank you."

The union rep says the worst-case scenario is that "they fire you, but you'll get your job back." Gonzalez heads back to Deming wondering what the hell just happened.

In the U.S. Border Patrol, like the U.S. military, there are many instances when people yell at you, many moments when people treat you like shit. This is how a Border Patrol agent is made or unmade. You must be able to perceive and understand clear, bright lines of division. There is no blurriness. You have to be made to defend the lines of division until you are breathless, even if they are coming at you from all sides, even if "they" are beating the shit out of you. But Gonzalez thinks that there is something about this whole incident that seems different.

The Red-Man-Suit Brawl

There are many rites of passage to become a Border Patrol agent, and Gonzalez passed them all with flying colors. Gonzalez tells me that he left the Border Patrol academy—sixty-nine days of intense training—enthusiastic about the job and in good physical shape. The rites of passage, however, are not easy.

One is called "the red-man-suit brawl." All the training officers dress in red, with excessive padding. Each wears a flexible chest protector with air in it, padding for the knees and elbows. Each wears a red martial arts helmet. They look as bulky as football players. They are at the Federal Law Enforcement Training Center in Artesia, New Mexico, a Border Patrol training center where civilians become federal agents or are broken and rejected.

Everyone is waiting in line. When you are in line, you can hear the wall shaking. Each training agent has to go in one by one. When they come out they are breathless, some have bloody noses. The instructors are not supposed to punch the prospective agents directly in the face, but mistakes happen. Mistakes happen, Border Patrol agent Baxter tells me, all the time.

Baxter is an Anglo agent from the Pacific Northwest. When they come out of the room, Baxter tells me, the training agents drop to the ground, relieved that it is over. This is happening toward the end of the sixty-nine-day training. There are more, Baxter tells me, but this is one of the Border Patrol "rites of passage."

When you enter the room, there are three Border Patrol instructors. They are big. The point of it, they say, is to overcome exhaustion. The point is not to give up. You are nervous, Baxter tells me, amped up. The three instructors give him a chance to approach. He kicks one of them before they throw him to the ground. They throw him against the walls. They punch him everywhere except in the face.

"Does it hurt?" I ask.

"It hurts, but I'm more worried about breathing." He flails back, almost blindly. They throw him to the ground. They kick him on the ground. One is behind him, choking him. They sit on him, smother him, and he can't breath. He starts to panic. The room they are in is small and has no ventilation.

"It is hard to breathe," Baxter stresses again and again. Then they let you up, but not as a break. You stand up and they punch and kick and throw you against the wall again. Three minutes is an eternity. And then it's suddenly over.

"This isn't even the worst rite of passage," Baxter tells me, "there's even worse." Some of the military guys, Baxter tells me, take the training in stride. He gets the sense that they've seen "some pretty horrible stuff" in Iraq and Afghanistan.

You arrive at Artesia, Baxter tells me, after a long ride from Tucson, or, in Bryan Gonzalez's case, from El Paso. Everyone is dressed in civilian clothing on the Border Patrol's rental bus; nobody has a uniform yet. You are just staring out the window, oblivious. The moment the bus comes to a stop a senior agent storms on board. He is wearing the Border Patrol's campaign hat. As Gonzalez puts it, this "big old guy in the ranger [hat], you know, the Smokey the Bear hat we have, he gets on the bus and starts yelling at you like a drill sergeant." It's a different uniform than the one used in the field. It has brass; it is the fancy, shiny, formal uniform used for funerals and award ceremonies.

He is yelling very loudly. He is telling the agents, who up to this point had been lounging, to get off the goddamn bus and to leave their stuff lined up on the goddamn sidewalk. They are directed to a classroom. The instructor walks up and down the rows yelling at everyone. He tells them how messed up they are. He comes to Baxter and pulls his hair and says his hair is too long. He tells him that he hasn't shaved well enough. This is the point, Baxter says, where you "lose your freedom."

You are quickly "learning to become part of the culture," he says. There isn't even time to regret your decision. There isn't even time to think. "You are immediately expected to conform to a certain look and standard," Baxter says, "and the point is that not everyone is meeting or conforming to it."

"It's like the military," Baxter tells me. The idea is that you subvert your individual self for the greater good of your unit. All ego must go out the door, and you are no longer yourself, rather a self in a role that you are told will be "heroic" later. But not yet. There are no first names, just last names. You can't just go from building to building. You have to get into formation and march. You chant while you march in two columns of twenty-five people. If you step out of line there is an instructor who will say, "Step in, you fucking moron." Each class has its own flag.

In the morning there are classes on nationality and immigration law. Cadets will learn to "[verify] the classification of aliens, determine the legality of status, recognize violations, and initiate appropriate action." There is the dreaded, at least by some, Spanish class where agents learn to conjugate verbs in the imperative, so that they can interrogate and give orders to people who have been detained or captured. "It's nothing like a conversational Spanish class," Baxter tells me. In the late morning there is the physical training—running, obstacle course, swimming. In the afternoon there is firearm instruction with assault rifles, shotguns, pistols, M-4s. Students will learn survival shooting techniques, judgment shooting, quick point, and instinctive reaction shooting. They will learn how to skillfully execute pursuit driving, vehicle stops (high- and low-risk), night driving, 4x4 off-road driving, and SUV/van evasive driving.

The most painful thing, Baxter tells me, worse than the red-man-suit brawl, is the pepper spray. It too is a rite of passage. The worst thing about it is that you know it is going to happen. An instructor says keep your eyes on me while you do jumping jacks. You are outside next to the track, and it is hot and you are beginning to sweat. You keep doing the jumping jacks, wondering when it will happen. The instructor begins to hose down your eyeballs with pepper spray. It takes a second to kick in, and when it does it is stingingly painful. This isn't over-the-counter pepper spray, it is law-enforcement grade, Baxter tells me. An instructor approaches you, carrying a fake baton. And he starts to fight you. He holds up fingers and you see them, blurry fingers, and he asks, "How many fingers am I holding up?"

If you make it through all this, you are assigned to your station. For Bryan Gonzalez it is Deming, New Mexico. Gonzalez is an ideal agent when he leaves the academy. He tells me that the Border Patrol boot camp was one of the most fun things he's ever done because he got paid to "work out, shoot guns, and drive cars. . . . I got into great shape. Never shot guns before. I fell in love with guns."

September 16
Almost two months have passed since Gonzalez's interrogation in El Paso, and now the field operations supervisor tells him that he needs to show up at the station at 6:00 a.m. on Monday, September 16, 2009. This is a big deal, because Gonzalez is working a "swing" shift that goes from 4:00 p.m. to 2:00 a.m. He knows it's a big deal. Getting there so early when you are working swings is a big deal.

He gets to the Deming station at 6:00 a.m. They aren't ready for him, and he sits at a table in the hallway near the door where everyone enters. He knows something is up, because the supervisors who would normally shake his hand and greet him walk by without acknowledging his presence. He begins to fret. He asks a passing supervisor what is going on.

The supervisor says, "Just sit there." He sits there for five minutes. Five turns to ten. Ten becomes fifteen.

September 16 is Mexico's Independence Day. The night before, every central plaza in every Mexican city from Ciudad Juárez to Tapachula celebrated by reenacting the famous 1810 *grito* of priest Miguel Hidalgo, the rebel yell that began Mexico's War of Independence from Spain. Gonzalez is in full uniform, as if he is ready to work. The field operations supervisor approaches him and says, "C'mon."

Gonzalez walks down the hallway. He's never before exchanged one word with Daniel Serrato, the Border Patrol chief of the Deming station. They walk into Serrato's office, a spacious office with an imposing desk. Serrato is sitting behind the desk. His combed-back hair is black, peppered with gray.

"Take off your gun belt," commands Serrato.

Those are the only words that Gonzalez hears.

They keep talking, but for a moment all he can see are moving lips. His whole world crashes. He thinks to himself: *What am I going to do? Nobody is going to hire me now. It's over.*

"I mean, I've always wanted to be in law enforcement," Gonzalez tells me, "so my dream ended right there."

Serrato reads the termination letter written by El Paso Sector Chief Victor Manjarrez. Gonzalez looks at the front of Serrato's cherrywood desk as he reads the letter in his hand with his reading glasses. "Dear Mr. Gonzalez,"

Serrato says. Gonzalez is blocking him out, but hears the flotsam and jetsam.

"The report of investigation revealed that on April 13, 2009, you entered into discussion with BPA Shawn Montoya and made the following comments." Serrato reads: "'Legalizing all drugs would end the drug war in Mexico,' or similarly stated words. You also told him that you were a member of an organization that is for legalizing drugs."

Serrato reads: "According to BPA Montoya, you told him that you were a Mexican and not an American citizen and that you were in the United States only to work. When BPA Montoya asked you why you were in the United States, you replied by telling him that 'there are no jobs in Mexico,' or words to that effect."

"According to BPA Montoya," Serrato reads, "during the conversation you referred to Mexico as your country and the United States as BPA Montoya's country."

Serrato continues reading on and on. He says, "Your personal views are contrary to the core characteristics of Border Patrol Agents, which are patriotism, dedication, and esprit de corps."

One month before Gonzalez would have ended his two-year probationary period, Manjarrez tells him he "will not be retained as a Border Patrol Agent."

"You are still my employee for the rest of the day," Serrato tells Gonzalez. So he says that what's going to happen is that one of the supervisors is going to take Gonzales to his house to give back "all my stuff," as if his government-issued uniform and equipment belonged exclusively to Serrato. You're going to have to clear out your locker, he says. "Give me your shirt," Serrato says. Gonzalez unbuttons and pulls off his green Border Patrol shirt for the last time. He hands over his shirt. He is just in a white V-neck

T-shirt and his Border Patrol pants. "They couldn't take those off me, "Gonzalez tells me, but "if they could've, I bet they would've."

They take Gonzalez from office to office where he signs papers. They take him to his locker, where he clears out all of "Serrato's stuff." "These fucking assholes paraded me around that station," Gonzalez says. He sees his former coworkers in the halls of the station. They keep asking what's wrong, what's wrong? Gonzalez doesn't answer, doesn't say a thing. His world is shattered and now he is deeply embarrassed. As he walks around the station in his T-shirt a supervisor follows close behind him, "like I was going to do something crazy." Gonzalez says, "I felt like a criminal. . . . literally, the guy was walking behind me as if I killed someone." He says they ordered him around for hours: "Go here. Go there. Go here. Go there."

Gonzalez says, "It was just the worst fucking day of my life. I can't even explain the hurt I felt." And that's the beginning of the depression. For months he doesn't want to do anything, he feels bad for himself. He hits the bars. "I mean that's a feeling that I had never ever felt before. I've always been good at everything I try. At least I try my hardest. And they told me I wasn't good enough. And in my heart I knew that I was better than good enough."

I ask him if he really thinks that they were telling him that he wasn't good enough, or if he thinks they are telling him something else.

Gonzalez responds: "You've got to think exactly the way we think."

Tonk

Benny Longoria and his partner are five miles west of the Baboquivari mountain range and three miles north of the

U.S.-Mexico border. They are on the Tohono O'odham reservation, located in southern Arizona. It is July and really hot—100-plus-degrees hot. They are on a normal patrol and driving down a dirt road when they see the footprints. They are fresh tracks. Longoria and his partner look at each other. His partner is an Anglo guy from West Texas. According to Longoria, like most in the Border Patrol, "he's a gun guy."

Whenever I see Longoria he asks me about Bryan Gonzalez's case, which is now before the U.S. District Court for the Western District of Texas. Gonzalez is the defendant against former El Paso sector chief Victor Manjarrez. Longoria monitors the case closely, because he knows he too is on the fringes of the Border Patrol. He is a firearms instructor and has impeccable aim, yet to the chagrin of his fellow agents, he hates guns and doesn't possess his own personal gun, which makes him quite an anomaly. He constantly critiques what he calls the "gun culture" of the Border Patrol.

Both Longoria and his partner get out of the vehicle and begin to follow the tracks. Every day, many hours are spent following tracks. They figure that the people have barely crossed. Maybe they're just an hour from the border, on foot. It is hot. It's as if you are walking in the inside of a light bulb. They have been following the footprints for about an hour when Longoria sees someone—a woman. She is hiding, he thinks. There's a giant mesquite tree, and she is resting on the ground beneath it. Her back is to the agents. Her arm is up over her head. She is trying to hide. She is trying to duck down. She is trying not to be seen. The agents creep up on her. They get closer and closer. She is wearing blue jeans, a striped navy shirt.

When they get ten feet away and she still hasn't

moved. Longoria says, "Oh shit. Why isn't she reacting?" She should be reacting by now. They are close. There is a shrub in front of her. The tall buffalo grass waves gently in the breeze. In Arizona in July you can hear the subtle sizzle of the heat.

The moment is surreal and suddenly, for Longoria, depressing. There they are, in the middle of nowhere. There's nobody around for miles. There is nothing. Maybe at night, Longoria says, you can see a light in the distance.

"Hey," Longoria says, "hello!" Nothing. He gets closer and closer. "Hello," he says, finally standing over her. He sees her face and spends a moment looking at her face. There is white stuff coming out of her nose. Her belly is puffed out. He looks at her shoes, her jeans, her striped shirt. She must have just died within the hour.

"How do you deal with it?" I ask Longoria, knowing that many of the more than 600 agents at the Casa Grande station have come across the bodies of people who perished trying to enter the United States. When you look at where bodies are recovered in southern Arizona, there is a thick red cluster of dots over the Tohono O'odham reservation, an isolated region of desert where many migrating people started crossing after operations sealed the urban areas. This was the third body Longoria had found in three years. Longoria says to deal with the death, the pain, you have to dehumanize it, you have to make it "less than human."

Longoria mentions "pseudo-speciation." He talks about an interview he'd heard with a Vietnam vet on National Public Radio. Longoria says: "You have to take a person and change their genus. Give them a whole different category. That's how he dealt with the combat in Vietnam. We could not stand to look at these bodies, he said, so you detach yourself. You give them a different name that then detracts from their humanness." According to the *Oxford English Dictionary*, "pseudo-speciation" refers to the tendency of members of in-groups to consider members of out-groups to have evolved genetically into different, separate, and inferior species relative to their own.

"What do you mean by that in a Border Patrol context?" I ask him.

"Tonk," he tells me. "The word 'tonk' expresses it all." It is a word that comes from a violent act. It describes the sound the butt of a Border Patrol flashlight makes when it hits the head of another person. In Border Patrol stations the word "tonk" is a commonplace description for the person whose papers are not in order. They are the people who most often receive the blow to the head.

Longoria gives me an example of how it is used in common, everyday Border Patrol. "This freakin' tonk wants something," he tells me, is the normal in-the-station lingo.

You would never hear anyone say: "This gentleman has a question."

I ask him if he's ever heard an agent say it that way, the polite way.

"I would be shocked." He pauses. "Super shocked."

Longoria thinks the evolving use of the word "tonk" parallels the deeper process of the border's militarization. He talks about the Border Patrol hiring Vietnam vets in the 1970s. He says that soldiers come with "certain predispositions." He talks about Timothy Dunn's book *The Militarization of the U.S.-Mexico Border, 1978–1992*, which offers a detailed analysis of U.S.-Mexico border policies in what Dunn describes as a "low-intensity conflict." Low-intensity conflict was developed in the 1980s for use in

Central American wars as a means of social control. It is not all-out war, but it does mean militarized responses to civilian problems.

The more the militarization, Longoria claims, the more frequent the use of the word "tonk," as if the two dynamics were indisputably intertwined. He remembers when he first heard the term in the 1990s, and how it increasingly became a part of the Border Patrol vernacular. With the late 2000s hiring binge that brought in more Iraq and Afghanistan war vets, "tonk" has become even more "culturally accepted."

In fact, the other day, Longoria was in the control room in the Casa Grande station, where all the radios are. An agent walked in and said: "I can't understand this 'tonk'; he's trying to speak English."

According to Longoria, the guy in the control room said: "I don't want him to speak English. I want him to speak white." Longoria says that at the root of the use of the word "tonk" is a certain acceptable racism of how a Border Patrol agent is socialized.

So it is a worldview in which the word "tonk" is a powerful part of Border Patrol vernacular, while the expression of pride in your Mexican heritage gets you fired. As Robert Lee Maril writes, "Anyone dumb enough to complain, criticize, or in any form convey a negative comment about the Border Patrol to a supe or higher-up may as well kiss his career goodbye. . . . A top-down hierarchy, the Border Patrol affirms, promotes, rewards, and compensates only those who follow orders, keep their mouths shut, and demonstrate personal loyalty to their immediate supervisors."[8]

Gonzalez says that finding a new job was tough. He had to repeatedly explain what happened with the Border Patrol, but he finally landed a job with Verizon.

Gonzalez first tried to fight his case through the Equal Opportunity Office. He claimed that he was discriminated against because of his Mexican heritage. But there are plenty of Latinos, many of Mexican heritage, in the Border Patrol, and the EEO judge ruled against him.

Anthropologist Josiah Heyman writes that Latino immigration officers "understand themselves as U.S. citizens who reject both domestic racism and ethnic loyalties that cross national borders."[9] In this sense, Gonzalez's gaffe is to proclaim his ethnic loyalty and to attempt to further understand serious political, social, and economic issues from a place where much of his family comes from. He never developed that clear bright line of division. He never, as Montoya said during their conversation, forgot his Mexican side. When I talk with Gonzalez, he fondly remembers visiting Mexico every summer for months, playing with his cousins at his relatives' farm. There is no doubt that Gonzalez considers his Mexican side to be not only a firm, but a beloved part of his identity. And that is the part that he needed to forget in order to become a true Border Patrol agent.

Longoria says his partner is a nice guy, even if he's a real "gun guy," into tactical stuff. Back at the Tohono O'odham reservation, when they find the body of the woman in the striped shirt, Longoria's partner is less fazed, although Longoria concedes that his partner might be feeling something that he isn't expressing. They call in the GPS coordinates. Headquarters in Tucson contacts the Tohono O'odham tribal police. The agents wait, with the body nearby, wondering what could've happened to cause her death.

When the tribal police come, they take her picture. They roll her over and take another picture. She is purple on one whole side of her body, a deep purple. The tribal police tell Longoria it is because the blood settles there. They bring out a big plastic body bag. The tribal police are used to this; it happens all the time. They work with stoic faces. They put the body on a cart and pull her out with an ATV. The body bounces up and down as the cart is pulled along the bumpy dirt road for a few miles. When they reach the paved road, Longoria helps to lift her, to put her in the back of the police truck parked there.

"I am nervous when I do it," he tells me, "I don't know why." After reporting it they continue to patrol, as they are expected to do. "Put that scene in Scottsdale," Longoria tells me, "and it is a tremendous event. If it were a white lady in Scottsdale, stop the presses."

After this, Longoria and his partner simply continue their shift. At the station there's no one to talk to about extreme or traumatic situations you face as an agent, except maybe the chaplain. If something hits you hard you just continue on with the proper dedication, patriotism, and esprit de corps. That is the lesson that Bryan Gonzalez never learned.

PART II

THE BOUNDARIES OF EMPIRE

> In our day, this global offensive plays a well-defined role. Its aim is to justify the very unequal income distribution between countries and social classes, to convince the poor that poverty is the result of the children they don't avoid having, and to dam the rebellious advance of the masses.
>
> —*Eduardo Galeano*

Galeano wrote this in the 1970s about U.S. family-planning campaigns throughout the world. He could've been writing this about post-9/11 U.S. boundary-building operations, both globally and domestically.

Like warfare, boundary-building relies on an enemy. Without the same explosiveness of war, it is waged slowly, until the original inhabitants of a place are enclosed by a seemingly permanent militarized zone. Officials tell the people who live there that they are surrounded by enemies and threats, maybe even their own neighbors, and that all the weapons and military hardware and surveillance make them more "secure." The enemy, in other words, must be perpetual.

Boundary-building is a very new dynamic of a very old imposition, and the following three chapters offer sharp glimpses of this in three very different places.

Border Patrol doing line watch just west of downtown Nogales. Since the mid-1990s, the Border Patrol presence in this community and many other popular urban crossing sites has increased dramatically. Photo by Murphy Woodhouse.

While it may seem that the days of killing or corralling Native Americans and annexing their territories are an ancient and forgotten chapter in U.S. history, the experience of the Tohono O'odham Nation show us that nothing can be further than the truth. Boundary-building on sovereign O'odham territory, which was bisected by the U.S.-Mexico border, has given us a post-9/11 Indian war, a renewed campaign of conquest against a quiet but indomitable force of community resistance.

Up north, U.S. officials say that the 4,000-mile Canada-U.S. border is more vulnerable to enemy incursion than the southern one, and since 2001 there has been a significant increase of Border Patrol agents and technological resources modeled after the prominent presence on the U.S. southern border. Unlike in the South, however, much less is heard about actual border-crossers.

Instead, Homeland Security forces with extra-constitutional powers are patrolling the 100-mile border zone, often targeting trains, buses, transportation stations, churches, and community centers from Port Townsend, Washington, to Detroit, Michigan, to Derby Line, Vermont. Maybe nowhere is the quiet but steadily advancing post-9/11 world of watchers and watched so pronounced as it is along the northern front.

This rapid expansion of "strong borders," however, is not limited to the United States. According to a member of the U.S. consulate in the Dominican Republic, the promotion of strong borders globally has been a part of the global war on terror. The reasoning is stated explicitly in the 9/11 Commission Report, which says, "9/11 has taught us that terrorism against American interests 'over there' should be regarded just as we regard terrorism against Americans 'over here.' In this same sense the American homeland is the planet."

Border Patrol agents are traveling throughout the world to train border guards in places like Iraq and Afghanistan. Often these are places where the United States spends an exorbitant amount of resources to project dominance and "protect its interests," such as the Haitian-Dominican border, an area that has long been considered "America's backyard" like most of Latin America and the Caribbean.

The next three chapters take a look at this boundary-building in places where divisions between good and bad, civilized and uncivilized, police and policed, watcher and watched, have become dramatically drawn and hardened, creating the blueprint of the post-9/11 nation and globe.

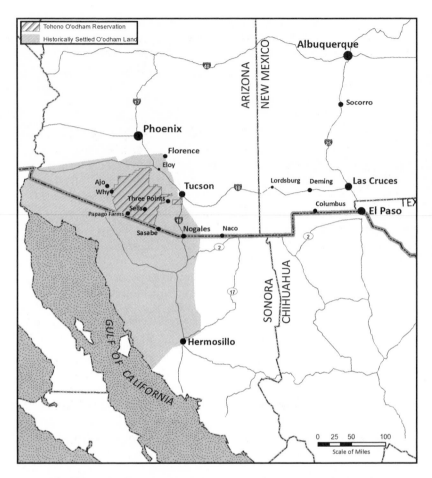

The Tohono O'odham traditional territory and reservation of today. Cartography by Louise Misztal. Data provided by ESRI and The National Map.

chapter five

UNFINISHED BUSINESS
IN INDIAN COUNTRY

When we stop the car, David Garcia opens the door, steps out, and walks straight to the metal border gate that officially separates the United States and Mexico. Garcia, an elder of almost sixty, has long graying hair that reaches to his shoulders. Without a word, the former Tohono O'odham tribal councilman opens the gate. He does this as if it were his automatic impulse. There is nobody on the other side waiting to come in, nor are we planning to cross into Mexico ourselves. Garcia opens it simply as if the barrier didn't belong, as if it were artificial and imposed, something to breach, something to open, something to resist.

Garcia stands in front of the open gate with Mexico's mountainous Sonoran Desert spread out behind him. There are the same gorgeous saguaros, arms extending upward to the sun, that one finds on the U.S. side of the divide. There are the same ocotillos, and cholla cacti whose spiny segments often puncture the shoes—and flesh—of people attempting to enter the United States unnoticed by traveling vast distances across the desert on foot.

With the border gate open to the world, I know it is

only a matter of time before the Border Patrol comes to investigate the area and close it.

We are in an isolated area near Papago Farms in late June, in the south western corner of the Tohono O'odham Nation in southern Arizona, the second-largest Indian reservation in the United States in sheer land mass. Though only a fraction of the Tohono O'odham's original land, today the nation's territory is the size of the state of Connecticut.

Up the rutted road about a mile from where Garcia and I stand is a Border Patrol Forward Operating Base. The base is more than just a center for mission communications and surveillance; it's a strategic presence demonstrating that the U.S. government is in a wartime posture that regards borders as front lines, whether or not they run through sacred Indian land or ruffle the locals' feathers. The Pentagon commonly used Forward Operating Bases in Iraq and Afghanistan as secure military positions to facilitate tactical operations in remote regions, essential for "gaining, maintaining, and expanding," as the Border Patrol's Ramiro Cordero told the *New York Times*.[1] Such bases are now commonplace along the U.S.-Mexico border, and there are two on Tohono O'odham territory. Never before has there been such a widespread presence of U.S. federal forces on the Tohono land.

Garcia is challenging the meaning of the closed gate. As many Tohono O'odham do in subtle ways every day on the reservation, he is also challenging those who impose and enforce that meaning: the U.S. Border Patrol. The border gate is between the vehicle barriers constructed by CBP after the Secure Fence Act of 2006, which called for 650 miles of fencing constructed along the 2,000-mile southern border. Set in concrete, the vehicle barriers are closely spaced posts spanning the seventy-five miles of border the Tohono Nation shares with Mexico. "Imagine a bulldozer parking on your family graveyard, turning up bones," nation chairman Ned Norris Jr. said describing the barrier construction in 2008. "This is our reality."[2]

With the opened gate provoking them, Border Patrol agents will be coming for us soon, but I see nothing but the heat waves coming up from the land under a scorching late-morning sun. Forecasters are predicting a 110-degree day, the hottest of the year. Even five minutes in this heat is enough to push us back into the air-conditioned car. One week later, it will be very close to here that agents will discover the remains of five people. This is one of those places, as mentioned earlier, that is supposed to be so isolated and dangerous that, according to Border Patrol strategy, nobody would dare to cross here.

We see the Border Patrol coming for us when we get back on the dirt road and head north. It is almost comical. There in the distance is the Homeland Security vehicle driving fast and kicking up a cloud of dust. The vehicle is coming toward us from the Forward Operating Base, backed by the bases's large antenna under a large sky and the empty desert behind it. Focusing on the scene, it was as if we could be anywhere—anywhere in the world that the United States attempts to occupy and control. However, we just look at the distant vehicle in silence; there is nothing we really need to say. We both know what is about to happen. The rumbling green-and-white SUV comes closer and closer. When it is thirty feet away, it skids to a dramatic stop with its sirens blaring. Two Border Patrol agents dressed in their quintessential green uniforms jump out of the SUV and rush at us.

"They don't have to do that," Garcia says, un-amused, as I stop the car.

One agent circles around to the back of the car to call in the license plate. The other approaches the window. When I roll down the window, I can see that the agent is far from calm. There is adrenaline snapping in the air. I wonder if the agent, his dark hair in a military flattop, is a combat vet who fought in Afghanistan or Iraq. Many of the new recruits are, and I assume he is too. He looks and acts like a soldier, but I can't be sure.

"What are you doing?" he asks us. His question is command-like, infused with the suspicion that we've done something wrong. His face, leaning into the car, is slightly red, as if he has been running, and round. Despite his authoritarian tone, he seems to be forcing a smile, squeezing out politeness.

"We went to look at the border," I reply.

"Why?" he asks without a pause.

"To report what's happening," I say, then add, "I'm a journalist from New York" (at the time I was living in New York City), hoping that would explain it.

Instead he leans into the vehicle, even more suspicious, as if that gave him a clue to some sort of unlawfulness.

"How do you know each other?"

"Through a friend," I reply.

"Oh, yeah, do you have a lot of friends in New York City?" the agent asks Garcia. His tone is laced with sarcasm, and this is the first time that he directly addresses the Tohono O'odham man who is in his home Chukut Kuk district, a place where his ancestors have lived for more than a thousand years. We are less than twenty miles away from where Garcia grew up, his family's land where they used to plant watermelon, squash, corn, and wheat, like most other Tohono O'odham people. This was well before armed federal forces, in the form of the Border

Patrol, installed and occupied permanent bases on the reservation.

Garcia's expressions and body language suggest that he has been dealing with the Border Patrol for far too long. And he has. As a former tribal councilmember, Garcia has had numerous dealings with Homeland Security. At one point he took it upon himself to go out to the borderline to monitor the men in green, much to the chagrin of the agents. Alone he would tail them in an old, beat-up car. However, as a former councilmember who is actively critical, Garcia is an anomaly. As with any other group of people, among the Tohono O'odham there is not one clear opinion regarding the Border Patrol. But the nation's official position, from its legislative council, has been one of collaboration. The tribal council has formally approved many Homeland Security projects, from more surveillance towers to more agents.

Like most Tohono O'odham, Garcia has been insulted by the Border Patrol before. This time the agent once again steps over a line by implying that the Tohono O'odham elder could not have friends in New York City. But Garcia gives him the benefit of the doubt and asks, "What?" just in case he didn't hear the agent correctly.

Instead of acknowledging Garcia's question, the agent orders him to produce some ID. Garcia pulls out his tribal membership card. The agent looks from the photo to Garcia several times, making a point of his doubt and suspicion.

"It's me," Garcia says, now visibly impatient.

"What is your citizenship?" the agent asks.

"Tohono O'odham," Garcia responds. This could get good, I think to myself. But the agent doesn't bite. He releases Garcia from his gaze and instructs me to state my citizenship. I tell him that I am a citizen of the United States.

"And who is this friend?" the agent asks, again. But this time I sense more in his voice than mere disbelief that we have a mutual friend. At first I can't tell what it is, but his tone and mannerisms—simmering with aggression and suspicion—seem to be another example of what everyday life can be like for the Tohono O'odham Nation when the U.S. Border Patrol imposes its authority. And this is what I have come here to learn.

Perhaps it is naive on my part to think that the agent would treat us better once he saw that Garcia was Tohono O'odham and that we are on his sovereign ancestral land. For one thing, even though I am a professional journalist, I am prohibited (by the Tohono O'odham Nation) from traveling off-road on the reservation without the accompaniment of a member of the nation.

However, the agent does not treat us any better. If anything, his suspicion deepens. Racial profiling seems to be in play: a Native and non-Native out in the middle of nowhere, but so close to the border, need to be examined closely. That the U.S. government recognizes the Tohono O'odham Nation as a "distinct, independent political"[3] community with a highly qualified sense of sovereignty seems to mean little to this agent. He doesn't appear to be aware that another body of laws, voted on by the O'odham and its legislative council, govern the land where he is standing. Or maybe it just doesn't matter to him.

According to the U.S. government, the international border that exists on Native American land is at many points "vulnerable"[4] to unauthorized entry. In the post-9/11 era, this sloppy, porous patch of border, in the government's eyes, is a full-fledged national security threat.

However, what I will learn is something that isn't explicitly stated in publicly accessible government documents: it isn't just the people who are searching for work or smuggling narcotics, but also the Tohono O'odham themselves who seem to be considered "foreign." This "messy" but ancient world of familial, social, political, economic, and spiritual cross-border community flies in the face of the black-and-white, good-and-bad nature of border security. The tone of the federal agent's voice makes everything crystal clear. He is in control, and he is just one of hundreds there to use borders, gates, guns, and a grid of global surveillance to enforce the hard fact that the United States of America trumps Tohono O'odham sovereignty and security—and anyone else's for that matter—like it or not.

The indigenous elder opened the border gate for a reason. Garcia was born on this land and is connected to this land, as was his father and his father's father and his father's father's father, going back centuries. The ancestral connection to the land, and the profound sense of dignity and autonomy with which it infuses the living Tohono O'odham community, arm it with something that is perhaps more powerful than any occupying force that has attempted to dominate these parts: perseverance.

Tohono O'odham Unconquered

In May 2010, six Tohono O'odham and Navajo activists chained themselves together inside the headquarters of the Border Patrol's Tucson Sector, 100 miles north of where Garcia and I are standing right now. They draped a banner in front of a receptionist who looked on helplessly through the plate glass and tried to command the activists to stop. His metallic voice said: "Don't touch the wall."[5] They touched the wall.

The yellow banner said: STOP MILITARIZATION ON INDIGENOUS LANDS NOW. They placed it directly below

framed headshots of President Barack Obama and Homeland Security Director Janet Napolitano. A man started to
sing a traditional indigenous song and kept rhythm with a
rattle. The Border Patrol receptionist clenched his phone.
He called for reinforcements. Approximately thirty con-
fused Border Patrol agents flooded the lobby in response,
but seemed uncertain how to react. This sort of full-force
bewilderment epitomizes the clash between Homeland
Security and those who, like the Tohono O'odham, have
been here long before the United States, Mexico, or Canada even existed.

With the presence of armed federal forces, things
have drastically changed for the Tohono O'odham on the
reservation. This has been the result of what Ed Reina,
public safety director of the Tohono O'odham Nation,
characterizes as the "funnel effect."[6] Border Patrol operations throughout Arizona, California, and Texas have
redirected heavy flows of migrating people onto the reservation, Reina told listeners on National Public Radio. Because the nation is "sovereign"[7] and remote, and because
there was less of a border-policing infrastructure, Reina
explained, starting in the early 2000s it saw an upsurge of
people entering to either search for work or to smuggle
drugs.

Migration has been the cause of people traveling over
O'odham land for a long time, but according to Tohono
O'odham Nation chairman Ned Norris, there were more
than 15,000 unauthorized border-crossers who traversed
the nation on a monthly basis in 2008, up from only a few
hundred per month in the 1990s. Norris complained that
the cost incurred by the already financially challenged
Tohono O'odham Nation, costs that included significant
health services and law enforcement, were more than $3

million per year. When Norris raised these issues with the U.S. Congress, he insisted that border policing was a federal responsibility, and that the federal government needed to help the Tohono O'odham with these costs. The 2008 timing of Norris's comments was impeccable, in the middle of the Border Patrol hiring surge that would bring thousands of additional agents to the force. Never in the history of Tohono O'odham contact with European powers had their lands been filled with so many armed federal forces, and Norris, pressed into a corner, was asking for more.

Norris's vision, however, contrasted with that of the anti-militarization activists in significant ways. The chairman told the U.S. Congress: "In response to the border crisis, the Nation has repeatedly partnered with Customs and Border Patrol and actively supported alternative strategies to walls, including vehicle barriers, towers, checkpoints, integrated camera-radar systems, and other measures that reduce negative impacts on tribal lands while still achieving the overarching goal of increased border security."[8]

The idea of border security is something new to the Tohono O'odham. Migrants and travelers have been passing through Tohono O'odham lands for hundreds of years. Semi-nomadic themselves, the Tohono O'odham, for the most part, have sympathized with the reasons people would choose to travel from one place to another, especially the need to eat. As has been stated again and again by O'odham people, their first instinct is to help a person along on the journey. "Some of this openness to migrants follows from generations of hospitality to newcomers and visitors to the desert," explains geographer Kenneth Madsen, "dating back to the point of Contact."[9]

Indeed, if in the 1600s the Tohono O'odham had not provided the Spanish with food, which only they knew how to gather from the desert, maybe the Spanish would not have set up its religious missions with their goals to convert, assimilate, civilize, and ultimately, along with the Spanish military's heavy hand, colonize and subjugate the indigenous people in the area. Some Tohono O'odham, whom the Spanish misnamed Papago, lived near the Spanish missions, participated in the rigorous courses of cultural indoctrination, and worked for food. At one point the Spanish even formed military auxiliaries of Tohono O'odham to help soldiers fend off attacks by the Apaches, a strange foreshadowing of the relationship the Tohono O'odham would have with the U.S. Border Patrol.

However, the Tohono O'odham were never entirely pacified by the Europeans' iron fist. Several uprisings by the O'odham—in 1695, 1751, 1756, and 1776—contested the authoritarian rule of the Spanish. According to Blake Gentry of the O'odham organization Gente de I'itoi, "O'odham rebellions during the early colonization (1535–1767) to intermediate colonization (1767–1835) reflect O'odham rejections of two manifestations of colonial society: unjust military and ecclesial punishment ranging from whippings to firing squads, and incessant land incursions which reduced their resource areas—due mostly to cattle in open range." Gentry characterized the 1751 Tohono O'odham uprising as the "largest and most well organized," which involved 1,000 O'odham with the intent of expelling the Spanish missionaries from their land. In some cases of O'odham revolt, "missionaries were killed and their missions burned to the ground."[10]

However, the most common form of O'odham resistance to the Spanish advance was more subtle, one of avoidance, a deep retreat into the desert, something that wasn't ideal, but was ultimately manageable for the ever-moving Tohono O'odham, whose name appropriately means Desert People. Historian Guadalupe Castillo—a long time professor at Pima Community College and cochair of the Tucson-based rights group known as the Coalición de Derechos Humanos—described this type of withdrawal to me as a "powerful type of resistance" that was used by the O'odham since the onset of the Conquest. This type of resistance is often not understood in the modern world, Castillo explained, because it does not involve direct aggression against the conquerors, but rather silence and a withdrawal to the autonomous and sovereign exercise of everyday life and indigenous cosmovision.

"The O'odham way of life is based on the land that held the remains of our ancestors since the creation of this world. The O'odham did not migrate from anywhere, according to our oral history," said nation member Ofelia Rivas, "Our creation tellings record our history and teach the O'odham principles of life. The survival of the O'odham today is based on our Him'dag," or traditional way of life. Rivas went on to say that the collaboration seen today between the nation and the Department of Homeland Security's inhumane border policies "is an outright violation of the O'odham Him'dag."

The Him'dag includes O'odham spirituality, arts, songs, storytelling (and the O'odham raucous and rollicking sense of humor), O'odham harvesting, medicinal plants, and family, to name some things. It includes freedom of mobility, freedom to travel throughout O'odham land to be able to practice Him'dag, and to visit sacred areas. During the era of Spanish domination, most O'odham were what Castillo now calls the "deep traditionalists" who moved deep into the desert—far from where the Spanish troops and missions frequented—in quiet yet powerful resistance to the subjugation of their land.

So it must have been quite the shock for the Tohono O'odham of the mid-1850s to find deep in their desert sanctuary a ragtag crew of U.S. soldiers and surveyors, there with the intent of imposing an international boundary between the United States and Mexico. This was after the Spanish empire dissolved, when Mexico gained independence in 1821. Before the boundary builders arrived, the Tohono O'odham were one of many indigenous communities whose land was within the Mexican republic.

An elderly Tohono O'odham man, bewildered at their presence, approached one of the soldiers in the surveying crew. Neither the old man nor any of the other O'odham knew that that this crew was coming. They did not know that an international boundary was going to be drawn, bisecting their land. The old man did not know about the 1853 Gadsden Purchase between Mexico and the United States that would draw the "final" international boundary between the countries, the one that established the shapes of the United States and Mexico that we see today. The Tohono O'odham did not know that their territory had been claimed by two nations, without a treaty.

James Gadsden, U.S. minister to Mexico, had negotiated nothing with the Tohono O'odham, so they would know nothing about his role in the brutal U.S. "Indian Wars" whose mission was to remove the resistant Seminole Indians from their home in Florida during 1818 and 1819. The Tohono O'odham also knew nothing about the concept of Manifest Destiny that motivated Gadsden, the worldview that led to U.S. westward expansion and the eventual annexation of more than 40 percent of Mexican territory, including all of the indigenous land therein, after the 1846–1848 Mexican-American War. From Mexico the United States seized all or part of what are today Texas, Oklahoma, Kansas, Nevada, Colorado, Wyoming, Utah, New Mexico, Arizona, and California. All that was left was a little chunk of land in today's southern Arizona—Tohono O'odham territory.

According to the nineteenth-century doctrine of Manifest Destiny, it was the God-given right of the United States of America to expand its territory over the whole of North America, and to extend and enhance its political, social, economic, and ultimately "civilizing" influences. That was exactly the march of the nation-state then, a mission that the Border Patrol, whether it is aware of it or not, continues today.

The old man spoke the Tohono O'odham language to the U.S. soldier, as related by historian Karl Jacoby in his book *Shadows at Dawn: An Apache Massacre and the Violence of History*, and the soldier did not understand. So the old man started to point in all directions. He was trying desperately to communicate to the soldier what were the Tohono O'odham aboriginal territories. He had no idea that the United States had threatened to seize parts of northern Mexico by military force if Mexico didn't allow "purchase" of Tohono O'odham land. The old man did not know that the United States saw this area as a perfect place for the construction of the east–west Southern Pacific transcontinental railroad, and that the country wanted to mine the mineral-rich areas of southern New Mexico and Arizona. He pointed deep to the south, into an area that is now considered Sonora, Mexico. He pointed as far as Hermosillo, 200 miles south of the boundary line the soldiers were constructing. He pointed west toward the Sea of Cortés, the only place in the world where saguaro cacti meet the sea.

The old man pointed north toward Phoenix, its population barely a smidgen of the two million people in what is today Arizona's capital.

In the soldier's recollection, according to Jacoby, the "old grey-headed Pimo [*sic*] took great pleasure in pointing out the extent of their domains. They were anxious to know if their rights and titles to lands would be respected by our government, upon learning that their country had become a part of the United States."[11]

The Tohono O'odham continued to cross the newly minted border after this, as if this surveying crew were a ridiculous hallucination. They visited family and their communities, went to religious and spiritual ceremonies. Even after the formation of the U.S. Border Patrol in 1924, the agents of what was then the Department of Labor left the Tohono O'odham alone. There were other forms of subjugation, particularly the massive theft of the Tohono O'odham land that resulted in a shrunken reservation in 1919.

Enclosing the Desert People in a reservation had long been advocated in newspapers such as the *Los Angeles Times*, which called the Tohono O'odham the "wild papago" in their "conical mud huts." They wrote that they were only mildly better than "gophers and prairie dogs in their habitations."[12] When several Tohono O'odham men kidnapped a local sheriff after a rancher seized O'odham land and one of their water sources (something that happened regularly during that time), the *LA Times* insisted that the O'odham needed to be more "closely monitored and controlled."[13] The indigenous people were clearly cluttering up the way to cash in on Arizona's expanding mining, agriculture, and ranching opportunities.

The Tohono O'odham were expected to assimilate and were sent to boarding schools where Anglos tried to teach

them about wage labor. They were paid pennies for working in the cotton fields and mines, and they were subjected
to deplorable conditions of severe poverty that have been
an aspect of everyday life on the reservation ever since. But
throughout this time the Tohono O'odham still crossed back
and forth over the Anglos' borderline as if it didn't exist.

The Tohono O'odham, thus, after surviving for more
than 150 years with a significant part of its land within
U.S. territory, were still not controlled. The rise of the
post-9/11 Homeland Security state has targeted this practice of freely crossing the international border. Indeed, a
post-9/11 battlefield was quietly set up, one that has received scant attention in the press. There are, of course,
important distinctions between U.S. presence on indigenous lands and U.S. military incursions in Iraq, Afghanistan, and other places, but at the same time there are also
striking similarities: deployment of armed forces, Forward
Operating Bases, mass surveillance and interrogation, and
regular use of growling helicopters and silent drones. This
calls to mind the words of StrongWatch's salesperson Drew
Dodds at the Border Security Expo: "We are bringing the
battlefield to the border."

The hybrid battlefield on the land of the Tohono
O'odham Nation is one of profound historic significance,
one that blends the Indian Wars of the eighteenth and
nineteenth centuries with a post-9/11 world of an increasingly militarized border armed with a technological arsenal developed, in part, at the nearby University of Arizona.
This battlefield pits the national security interests of the
United States versus impoverished indigenous communities that seem to be perceived, though it is never explicitly
stated, as something akin to a terrorist threat.

In his book *Mexico Unconquered*, John Gibler quotes

Mexican philosopher Bolívar Echeverría, who wrote: "If we take a long-term view of things, then we should keep in mind that the process begun in 1492 . . . the Conquest, is an enterprise that has *not* finished. I think it is important to start from this idea: that the Conquest of America is still ongoing." Gibler writes that if it is indeed true that the conquest continues, "then there are people and places that remain unconquered."[14] Case in point: the indigenous youth briefly, yet dramatically, taking over the biggest Border Patrol headquarters in the United States, in Tucson. Case in point: the O'odham continually crossing the international border to visit family and practice the Him'dag.

This border, witnessed in its nascent form by the old man, was not fully perceived as a line of domination and control (either by the old man or by the soldier). But it would become one that would, as explained by Jacoby, lay "the groundwork for dramatic transformations to come."[15] For what was being explained to the old man was, to him, ludicrous. It was as if a foreign force arrived in Kansas and drew a line through the center of the state—through cemeteries, schools, community centers, and churches— transforming it into two countries without consulting the Kansans. It was as if you were suddenly told that your community, family, and neighbors now were being separated into two different nations—two different nations to which you had no affiliation at all.

Occupied Territory

One hundred fifty years later, when Arturo Garcia, a Tohono O'odham man—no relation to David—leaves a local watering hole, he decides to go up Trading Post Road along the mountains, instead of Highway 86, where everyone in the nation complains about the Border Patrol driving at high speeds. Because of these high speeds, Arturo is convinced that a Border Patrol vehicle killed his cousin, Barney Garcia, though the agency claims otherwise; it claims the accident was Barney's fault. Arturo has been working at building a fence around the watering hole. He is looking forward to getting home and having dinner with his wife and children.

In his truck, Arturo is crossing one of the dry washes heading south on one of the Nation's many rugged roads, a testament to the endemic poverty throughout the reservation where more than 35 percent of the people are unemployed and the annual per capita income hovers around an abysmal $8,000. A Border Patrol vehicle rumbles at him from the other way. When the agent sees Arturo's old truck, he flashes his lights.

Arturo hasn't had good experiences with the Border Patrol. He remembers after Barney's death when he and others were cutting mesquite logs and peeling them to put on top of Barney's coffin. A Border Patrol vehicle drove into the area, but Arturo cut him off, blocked his path, and told him that he couldn't pass. The agent responded by stepping out of his vehicle, slamming his door, and walking at him with a pistol drawn. The agent remembered Arturo, said he had dealt with him before on Trading Post Road. He said that he could take him out, there and then, according to Arturo's telling. After a thirty-minute standoff, the agent drove off.

The incident is fresh in Arturo's mind as he watches the Border Patrol agent get out of his truck. When he is about twenty feet away from Arturo, he shouts at him to state his nationality.

"Native," Arturo says.

There is a pause. Silence.

"Why, what's up?" Arturo asks.

The agent doesn't say anything, and is looking around Garcia's truck.

"What are you looking for?" Arturo asks.

"Stuff," the agent responds.

Arturo can barely see what the agent looks like in the cool darkness. Garcia hears metallic clanks behind him as the agent searches his truck without a warrant.

Finally the agent approaches the driver's side of the car. The agent is wearing glasses. He says: "Can you turn off your vehicle?"

Arturo is mad that the guy is messing around with his truck. The guy never tells him that he's a Border Patrol agent, that he's a federal authority or anything, "so I didn't comply." The agent radios for backup.

Soon after, another Border Patrol vehicle pulls up, and its bright headlights bear down on the backside of Arturo's truck. The first guy continues searching around, banging on the truck bed, looking underneath.

The new agent steps out of his vehicle and walks over to the passenger side. The agent tells Arturo that he is a federal officer. He tells Arturo to shut off his vehicle.

"As you can see," Arturo says, "your partner isn't finding anything in the back so there's nothing here, there's nothing."

"Please turn your car off," the agent says.

"There's nothing in the back of my seat so I'd rather not."

"Turn your car off."

"My steering helm is loose and if you get in the wrong way it don't start sometimes," Arturo tells him.

"If you don't turn off the vehicle, I am going to pepper-spray you."

According to Margo Cowan, former general counsel to the Tohono O'odham, "as recently as 1993" there was little Border Patrol presence noticeable on O'odham land.[16] Now their presence has increased significantly. Their all-terrain vehicles, horses, and mobile surveillance trucks can be seen patrolling the border by land. Blackhawk helicopters with blinding floodlights, fixed-wing aircraft, and Predator drones patrol from the sky. Scope trucks and surveillance towers have become a regular part of the landscape and most of it has been approved by the tribal legislative council. As expressed by Norris in his 2008 testimony to the U.S. Congress, the council views the relationship with the Border Patrol as a partnership, a viewpoint not necessarily shared by the general population, especially as incidents of abuse against the O'odham, like what is about to happen to Arturo Garcia, become more well-known.

On all sides of the nation are some of the largest Border Patrol stations in the country. To the north, near Phoenix, the Casa Grande station has 600 agents,[17] most of whom patrol the reservation. To the east, 650 more agents work out of the Tucson headquarters, and ninety more are stationed at Three Points, right on the edge of the reservation. The Three Points substation commands the vehicle checkpoint that stops all eastbound traffic on Highway 86 leaving the reservation. Border Patrol has located other checkpoints on all roads departing the reservation, north to Casa Grande and west to Gila Bend, guaranteeing that the Border Patrol will have the option to inspect and question every single vehicle leaving or entering the nation on the major roads. Effectively, a separate layer of border divides the nation from the rest of Arizona, as if the nation itself were a foreign country under a new, post-9/11 form of military occupation.

In 2013, the Border Patrol christened one of its newest stations in Why, Arizona. The solar-powered state-of-the-art station is located less than a mile from the reservation's border. Its mall-sized parking lot holds a fleet of green-striped vehicles to be used by 360 agents. So many Homeland Security agents have moved into the area that CBP has built a subdivision of houses in the nearby town of Ajo due to "lack of available or suitable housing"[18] for their growing ranks. And this shiny new Border Patrol station is practically in the shadows of a defunct copper mine where segregated Tohono O'odham laborers used to earn bottom-of-the-barrel salaries in a racialized wage-stratification scheme. It is as if one oppressive industrial system were replacing another.

As the Homeland Security complex expands into the farthest reaches of O'odham territory and reservation, it, like the mining empire, brings its own logic and worldview. Arturo Garcia knows that contact with the Border Patrol, unlike previous O'odham experience with the Spanish, is difficult to avoid. But the confusing question is, why does he think he has to avoid them, if indeed he is a U.S. citizen?

On the one hand, dark-skinned Tohono O'odham do provide a confusing panorama for the Border Patrol. There are a number of U.S.-born members who are "undocumented" because they were born at home and never received a birth certificate. There are Tohono O'odham who were born on the U.S. side and are U.S. citizens, but grew up or live on the Mexican side, and thus, in the eyes of the Border Patrol, are suspicious. There are those who were born in Mexico and live south of the border but come to the United States for a variety of reasons, including education and other basic services. And there are others who were born in Mexico but live on the United States side.

"Too much harrassment," Tohono O'odham Priscilla Lewis says, summing it up in a 2011 open hearing with the Tohono O'odham Legislative Council: "following the wrong people, always stopping us, including and especially those who look like Mexicans when driving or walking in the deserts. . . . They have too much domination with or over us."[19]

While there have been many complaints of racial profiling from this binational tribe, there is much evidence to believe that the Tohono O'odham, regardless of their citizenship, are being victimized by North American demand for marijuana and hard drugs. Ed Reina estimates that there may be as many as 150 drug crossings per day, and that 5 to 10 percent of marijuana grown in Mexico travels through the O'odham Nation. Reina says that in 2009 the Tohono O'odham Police Department seized 38,000 pounds of marijuana; he estimates that the Border Patrol seized probably five or six times that amount on the nation's land.[20]

One of the most unfortunate aspects of drug flow across the territory, according to Reina, is that smugglers constantly entice people from Tohono O'odham communities to get a taste of the profits to be pocketed from transporting or storing contraband. On occasion, however, some Tohono O'odham are coerced, rather than persuaded, to get involved.[21]

It is not easy to estimate the number of local people involved in smuggling, but according to geographer Kenneth Madsen, it is "surprisingly high."[22] Madsen says that early in his field research a Border Patrol agent informally told him that he thought that up to 80 to 90 percent of the population was involved with smuggling. The agent said that he became extra suspicious when tribal leaders asked the Border Patrol to move a vehicle checkpoint or be more sensitive in their enforcement in certain areas. Madsen stresses that for the perceived level of local involvement to be anywhere near 90 percent, it must be due to a high number of people who do "humanitarian" solidarity, rather than "smuggling." However, many Tohono O'odham he interviewed told him he "would be surprised" at the number of people who were involved, including "grandmotherly-types, neighbors, relatives, people in important positions."[23]

One person Madsen interviewed was once offered $15,000 by smugglers for use of his shed. Another young man would cook up huge amounts of food. An older woman always had lots of tortillas and a pot of beans on the stove for the groups of people who passed, no questions asked. She would never ask for money, but if offered a donation she would accept it. The Department of Homeland Security says that transnational drug cartels are targeting youth in the Tohono O'odham Nation. In one television news story, they profile a kid, blurring his face, who was offered $2,000 (one-quarter of the average annual wage in the nation) to transport a load of marijuana from the nation to Tucson. "I was thinking I could do a lot with that money," the youth told the television reporter.[24] He was caught by Homeland Security, and now has four years' probation. Others are incarcerated. One town estimates that one out of every ten its residents are in prison.

Although smuggling is roundly condemned by the Tohono O'odham tribal council, Madsen says that many individuals he interviewed "expressed empathy, explaining that they understood the issues motivating members who participated in the smuggling process." And, Madsen wrote, "almost all the members of the Nation" that he talked with understood "the economic motivation for migration."[25]

In Arturo Garcia's case, however, he does not understand why Border Patrol detained him without informing him why. If the Fourth Amendment seems tenuous in other parts of the borderlands, it is metaphorically torn to shreds on the reservation. The Border Patrol's aggression, however, could easily be rooted in a perception that the Tohono O'odham are part of the "enemy" that undermines the Border Patrol's mission to thwart the flow of unauthorized people and drugs.

The agents have not accused Arturo of anything, and now the dispute is that he has yet to turn off the engine of his idling truck. There are now two agents, and the first agent with the glasses comes around from the back with the air of having had enough of this. The agent reaches into the truck to force off the ignition. Arturo sees his hand, then his arm. The other agent then points the pepper-spray gun at Arturo's face and squeezes the trigger. Arturo raises his arm in a futile attempt to block the burning spray. He hits the arm of the agent who is reaching into the car.

"You touched me. You touched me," the agent yells, standing up. The other agent reaches in and pulls Garcia's arm. They are trying to pull him out of the vehicle. But the standard-transmission truck begins to roll.

"Put it in gear," one of the agents shouts.

"How the hell am I going to do that if you are pulling me out?" Arturo asks. His eyes and face are burning with pepper spray, his eyes involuntarily shutting. When he opens them, they water up. It feels as though there is sand underneath his eyelids. The agents give him a little slack and he throws the truck into gear. Because the engine is still running, the truck lunges forward. The side-view mirror snags a branch of a mesquite bush and pulls it back like a slingshot. Then, as the truck rolls back, it releases the branch, which snaps forward at full force and whips the agent directly at eye level, smashing his glasses. The agent, trying to shake off the intense pain and groping for his glasses, is furious.

Arturo, now outside the truck, is holding the side of the vehicle. Seeing is impossible while his eyes burn with excruciating pain. He is afraid that the agents want to take him down. "Get on the ground," they keep yelling. But Garcia is gripping the tailgate. He hears the click of the baton on the ground. One of the agents says: "If you don't get down on the ground I am going to hit you with this."

Nation member Ofelia Rivas claims that all the people in her community of Ali Jegk (fifty households)—and a majority of Tohono O'odham in general—have experienced human rights violations perpetrated by the Border Patrol. This includes physical and bodily injuries and verbal threats. It includes unjustified interrogations on people's property or in their vehicles. "There have been numerous unwarranted home invasions and searches, and trespassing on their property (yards, fenced and unfenced areas around homes)," she told the Tohono O'odham Legislative Council in 2011.[26] Rivas also mentioned tailgating, blinding spotlights, arrests and deportations, and confiscation of legal documents. Amnesty International's report "In Hostile Terrain" corroborates Rivas's claims, documenting case after case in which "Tohono O'odham citizens point to a history of abuses by CBP agents including cases of verbal and physical abuses."[27]

Many, like Arturo, have been assaulted with pepper spray. Others have been threatened with lethal weapons, or subjected to Border Patrol home invasions. During an interview with Tucson's KVOA, a television station, "Anthony" from the far western Gu-Vo district, said: "I feel like have no more civil rights."[28] Joseph Flores, from the same area, told KVOA that it "feels like we are being watched all the time."[29] And Ruth Ortega, who doesn't have a birth certificate because she was born at home, testifies in the book *It Is Not Our Fault: The Case for Amending Present Nationality Law to Make All Members of the Tohono O'odham Nation United States Citizens, Now and Forever*, "Even though I am a great-grandmother, the Border Patrol still chases me."[30]

Like many places on the U.S.-Mexico border, the O'odham land has been permanently altered. Tohono O'odham Mary Narcho says that in the past, "we did not have any hesitation about going south. It was very normal. There was no Border Patrol. . . . We traveled freely through O'odham lands. Today, the U.S. Border Patrol occupy our lands. O'odham are afraid to walk in the mountains, gather the fruit of the sahuaro."[31]

Another tribal member, Mike Wilson, told journalist Margaret Regan that the Border Patrol was an "occupying army."[32]

This perception has been felt for many years, even before the significant increases in Border Patrol forces and their surveillance technology. In a 2001 letter to the U.S. Congress, Edward D. Manuel and Henry Ramon, chairman and vice chairman respectively of the tribal council, said: "Our Nation's lands north of the boundary are occupied by the United States Border Patrol. All of us are stopped and asked for documents."

They told Congress: "We view our desert lands as a great gift to us from our Creator. Since time immemorial . . . Tohono O'odham have traveled freely, worked, lived, ranched, hunted, gathered, and practiced our religious customs throughout our desert lands without regard to the [Mexico-U.S. boundary]." [33]

While these words underscore the widespread perception that the nation's land is occupied territory, they also underscore an important contradiction. The Tohono O'odham Legislative Council has approved of many Border Patrol projects and the Homeland Security presence on its land. It is an occupation in which, indeed, the council participates.

Arturo Garcia can't say for sure if they hit him with a baton or not, because he blacked out momentarily, but he assumes that he was hit hard. When he wakes up, he is on the ground and handcuffed. The agent with smashed glasses is pinning him down, his knee in Arturo's upper back. However, as in the O'odham revolt of 1751, Arturo resists not only the agent who is pinning him, but also the agency's overall attempt to monitor and control everything that moves in O'odham territory.

Collaboration

The receptionist is a friendly guy, and I am truly surprised when he places a visitor sticker on my shirt. My ploy to just drive to the Immigration and Customs Enforcement (ICE) facility without an official appointment is actually working. I am in Sells, the seat of the Tohono O'odham Nation, home to the nation's legislative council.

Kevin Carlos of the Shadow Wolves, a Tohono O'odham man, greets us in the hallway. Carlos is dressed in a brown jumpsuit, almost symbolic of what I imagine to be his disdain for office work; he guides us to his barren office that reinforces the impression. There is only a desk, phone, and computer, and nothing else. Indeed, his real work is outside, tracking the "bad guys." Certainly, on one level I am anxious to talk with him about the Shadow Wolves, but on another level I want to learn more about the collaboration between Homeland Security and the Tohono O'odham, especially when so many communities here report the Border Patrol acting dishonorably, routinely committing rights violations and acts of abuse. How could many in the Nation simultaneously say it is a military occupation and collaborate with it? How sovereign is their sovereignty? The name Shadow Wolves, according to ICE, "refers to the way the unit hunts, like a wolf pack."[34] They only work on the Tohono O'odham Nation to carry out border-security or drug-enforcement missions.

We sit down, but Carlos tells us that he must first call the ICE Public Information Officer in Phoenix. I watch Carlos dial and have a feeling that the meeting will turn sour, even though it is quite apparent that Carlos has the time, energy, and will to meet with us. He talks for a minute, and I can tell by his tone and his face that things are not going well. He hands the phone to me. Amber Cargile, the public information officer from the Phoenix Regional Office, is on the other line.

"That's just not the way we do things," she says right away. "You can't just show up and have the interview."

I'm looking across the table at Carlos. I can tell by his eyes that he knows.

"Of course the Shadow Wolves will tell you yes," she explains, "because they are really nice guys."

Besides, she says, "there has been a deluge of requests to meet with these guys. I just had to turn down *60 Minutes.*"

It's true, there are many gushing stories that praise the Shadow Wolves as a border-security success story. The unit is entirely Native American, though not all are Tohono O'odham, and it doesn't take the media long to fall into easy stereotypes: the *Telegraph* of London calls them "the best hunters of humans in the world"[35] and National Geographic Channel calls them "border warriors."[36]

In one article, Carlos tells the *LA Times* that he hates the drug smugglers' practice of running roughshod through the ancient cemeteries and holy places on the Tohono O'odham Nation.

"That peak up there," he tells the reporter pointing to the majestic Baboquivari Peak that can be seen throughout the reservation, "that's where The Creator lives. His name is I'itoi, The Elder Brother. He created the tribe out of wet clay after a summer rain. Tribe members still bring Him offerings—shell bracelets, bear grass baskets, and family photos—and leave them in His cave scooped out of the peak."[37]

But now, the reporter writes: "On their way to supply America's drug markets, they use these sacred hilltops as lookouts, water holes as toilets and the desert as a trash can."[38]

"I like to think I am protecting not only the U.S.," Carlos tells the reporter, "but my area as well, my home."[39]

But Carlos will share none of this with me that day. "I have to speak frankly with you," Amber Cargile says to me. "We can't have them speaking about policy issues—such as immigration." When I hang up the phone, Carlos and I stare at each other awkwardly. I can't shake out of my head that I'm witnessing an ancient colonial relationship in its most modern form. The Shadow Wolves were the most useful narrative presented to the world about what is going on at the rez, however the Native American paramilitary group can't speak themselves about their own experience. Did this offer a portal into the delicate power imbalance between the U.S. government and the Tohono O'odham Nation's homeland security?

Indeed, the Tohono O'odham Legislative Council's cooperation with U.S. federal authorities has been a contentious issue. Ofelia Rivas contends that the nation "has allowed the Federal government to control the northern territory [the territory located in the United States] and allows human rights violations to occur." She says that it doesn't "oppose the harassment, home invasions, tailgating at high speeds and deaths of the O'odham caused by the United States Border Patrol and other agencies." Rivas says that not only does the Tohono O'odham Nation publicly support the presence of the Border Patrol, but it has also "made requests for aid and has received 'surplus equipment' including weapons and an increase of agents in the territory."[40]

When asked what interest the Tohono O'odham tribal council would have in working with the U.S. government, Rivas responded that "the tribe was not equipped to handle this onslaught of people coming through O'odham lands. The tribal government then accepted federal assistance not only to increase its police force, but also to increase agents on the reservation to 'assist' efforts to monitor the border."[41]

At times the legislative council has been explicitly outspoken against Border Patrol presence. In 2007, chairman Ned Norris said that a wall would be built "over my dead body."[42] When asked about the increasing Border Patrol presence, Norris was quoted in the *New York Times* saying: "Quite frankly, the people are getting sick of it."[43] And in 2008, Norris had a very public dispute with DHS Secretary Michael Chertoff after Homeland Security waived thirty-seven environmental and Native American cultural heritage laws to build vehicle barriers on the nation's seventy-five-mile border with Mexico. When Chertoff did not visit Norris or the nation on a 2008 tour, Norris told *Indian Country Today*: "It's a total disrespect for the sovereign authority that this Nation has and enjoys with the United States government."[44] To make matters worse, the Department of the Interior—the federal department that was mandated to recognize tribes' "inherent sovereign powers over their members and territory"—supported DHS's "border security infrastructure" project, said Norris. The nation was not consulted either by Interior or by DHS, provoking the question from Norris: "Has the Nation's sovereign power to make laws also been waived?"[45]

However, the Tohono O'odham Legislative Council has cooperated so extensively with the Border Patrol and its projects, including the installation of sophisticated surveillance technology on O'odham land, that to many there seems to be a tacit collaboration. In 2012, the Tohono O'odham Nation received a $285,000 grant from DHS under a program called Operation Stonegarden, a CBP program that consolidates the relationship between the agency and local police. The nation has been receiving such grants for years. This funding is for overtime, equipment, and the Tohono O'odham Police Department's "high visibility uniformed patrols that enhance cooperation and coordination with . . . Border Patrol in a joint mission to secure the Arizona-Mexico border."[46] The nation's police department has received other Homeland Security grants to enhance the tribal police's SWAT team. Another grant was to increase preparedness in the face of a national emergency or acts of terrorism. All together, according to Norris, the nation's police receive about $1 million annually.

I pose this question of cooperation and contention to

legislative council chair Timothy Joaquin in his office in Sells in March 2012. He says that many in the nation are interested in "protection and safety" of their people, and because of that there have been many joint resolutions between CBP and the nation, such as the San Miguel substation and the Forward Operating Bases. These resolutions have enshrined the relationship between the Border Patrol and the Tohono O'odham police.

Joaquin says that many in the nation, like Arturo Garcia (though he doesn't mention him by name), complain about the aggressive tactics Border Patrol uses against the indigenous communities—the "get out of the vehicle!" the "get on the ground!" Joaquin suggests that coercive, threatening, and abusive behavior has become part of the occupied landscape. Agents will "hold people until a dog comes to check out the vehicle." Some O'odham, Joaquin says, will demand to see a warrant. Joaquin speaks slowly and deliberately, as if he has put a lot of thought into the issue.

When someone gets pulled over by the Border Patrol, "there's the whole twenty questions," Joaquin tells me in his small office. "But I do it," he says, implying that he answers all Border Patrol questions without complaint, "because I have nothing to hide."

Joaquin says Border Patrol agents get aggressive when you try to question them. Maybe, he says, if a Border Patrol agent did a "throw-down" of a person, that person was involved with "illegal activities." He shrugs his shoulders. Joaquin tells me that about 30 percent of the people on the reservation are involved in "illegal activity," such as drug or human smuggling. Although much less than the previous Border Patrol agent's perception of more than 80 percent, Joaquin was validating that fact. Homeland Security is targeting the indigenous communities.

We Don't Have To Tell You Anything

Border Patrol agent Benny Longoria, who discovered the body of the woman on O'odham land, describes a scenario to me at muster in the Casa Grande station, located just north of the nation, where he works. Muster is where agents meet before their shifts to divvy up their tasks for the day. In Casa Grande, this involves a gathering of about thirty or so agents, several supervisors, and one field operations supervisor who now is called a shift commander. The brunt of the patrolling work from this station takes place on the Tohono O'odham land. Muster sessions are often filled with recountings of things that have happened on the reservation.

Longoria shakes his head trying to recollect what they were talking about that day, but he can't remember the exact details. It doesn't matter, he says. "The point is we were talking about something on the reservation."

While the supervisor was talking about the incident that involved a particular person, one of the agents yelled out: "Was he human or an Indian?"

Everyone, Longoria explains, "cracked up." But it wasn't even the "hard joke," he says, that "got to me." It was the fact that everyone, all of the dozens of agents sitting there, laughed. It is how accepted these sorts of thoughts are, Longoria tells me. It is how ingrained this sort of racism is, without even a bit of self-reflection, the present within the ranks of the agency.

At same time, as in many other places, the Border Patrol has an intense public relations campaign on the rez. Specific agents are designated to work on community relations. Sometimes a Border Patrol trailer will go from community to community to provide information, hear complaints, and recruit for its Explorer posts. During the

hiring surges, they also look for potential ready-made recruits for the Border Patrol itself, though few O'odham
make it that far. They have a Kid Print program in which
the Homeland Security agency takes children's finger-
prints and then returns copies of the prints to their parents for safekeeping. The Border Patrol has participated in
back-to-school events where, the agency claimed, children
were "excited to receive a Junior Border Patrol sticker and
learn about firearms safety."[47] The Border Patrol is present at large events such as rodeos and job fairs. The Border Patrol says that it is trying to establish a "safe border
environment while improving the quality of life in border
communities."[48]

Sometimes, Longoria tells me, O'odham leaders come
to talk to the Border Patrol at the Casa Grande station.
They come to explain different things that might be happening on the reservation—a ceremony, a procession—so
the agents are aware. One time, Longoria says, an O'odham
official told the agents, who were all grouped in muster:
"We pray for you. We know what a tough job you have."

After that, Longoria says, the "negativity" of the
agents in the room felt as if it were going to explode. He
says he knew that he was going to hear about "the Indian
praying for us" all day long and the next day as well. He
describes that as a mixture of racism and "exceptionalism."
American exceptionalism, what historian Guadalupe Castillo calls the new "Manifest Destiny," is the idea of U.S.
superiority and moral authority over every other country
in the world—that the United States can impose, police,
and enforce its interests globally with virtual impunity.
Underlying the negativity that Longoria describes is a
knowledge, even among rank-and-file agents like the one
who questioned David Garcia and me about our relation-

ship, that they have absolute power. It was as if, in the logic of Manifest Destiny, the Border Patrol were in the hands of God and on the right side of justice.

David Garcia tells me that although there was initial support for the Border Patrol when there was an upsurge of unauthorized traffic through O'odham land, if they had known what was going to happen they would have never supported the increase of federal forces. In early 2013, in David Garcia's Chukut Kuk district, community members noticed that there was a lot of unexplained Border Patrol traffic through the area. So a community member followed an agent up a hill and discovered that they had installed surveillance equipment and two or three generators, with wires squiggling all over the place. The locals complained that they never asked permission to install an intelligence post there. The Border Patrol claimed that chairman Ned Norris authorized the project, which Norris then denied. The whole thing blew up, and in February 2013 the district had a meeting with the Border Patrol.

Garcia called Carlos Escobar, the Border Patrol community liaison, to see if he would be at the meeting. When he got Escobar on the line, Garcia asked him if he was aware of the meeting. Are you attending? No, Escobar responded, but an agent would be there as his representative. Are you aware of the surveillance system in the Alvarez Mountains? Garcia asked. Yes, Escobar responded.

And then he said, according to Garcia: "You know, David. We don't have to tell the nation anything about our operations."

Garcia asks me, rhetorically: "If this is true, why all the meetings for support?"

And there they are on Tohono O'odham land, like the surveyors and the soldier and the old man; the Border

Patrol just shows up and sets up shop, without showing respect or proper protocol, to occupy yet more sovereign land with yet another federal installation. When the community questions their presence, agents say that Norris gave his approval. When Norris denies this, Escobar says they can do whatever they want. Which, with the national security mission Border Patrol has, is the most accurate statement of them all.

Which brings me back to that moment again, right after David Garcia opened the gate on the U.S.-Mexico border.

During the last 400 to 500 years, the Tohono O'odham have lived through many different attempts at territorial domination of their original lands by many different men in uniform. From the Conquest made by the guns, germs, and steel of Spain to the border-building operations of the armed agencies of the United States of America, foreign powers have imposed themselves on the O'odham people and their land time and time again. When we look at the agent, leaning down, his face in the window, looking at Garcia and wondering out loud how the O'odham man could have a friend in New York City, I realize that I am getting only the smallest glimpse of the nation's long, anguished contact with European empire-building, and that the Border Patrol is the newest manifestation of something very old.

As the two agents talk about our situation behind the car, I look to the antenna of the Forward Operating Base in the distance, and I see the ancient colonial relationship of cooperation, cooptation, and violence. At the same time, I have one of the rawest views into today's post-9/11 United States and the wars it wages in the name of border security so far away from the public eye. I don't see the elder David

Garcia liking it one bit. While sitting there, waiting and looking at the Border Patrol vehicle, still parked askew after sliding to a stop, I ask the agents if I can take a picture of the distant base.

"No," both officers say without hesitation.

"Why?" I ask immediately, not sure why they would reject the request.

"National security," the other blond agent replies.

When they finally let us go, Garcia looks at me and says: "They think they can do anything." After we drive off, I wonder if the agents shut the gate that Garcia had opened. But somehow I know, as we drive on the rumbly road, that if I were to turn around and drive back to the border, Garcia would, without hesitation, open the gate again. Although it's been a long time since there has been a large-scale revolt like the one staged in 1751, the Tohono O'odham Nation persists and still enacts the subtle yet powerful forms of resistance like those of David Garcia, Arturo Garcia, and Ofelia Rivas every single day. The Tohono O'odham Him'dag has held its ground for over one thousand years, from the Spanish bayonets and whips, to the tasers, surveillance walls, drones, and bullets of the U.S. Border Patrol. "My resistance is my language," said Rivas about the Homeland Security incursion on O'odham land, "and I survive in living the Him'dag."

chapter six

THE NOT-SO-SOFT UNDERBELLY OF THE NORTH

Up until the mid-2000s, the rural town of Sodus, New York, seemed a long way away from the U.S. border with Canada. Sure, the town is on the shores of Lake Ontario, but looking across this lake's endless blue waves gives a feeling of looking into an expansive ocean rather than an international divide in need of policing. Rows and rows of apple trees in orchards are seen throughout the region, many reaching the lake's shoreline, where the soil is particularly rich. Wayne County is the second-largest apple-producing area in the country. During harvesting season, 8,000 people show up to work and will crowd into rudimentary housing on the edges of the orchards. They will pick the apples that will fill produce aisles across the country, be turned into juice or cider, or become applesauce at the nearby Mott's plant just down the road on Route 104.

On one lonely two-lane road leading to the lake in Sodus, Primitivo Vásquez opened a grocery store called Mi Ranchito in 1992. It was a typical Mexican *abarrotes*, a small neighborhood shop that sells tortillas, tostadas, salsas, and all kinds of Mexican brands, including, much

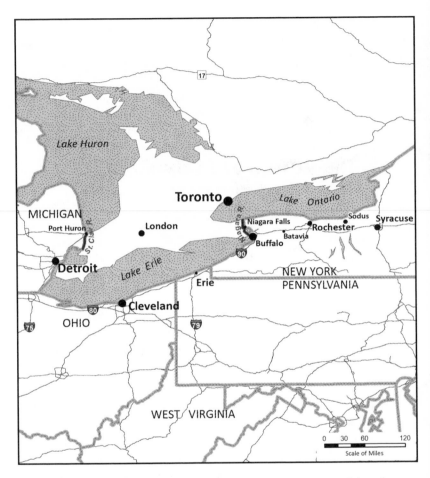

A slice of the U.S. northern borderlands. Cartography by Louise Misztal.
Data provided by ESRI, The National Map.

to my elation, Boing juices, made by a workers' cooperative outside of Mexico City. Up until 2008, Mi Ranchito bustled with business. Many of the people working on the farm were undocumented Mexican nationals, and the store became a center of activity for them. He was friends with one of the U.S. Border Patrol agents, Vásquez told me, at the nearby Oswego station, where they had a meager three-person staff. One Latino agent would regularly stop by Mi Ranchito for snacks and a chat.

Then, in 2004, Customs and Border Protection opened its Rochester Border Patrol station just down the road from Sodus. CBP said that this station would address potential problems with a ferry service that was to travel between Toronto, Ontario, and this western New York city, across Lake Ontario. When the ferry service was suspended in 2006, CBP did not close this Border Patrol station. Instead, Homeland Security increased the number of agents from seven to twenty-seven, on par with the significant growth of Border Patrol across the northern frontier following 9/11. Since 2001, the number of agents has grown from 340 to 2,300, a sixfold increase that outpaces even the growth on the southern border.

And like that, "the world's longest undefended border," what the *Toronto Globe and Mail* has called a "point of pride"[1] between two friendly countries, became a point of contention—all 4,000 miles of it. Geographer Geoffrey Boyce contends that more and more it is "Arizona everywhere"[2] and that this heavy-handed post-9/11 expansion is going unnoticed by the general public yet is happening with lightning speed, especially along the northern U.S. frontier.

These sudden, controversial (and, to some, illogical) changes can be seen most sharply between the towns of

Derby Line, Vermont, and Stanstead, Quebec, where the international border bisects the local library with a thick black line on its floor, yet has 20,000 books in French and English that citizens of both towns—and countries—share. They also share the same water service and sewage system, which, unlike the library, are both are out of sight and inaccessible to the public. The library's front door is in the United States, but the majority of the backside, and all its books, are in Canada. Canadians can use the entire library, but they have to return to their country after checking out a book, or risk arrest. The same goes for the opera house, located in the same historic building, where a brochure encourages all visitors to return to their country of origin following performances. There are no walls yet, but Homeland Security has started blockading some streets with gates, flowerpots, and large signs that say with red letters: YOU MAY NOT ENTER THE UNITED STATES ON THIS STREET. Now friends and neighbors in both towns express the same astonishment at these sharp, policed lines of division that people in many small U.S.-Mexican border towns once did in the mid-1990s.

In Sodus, it was in 2008 when this international border, in its own peculiar way, started showing up in the parking lot of Primitivo Vásquez's store, Mi Ranchito. Located on the shores of Lake Ontario, Sodus is still a border town, even though the closest Canadian town is more than fifty miles away across the lake. Nevertheless, the green-striped U.S. Border Patrol vehicles started to stake out Mi Ranchito, sometimes two at a time. The agents are from both the Rochester and the Oswego stations. They increasingly cruise through the area, vigilant of the "vulnerable lakeshore." They order arriving customers, mostly people who work on farms, to show their papers. Because of this, Vásquez says his business has declined so much that he might have to close up shop.

Given this climate, what happens to Sodus resident Gabriela Gutiérrez when she goes to the grocery store with her three-year-old daughter Lucy is no surprise. In Sodus, if you are undocumented, even going to the grocery store can be a high-risk activity. There are stories about the Border Patrol and ICE pursuing people into stores and pharmacies such as Market Place, Dollar General, and CVS. There are incidents of the Border Patrol arresting people in front of, and, in another incident, on the steps of, the local Catholic church during a Spanish-language mass. Sometimes New York state troopers set up a checkpoint in front of Sodus's only laundromat, as they did on Sunday afternoons during the 2011 harvest season. A Border Patrol vehicle is parked alongside the dark blue state troopers at one of the only places in the town where working people, mostly non-citizens, can wash their clothes on their day off.

Gutiérrez is halfway to the store from her mobile home park when the police pull her over and arrest her. Suspecting that she does not have papers, they turn her over to the Border Patrol. To three-year-old Lucy, her mother has been kidnapped, and she will experience the indelible trauma of suddenly having a parent taken away from her by armed men in uniforms.

According to John "Lory" Ghertner of Migrant Support Services of Wayne County, there have been more deportations of people from Sodus, New York, than the ones resulting from the infamous ICE raid in Postville, Iowa, in 2008. The Postville raid was an operation that arrested nearly 400 undocumented foreign nationals—mostly from Guatemala—at a kosher slaughterhouse and meatpacking plant. "It just hasn't happened at the same time," Ghertner says, referring to the number of arrests and deportations since 2009.

In places like Sodus, one might be forgiven for forgetting that the United States has long had very friendly relations with Canada, its largest trading partner and now the given reason for the sharp increase in Homeland Security's soldiers. While a militarized surveillance and enforcement regime has long existed in the U.S.-Mexico borderlands, its post-9/11 version is far more geographically expansive, encompassing the entire U.S. perimeter, as seen in Sodus, and across the northern divide from Washington to Maine. What the *Washington Times* has described as "the soft underbelly up north,"[3] isn't so soft any more.

"This is just like 1955 Tennessee racism," Ghertner says. "You may've survived the Southwest. You may've survived the border, the Border Patrol, the checkpoints. But unless you were born here, you are not going to survive Sodus, New York."

The Canadian Threat

U.S. Army War College's Homeland Defense and Security director, Bert Tussing, realizes that when people think of border policing they immediately think of the U.S.-Mexico border. After all, when I see Tussing in October 2012, he is speaking in El Paso, Texas, only a few blocks from the site where the creation of the modern border-enforcement apparatus had its launch in the 1990s. Earlier that day, Operation Hold-the-Line's architect, Silvestre Reyes, spoke at the same Border Management and Technology Conference. Tussing's focus, though, was not on the Southwest, but on the U.S. North.

Tussing, a white former marine with close-cropped brown hair, has a Napoleonic stature and despises being stuck behind a podium. "I kind of like moving around," he quips before starting his talk, "The Changing Role of the Military in Border Security Operations." "As they say in the Marine Corps," Tussing continues, "a moving target is harder to hit." We are in the El Paso Convention Center, and Tussing talks to a group comprised mostly of men, almost all of them in jackets and ties, sitting in folding chairs in front of the podium. Tussing must have realized that he was talking to a new breed of border-security entrepreneurs when his army-marine joke at the beginning falls flat, eliciting no laughs. Behind the small audience are booths from seventy-four companies selling border-security wares, one of many border-security expos that operate out of convention centers across the United States. Hanging from the high ceiling is a white surveillance aerostat made by an Israeli company. Latched onto the bottom of this billowing balloon are cameras that can, from 150 feet away, zoom in and read the notes that I'm scrawling in my notebook. RT Aerostat Systems Inc. is one of several Israeli companies with products to pitch, and Israeli Brigadier General Roie Elkabetz will speak after Tussing, following lunch.

Underneath the balloon sits a mannequin in a beige bodysuit, equipped with a gas mask. Behind him, Lockheed Martin is showing off its new desert-ready armored jeep; a salesman in suit and tie talks to a couple of ornery-looking guys. Off to the side of Tussing's despised podium more members of his audience sit around large round brown tables, including a group of eight Border Patrol agents, all in uniform. Tussing will reference them often during his talk. He will look their way and call them the "men in green," even though there is one woman in their group.

Tussing begins by offering a panorama: 1.1 million

people coming across the border each day and 79,000 shipments of goods, all legitimate.

But according to Tussing, it's the "other things" that are our "greater concern," the products and people, "illegals if you will," who are also crossing our borders. He homes in on a 2010 statistic that says that 59,000 people were trying to enter the United States per year, without proper documentation, from countries "other than Mexico." Tussing says, enunciating each word again: "the euphemistic OTMs."

Six hundred sixty-three of the OTMs were from countries "that we categorize as special-interest nations, such as Pakistan, such as Afghanistan, such as Somalia, and beyond those, countries that we have identified as state sponsors of terrorism—Cuba, Iran, Sudan, and Syria."

Having painted a picture of threats emanating from without, Tussing makes his case for more military support for border control operations. He sets his geographical sights on the U.S.-Canada divide. Now he focuses on the 1999 attempted crossing of Ahmed Ressam, who would have become "the millennium bomber," Tussing explains, if it weren't for an astute U.S. customs agent in Washington State.

In the case of Ressam, Tussing identifies what he considers to be the crux of the problem: "We found over time that he was able to do what he was doing because of the comparatively liberal immigration and asylum laws that exist today in Canada, which allowed him a safe haven. Which allowed him a planning area. Which allowed him an opportunity to build bombs. Which allowed him an opportunity to arrange his logistics."

Tussing pauses to clarify: "This is not to say that Canada's laws are wrong, but they are different from ours."

He quickly moves to how his views are supported. Referencing a U.S. Government Accountability Office (GAO) report,[4] he says, "and here's a shot for you [showing that] the risk of terrorist activity is high along the northern border." Of the 4,000 miles of territorial border between the United States and Canada "only thirty-two of those miles are categorized as what we say are acceptable levels of control." But the coup de grace for Tussing was a quote from Alan Bersin, former director of U.S. Customs and Border Protection who, according to Tussing's paraphrase, said that when it comes to terrorist activities, "common knowledge is that the greatest threat, the most significant threat, comes from the north."[5]

What Tussing is pushing is something very new compared to the reality of the northern border described by North Dakota senator Byron Dorgan in 2001. Dorgan held up an orange cone at a congressional hearing and said: "This is America's security at our border crossing. . . . America can't effectively combat terrorism if it doesn't control its borders."[6]

While the kind of northern border Tussing is pitching might not look exactly like the southern U.S. border in massive militarization, the steady buildup of armed authorities and technology will have a profound impact on the region.

Yet Tussing also describes a process that is old. His focus on exclusionary practices based on nationality along this "friendly border" is as old as the Chinese Exclusion Act of 1882. According to historian Erika Lee, at the beginning of the twentieth century U.S. officials complained, like Tussing, that Canadian laws, "practically nullified . . . the effective work done by the border officers."[7] Chinese nationals simply evaded immigration at U.S. seaports and crossed into the United States from Canada or Mexico.

Lee writes that with the Chinese Exclusion Act "they laid the foundations for racialized understandings of the 'illegal immigrant problem' and of American border enforcement and nation building at the beginning of the twentieth century." It was this act, Lee says, that signified the change in the United States from a nation that welcomed immigrants, to a "new type of nation, a gatekeeping nation."[8]

It was a gatekeeping nation in which there were more Border Patrol agents on the northern boundary than on the southern one. In fact, when the Border Patrol formed with two stations in 1924, there was only one in the vicinity of the Mexican divide—in El Paso. The other one was in Detroit, Michigan.

Motown

Detroit is a city of many idiosyncrasies. One of them is that if you cross the Ambassador Bridge from Windsor, Ontario, into Detroit, you are entering, as CBP spokesperson Kenneth Hammond tells me by phone while giving me directions, "the Mexican part of town." In a way it's as though you miss the United States all together. If you continue driving on the West Vernon Highway into the southwest part of a city that has a certain notoriety for blight—you will find a neighborhood full of *taquerías*, *tortillerías*, and *lavanderías* (laundromats). There are red-green-and-white Mexican flags in the windows. There are businesses where you can send money south. There is a large, well-kept park that stands out from other parks in Detroit in various stages of official neglect. The park almost reminds me of the many city plazas I've been to in Mexico, with their wrought-iron benches where people are sitting and chatting. It is through this neighborhood that

Hammond is directing me to the CBP offices. He says it is near the Mexican Village Restaurant.

Detroit has suffered one of the steepest population declines of any U.S. city—from a high of two million in the 1950s, when it was the fourth-largest city in the country, to a little more than 700,000 in 2013. However, since the 1990s, the Latin American (and mostly Mexican) immigrant population has grown 70 percent, reaching 48,679 in 2010. Elena Herrada, director of the Detroit-based Centro Obrero, said, "People started coming to Detroit after NAFTA," referring to the impacts of the free trade agreement on the state of Jalisco, the geographic source of much of the recent Mexican migration. But Herrada, whose claim to national fame was evoking the ire of Glenn Beck when she compared ICE to the Klu Klux Klan, is herself testament to the long-standing presence of the Mexican community in Detroit. Her family's historical roots are so deep here that when I used the name "Mexicantown" to describe the area, she said: "We don't call it Mexicantown; that's the commercial name. The older people were infuriated when they heard that name initially." When I asked her what they preferred, she said simply: "Southwest Detroit."

Herrada's family was in Detroit long before 1931, the year Henry Ford commissioned world-renowned Mexican artist Diego Rivera to paint a mural portraying industrial workers and the River Rouge Ford plant, the largest automobile plant at the time, which is now just a shell of its former self. The mural is twenty-two feet high and seventy-three feet wide, and when you view it in the Detroit Institute of the Arts, you enter the intestines of the auto industry that once dominated Detroit. On four walls appears the dank and muscular world of car manufacturing portrayed, as only Rivera could do it, from the perspective of the worker. What the communist muralist was depicting was the same industry that attracted thousands and thousands of people worldwide—including many workers from Mexico—in the early twentieth century.

Rivera was painting the mural when the Great Depression hit hard. And he was painting the mural when U.S. officials targeted his compatriots in an economic scapegoating program most commonly known as "Mexican repatriation." Approximately one million people of Mexican descent, including U.S. citizens, were expelled from the United States.

Jose Lopez, a U.S. citizen, was one example of many. When he was five years old, in 1931, officials in Detroit forced his family to take a one-way train trip to the Mexican border. Throughout the country, police executed armed raids in search of Mexicans, even bursting through doors into people's homes. Trains to the Mexican border were made available with, ironically, pre-paid fares. "It was an injustice that shouldn't have happened,"[9] Lopez said in 2006 at the age of 79, when many were pressuring the U.S. government to apologize.

In the 1930s, even the muralist Rivera played an odd role, encouraging his *paisanos* to return home and form revolutionary committees in Mexico (though this was ten years after the Mexican Revolution). In the Herrada family's case, although the U.S government deported them, like many others they came back to Detroit during the World War II industrial boom. Motown had become "the arsenal of democracy." Automobile factories were converted to manufacture weapons and hardware for the war. This was the beginning of the same industrial complex to which Eisenhower would sound the alarms twenty years later.

Migration didn't spike again until the post-NAFTA era. Herrada tells me that many people came here because they were trying to get as far away from the southern border as possible, "as far away from the Border Patrol as possible. . . and then they hit up against *this border*."

When I first arrive in Detroit, I immediately check out the U.S. Border Patrol station located close to the shadow of the city's quintessential silver General Motors headquaters building. Across the river is Windsor, with its enticing casino, trying to lure people from the "Ciudad Juárez of the United States," as Jonathan Contreras calls his hometown, Detroit. Indeed, for the cash-starved city that has declared bankruptcy and is constantly cutting basic services due to a perpetual budget crisis, seeing the shiny Border Patrol vehicles, including the sporty green-striped Dodge Chargers, was a sight to behold. This post-industrial city has become a showcase for an unadvertised side effect of global capitalism: urban collapse, which is so advanced in some places here that forty square miles of the city have devolved into a kind of urban prairie. Because of this, Detroit has also been deemed a showcase for urban farming that utilizes this land, a place where a new form of community can be imagined and practiced.

In 2013, control of the city was given over to an unelected emergency manager. Margaret Kimberley writes that "Detroit as a sovereign public entity no longer exists. It is completely powerless, having been taken over by the 'lords of capital.' . . . There is quite literally no one in Detroit's government with the power to stand up to"[10] powerful corporate interests such as the Koch brothers, who in 2012 dumped a forty-foot-high mound of toxic contaminants along the Detroit River.

Detroit has become a showcase for another way to

envision the world: a contaminated and foreclosed society under constant watch by the ever-expanding U.S. surveillance state.

Everybody in Southwest Detroit has a story. There was the guy from Mexico arrested on his way to work at 4:00 a.m. at a bus stop. There were the two other Mexican men fishing on the banks of the Detroit River whom Border Patrol agents approached and arrested as they were casting their lines into its greenish-blue water. People say Border Patrol agents loiter outside the stately Ste. Anne de Detroit Catholic Church during Spanish-language mass. They say that the Border Patrol sometimes stakes out the Latino Community Development Center. Mexican American Jonathan Contreras described to me his detention by a Border Patrol agent who pulled a taser on him when he refused to get out of his truck one cold November night. Contreras was attempting, and failing, to assert his rights. He saw the red laser line pass through the window and a red targeting dot dance on his chest. Needless to say, he got out.

Lidia Reyes, the executive director of Latino Family Services, told me that on April 27, 2011, as she arrived at work on a cold morning, she saw a U.S. Border Patrol agent questioning one of the center's volunteers, a man named Clemente. They were on the sidewalk in front of the gray two-story building, which offers various services to the Latino community, including a food pantry, youth tutoring, and English-language classes. When she asked what they were doing, another agent boxed her in with his green-striped Dodge Charger in what Reyes claims was a blatant act of intimidation. The agent arrested Clemente, and Homeland Security later deported him. This was only one, Reyes said, of a long list of incidents that both she and her husband had undergone with the Border Patrol.

Once, she said, a half-dozen agents on bikes surrounded Latino Family Services during a women's forum (when "I had about fifty moms here"). Reyes went outside and asked them to leave.

"Up until this," Reyes told me, "I took the side of the law. I figured that their rationale for doing this was A, B, or C. But now since I've been director of Latino Family Services [since 2010], the stuff that they do is just horrible." Reyes said that this was the first time that they targeted her, her family, and her community. Despite the agency's long-standing presence in the city, Reyes, like many people in Southwest Detroit didn't start noticing the Border Patrol until 2008. This was after its forces—over a period of time in the Detroit sector—increased from 40 to more than 400.

Even with such increases, compared to the U.S.-Mexico border it is hard to notice, especially if you are not part of one of the targeted communities. It is obvious, yet not obvious. It is nowhere, yet everywhere. This is what I want to learn when I finally get a meeting with CBP spokesman Ken Hammond.

My meeting with Hammond in Southwest Detroit does not start out well. When a colleague and I first get to the parking lot near the CBP offices under the Ambassador Bridge, there is no sign of him. Hammond had told me that my colleague could come "as long as he didn't ask any questions." Above us is the gigantic suspension bridge packed with trucks crossing to and from Canada. There is no other bridge on the U.S.-Canada border that has more commercial traffic. Hammond is not in the parking lot. When I call for a second time, he says: "I am right behind you." I turn around. I see a tall man in a blue CBP Field Operations uniform. I wave to him. He stands there. I wave again. He slowly raises his arm in a wave. When we get out of the car, he is standing there stiff as a statue. We shake hands. He looks me up and down, as if he were determining if I should be admitted into the United States of America.

"I'm sorry to have to do this," he says, "But can I see some sort of identification—something identifying you as a journalist, a press credential."

I look at him. I take a deep breath of Detroit's humid June air. I have been trying to arrange this meeting for a month. I have called Hammond at least a dozen times. I have left him messages. I want to learn not only about CBP on the northern border, but also about its Explorer post and programs with youth. It is my last day in Detroit, and I know that he wants to hear me stutter. And I stutter, worried he won't believe me. "I have one," I say, "but it's not on me."

Hammond, an African American man who, I find out later, is originally from Detroit, slightly smiles. "Okay, c'mon," he says. Now he has a tone like he is doing me a favor, despite his distrust. We enter a small building that smells of border bureaucracy. There is a maze of computers on desks and piles of papers as we enter the office of CBP officer Eric King.

King is also a Detroiter and also African American. He has a much friendlier face than Hammond does and more meat on his bones. He is an advisor of the youth Explorer Post 306.

Hammond immediately assures King—"Don't worry, I've already scared him with the security question." King looks at Hammond with an inquisitive look, like he himself doesn't understand. Hammond leans against the counter, to the side of King. I sit in front of them both, thinking that we are reaching a state of relaxation and that we are going to start the meeting, but then Hammond asks:

"Can you name one of your most prominent pieces?"
I hem and haw, not wanting to play his game, but feeling
forced to, as if I were actually pulled over by Border Patrol.
Hammond looks at his smartphone. He must be googling
my name on the spot, I think. I ask them if they can give a
general overview of what they are doing on the northern
border.

"Deterring terrorists and their weapons of mass destruction," Hammond says, as though he has said that
line one too many times. "And promoting lawful trade
and travel. We are stopping illegal entry into the United
States." Little do I know that this exact cut and paste from
the CBP mission statement is all that I am going to get for
the next forty-five minutes.

Eric King introduces himself—fourteen years in CBP.
King realizes that everything he says is monitored by Hammond, who continues to lean against the countertop and
monitor incoming communications in his handheld gad-
get as if he were an embodiment of the National Security
Agency. King knows that he can talk about the Explorers
and only the Explorers. He asks Hammond to tell him if
he goes off course.

There are twenty-five Explorers and nine advisors in
Post 306, he tells me. They meet every two weeks. There
are elected officers and a structured learning process. They
learn handcuffing, the apprehension of subjects, the laws
of entering the United States, how to process people, how
to interview them, including the "violent noncooperative
sort." They go to the shooting range and fire pistols.

The upcoming four-day academy is going to be a
new piece to it all, he tells me. "It's going to be intense."
They will be in a camp in Metamora, Michigan, located in
the woods north of Detroit, near the city of Flint. They

will learn about immigration, criminals, firearms, ports of entry, checkpoints, vehicle stops, and the history of the U.S. Border Patrol. They will sit in front of long tables and inspect passports and interrogate each other as if they were CBP agents in Detroit or Port Huron. They will also take kids on "ride-alongs"—little excursions during which young people accompany officers policing the international border.

Although King doesn't say this, the kids will most likely drive along the thirty-seven-mile stretch of border on the St. Clair River (very close to Metamora) that Michigan congresswoman Candice Miller calls "a hot spot for illegal activity." Along the river, the kids will see the eleven surveillance towers that were constructed in 2010 by the Boeing Company, an example of the type of virtual, technological "wall" that is becoming a basic component not just of U.S. boundary enforcement efforts but of the national surveillance state. The kids might get to see the $30 million "war room" on the Selfridge Air National Guard Base (just north of Detroit), where the Border Patrol headquarters is located. In this "gold standard"[11] for border protection, as the CBP dubs it, the kids will get to see the prized "video wall" that looks like it comes straight from a Hollywood action flick.

Imagining that this is what the kids might see on their ride-along, I jump in with a question. I ask about CBP's northern border strategy. I ask about how it has changed and grown since 9/11. I ask how this has impacted the Explorers. Hammond looks up at me from his smartphone like I'm trying to get him to leak something that would shake the foundation of the national security state. He says he can't talk about strategy, even though it is public. The 2001 USA PATRIOT Act mandated a 300 percent increase in Border Patrol personnel on the northern border and more surveillance technology placement there. Further legislation in 2004 required that 20 percent of the agency's new recruits be stationed there. The number of federal agents went from 340 in 2001 to 1,008 in 2005 to 2,263 in 2010. Now the number is approaching 3,000. The strategy stresses increased information sharing with Canada, increased personnel, increased technology, better infrastructure.

Although CBP forces were increasing at a higher rate on the northern border than at the southern border, Hammond does not tell me any of this, nor does King. They concede that there is more territory to cover. They concede that maybe only in the Caribbean or Alaska is there more water. "If we had a reality TV show about us," they say with swagger, "we'd kill CSI." But they go no further. Then they return to the Explorers. They talk about doing "perimeter-greeting duties" at sporting events, the way they patrol for lost children, and their outreach efforts at local food banks. "What the kids get goes a long way. A whole bevy of things they would not have seen."

What sorts of things? I ask. Again, Hammond gets that same look in his eye, like I'm after something. It's also a look you might expect to see if we were in a chess match that I was going to lose. Hammond's terseness and silence, even about the most public information, was creating its own provocative language, with its own message. Oddly, it fit the Motor City, a place where the border enforcement apparatus felt everywhere and nowhere at once, like a loud secret.

Questions about the new northern border are answered with stories about career fairs, recruitment fairs, citizen academies. The questions are redirected to talk about the kids doing gardening at the Kathryn Ferguson Academy, an inner-city high school for pregnant and mothering students. But even here you find that other reality of Detroit, as the Explorer post notes in its blog after explaining a day of irrigating, pruning, and replacing decomposed mulch in this decaying neighborhood. They are only trying to help a city "that has been stricken with the closing of auto plants and a major mortgage meltdown," it says.

There have been many complaints by Detroiters that outsiders flock to the city as tourists of urban collapse, attracted to real post-apocalyptic scenes of Western civilization as wasteland. Yet there is something in Hammond's silence about the costly border apparatus's movement north that makes the city's dire needs seem more pronounced. There is something about the shiny Homeland Security vehicles that make the collapsing buildings seem even more jagged, more decomposed. In his silence I think that he knows what I can only suspect: in this world of chronic inequality, Homeland Security is welcomed by the haves and keeps the have-nots from getting any big ideas.

A Constitution-Free Zone

Before September 11, 2001, more than half the border crossings between the United States and Canada were left unguarded at night.

Now Predator B drones, sometimes in the air for twenty hours at a stretch, are doing surveillance work from Grand Forks, North Dakota, to Spokane, Washington, with plans for more. The CBP's Office of Air and Marine—essentially Homeland Security's air force and navy—has established eight U.S. bases along the border from Plattsburgh, New York, to Bellingham, Washington.

While such bases are commonplace on the southern border, they are new on the Canadian frontier. In addition, new state-of-the art Border Patrol stations are popping up in places like Pembina, North Dakota (at a cost of $13 million), International Falls, Minnesota ($6.8 million), and other places. This advance of the Homeland Security state in the north, funded and supported by Congress, seems both uncontroversial and unstoppable.

After ordering fourteen additional unmanned aerial vehicles in November 2012, with a plan to increase its fleet to more than twenty-four over the next several years (more than doubling its fleet), surveillance drones could be flying over major U.S. urban areas like Detroit, Buffalo, Syracuse, Bangor, and Seattle, places the ACLU has classified as "Constitution-free zones."[12]

Each zone—up to 100 miles from any external U.S. border—is the area that the Justice Department deemed a "reasonable distance" in 1953. (How they made the decision was "completely unclear," according to Arizona ACLU attorney James Duff Lyall, but it now has huge ramifications, given that CBP "has since expanded to become the largest federal law enforcement agency in the country.") This 100-mile area has since been reaffirmed by the Supreme Court[13] as the legitimate zone of operations for border policing, including warrantless searches. As in the Southwest, expect more interior checkpoints where federal agents will ask people about their citizenship, as they did to Vermont senator Patrick Leahy in 2008 when he was traveling 125 miles south of the border in the state of New York.

"What authority are you acting under?" Leahy asked the agent, after he was stopped and told to get out of his vehicle.

The agent pointed to his gun and said: "That's all the authority I need."[14]

These sorts of things are not only happening in Vermont and New York, of course, but across the entire northern divide. In response, people in the Olympic Peninsula of Washington State have created a group called Border Patrol Free, demanding an end to checkpoint stops such as Leahy experienced. "All of a sudden," said Scott Wilson, publisher of a Port Townsend, Washington, newspaper called *The Leader*, "we have these random searches and seizures of everybody, and this is happening within a hundred miles of our borders. It just shocks me that this is legal; it strikes me that it's immoral, and it violates our sense of community."[15] In the zone, there is a blueprint of a country under increasing surveillance.

It's October 2007 at a Greyhound bus station in Buffalo, New York, when I get my first glimpse of these emerging Constitution-free zones in action. I'm with Miguel Angel Vásquez de la Rosa, a Mexican lawyer who is brown-skinned, of Zapoteco descent, and only speaks Spanish. As we enter the station, we spot two beefy white Border Patrol agents in their dark green uniforms monitoring the waiting area. They have the physiques of linebackers from the Buffalo Bills.

I have to blink to make sure I'm not seeing things, to remember where I am. I'm originally from this area but have lived for years along the U.S.-Mexican border, where I've grown used to seeing the "men in green." I can't remember ever seeing them here.

The two agents make a beeline for Miguel to check his visa. After seeing his visa, the hulking agents walk over to another brown-skinned man who begins to rifle through a navy blue duffle bag, desperately searching for his documents. Not long after, handcuffed and flanked by the two agents, he is marched off to the ticket counter. Somehow, cuffed, the agents expect him to retrieve his ticket from the bag, now on the counter. There are so many people watching that it seems like a ritual of humiliation, much in the same way that Bryan Gonzalez was paraded around the Deming station when he was fired (see chapter four).

Since 2007, this sort of moment has become ever more routine across the northern border region in bus and train stations within the 100-mile zone, as "homeland security" gains ever more traction and an ever wider definition. The Border Patrol is "an agency that doesn't have limitations," says Joanne Macri, director of the Criminal Defense Immigration Project of the New York State Defenders Association. "With police officers, people have more due process protection." Since 9/11, she adds, the Border Patrol has become "the national security police." A damning report corroborates Macri's grim observations. "Justice Derailed: What Raids on Trains and Buses Reveal about Border Patrol's Interior Enforcement Practices," say its authors, raises "serious concerns about an agency that appears to be driven by the belief that the regular rules of the Constitution do not apply to it."[16]

In "Justice Derailed," the authors examine Border Patrol arrests conducted during its operations on trains and buses, a prism through which you can see today's emerging evolution of the national security state. Just via the Rochester, New York, station, between 2005 and 2009, the CBP classified, according to by skin complexion, 2,776 people arrested during what it terms "transportation raids." The results: 71.2 percent of medium complexion and 12.9 percent black. Only 0.9 percent of their arrests were of people of "fair" complexion. If you are brown, the report suggests, you are a target.

Another report, "Uncovering USBP: Bonus Programs for United States Border Patrol Agents and the Arrest of Lawfully Present Individuals," revealed that agents have been given incentives to increase the number of people they sweep up, including Home Depot gift certificates, cash bonuses, and vacation time. The Border Patrol, they say, "should not be allowed to transform the areas of the United States that are adjacent to the border into a police state in which persons are forced to carry papers at all times."[17]

Macri tells me that it is now ever more common for armed federal authorities, in the name of national security, to pull people "who don't belong" off buses and trains. She doesn't mince words: "This is like Nazi Germany. What other image comes to mind?" In 2011, according to Immigration and Customs Enforcement director John Morton, the country saw more than 47,000 deportations of undocumented people along the northern border.

Without a Clue

Down the road from Rochester in Sodus, Gabriela Gutiérrez sits on her couch in her mobile home, stroking the hair of her daughter Lucy, now six years old, as she tells me how her trip to the grocery store ended in her deportation. Although Gutiérrez says she was not treated badly during a month-long incarceration at the county jail, her voice rises with emotion when she describes her deportation, starting from Batavia, New York, just outside Buffalo. "I was shackled like a murderer," she says. They cuffed her around the wrists, around the waist, and around the ankles before she was boarded on an ICE aircraft.

ICE has its own fleet of nine airplanes engaging in daily international flights, what ABC *Nightline* calls the "the busiest airline you've never heard of."[18] The cuffs around her ankles were so tight that they started to scrape, then rip through the tender skin on her leg right above her feet, and she began to bleed. The blood dripped into her sandals, so much of it that her feet slipped around when she tried to walk. "I told them, but they didn't do anything." She couldn't go to the bathroom chained like that, and although ABC's story boasts that it is the only airline that serves a complimentary meal, she couldn't eat.

"I arrive in Nuevo Laredo, Mexico, where I know no one—with no one. And my children are back in Sodus." From that point on, with the help of her also-deported husband, all of her energy would be dedicated to crossing the Arizona desert again to return to her family. Her fifteen-year-old daughter Mari, suddenly motherless, had to become a de facto mother herself.

As dusk falls over the mobile home park in Sodus, Mari, who is now seventeen, describes to me how Lucy would run to the back of the house and turn off the light if someone knocked on the door, thinking it was police or Border Patrol. Lucy thought they were coming to take another loved one away, maybe Mari. Many people in the house assure me, and some at this point are in tears, that there are many children like this now.

A flickering yellow candle offers the only light. Seventeen-year-old Gerardo starts to talk. He has a soft, level voice. He speaks slowly, articulately. He says that people don't trust police; they won't call 911. He says the Border Patrol sits next to the state troopers. He says people are afraid to go to the store. Although he is undocumented, Gerardo tells me that they don't bother him at the checkpoints because he speaks English so well. But they also took his mother away. And they took his father away. And his voice doesn't start to crack until this point. And then he mentions the kids. His younger cousins telling him how scared they are that some one is going to take their parents away. And his younger brother and sister ask him, "Where are my parents? How long will they be gone? Why?"

Gerardo tells me that he did a poll at his high school in Sodus to see how many of the white kids knew what was happening. He looked at me and said: "They don't have a clue what is happening to us, to the Hispanic population."

By the look in his eyes, that didn't sit well with Gerardo. Outside, the sky is a dark gray as night settles over the trailer park. Less than a mile away is Primitivo Vásquez's struggling *tienda*, so close to the shores of Lake Ontario that you can almost hear its surf. The shoreline of this lake, once a place to appreciate natural beauty, has now become a post-9/11 front for the war on terrorism and border control. There is no documented case of a "terrorist" attempting to cross the lake in order to attack the United States. But there are plenty of brown-skinned people who pick our apples.

chapter seven

AMERICA'S BACKYARD

The first thing that I want to do when I arrive in Dajabón, one of the Dominican Republic's border towns with Haiti, is find a good place to eat. After all, it is a five-hour bus ride from the capital of Santo Domingo, through a lush, mountainous landscape with many small towns, all with baseball fields on their edges. As soon as I get off the bus it's obvious that I'm in borderlands again. There is the roar of a cumbersome green helicopter that will circle the town for hours. A mere three blocks away is Haiti, a nation where more than nine million people earn less than a dollar per day. Between the spot where I step off the bus and Haiti is the Massacre River, representing the border that divides the island of Hispaniola into two countries.

I find a Chinese-Dominican restaurant and take a seat. Before I order, a man enters the restaurant and approaches an empty table where another man has just left. A white paper plate, still with a heap of rice, rests on the table amid a scatter of used plastic ware. The man stares down at the plate for a split second. He carries a blue pole under his arm. The man, who I think must be Haitian, grabs a half-eaten piece of chicken. He eats it with ravenous intensity, small bits of chicken exploding off the bone. It's

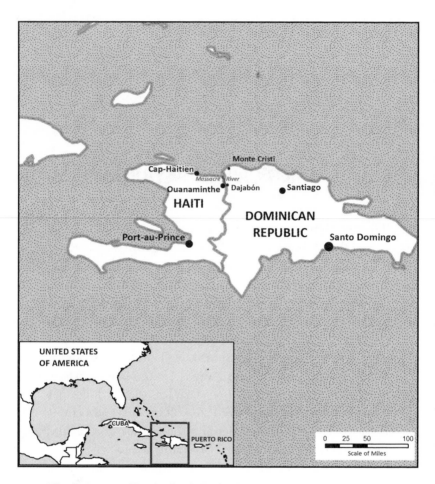

*The Dominican-Haitian borderlands. Cartography by Louise Misztal.
Data provided by ESRI, The National Map.*

as if he hasn't eaten for days. With his bare hand he grabs a handful of rice and shovels it into his mouth. Overhead, the green helicopter continues to circle. You can feel its propellers ripping through the atmosphere. As always in the borderlands, there is an impression that something is happening and that something is wrong.

The man grabs another handful of rice and stores it in a napkin he finds on the table. He grabs the fried plantains and pops them into his mouth, one by one. Behind the counter, four women casually watch the scene, unfazed, as if this happens every day. The Haitian man grabs a small plastic cup with a pool of red soda in its bottom and gulps it down in one fluid motion. He then walks out into the street carrying the napkin full of rice in his cupped hands. I have never, I realize, seen such forceful and aggressive hunger.

But then I ask myself: how do I even know he is Haitian? I realize that it's possible he's Dominican, or even Haitian-Dominican. There is hunger in the Dominican Republic too, so why should I assume this guy is Haitian? Like the Haitians who come across the 320-kilometer divide between the two countries, many Dominicans choose to leave their country, usually to the United States or Puerto Rico, packed into rickety boats called *yolas*.

Indeed, right there in Dajabón and the larger province you find all the typical characteristics of a migrant-sending region. The home region to Major League Baseball player Rafael Furcal includes chronic poverty, lack of basic services, and hunger. In 2007, a tornado that destroyed part of Dajabón was deemed a "blessing" by local authorities. The government finally came in and "resolved a lot of problems in the community," according to the newspaper *Diario Libre*, "including fixing the roads, potable water, food, and other basic services."[1]

As if epitomizing this local reality, another man then walks into the restaurant. The bottom of his worn brown pants are cut open and shredded, the skin around his chin split open in a wound, slightly discolored. He walks through the restaurant speaking loudly in Spanish, asking people for money. He arrives at a table where two men sit eating their meals. The wounded man points down to the plate, and the eating man, whose fork is already midair for his next bite, stops what he is doing. He slides his plate over.

This is the Dajabón that is in one of the key places in charge of policing the Dominican border with Haiti. And that is why I am here, to learn more about the Dominican Republic's border police. While Dajabón is more than 1,000 miles from Miami, the U.S. Border Patrol and the Department of Homeland Security have a presence of sorts there. The U.S. government has helped to fund the Dominican border policing agency and provides it with training. This speaks to Dajabón's strategic location within something that is larger and more complex than the United States proper but is part of its sphere of interests and influence, and thus equally "vulnerable." It is the place that the United States has long considered its "backyard."

Violence of Origins

The first time I see Colonel Juan de Jesús Cruz on the bridge connecting Dajabón and Ouanaminthe, Haiti, I am not sure what he is doing. Cruz is Dajabón's border chief for the Dominican Republic's version of the U.S. Border Patrol. Known as CESFRONT (Cuerpo Especializado de Seguridad Fronteriza Terrestre), the Land Border Security Special Forces Unit was first formed in 2006. Cruz clenches a purple umbrella with his right hand in an attempt to fend off the sun on this sweltering day. He is wearing the standard brown camouflage CESFRONT uniform, with black combat boots and a floppy hat. It is market day, as it is every Tuesday and Friday in Dajabón.

The bridge is crowded with hundreds of Haitians moving back and forth to and from the crowded binational market area on the Dominican side. Although most of the people come from Haiti's Ouanaminthe—a city of 100,000 people—the market attracts people from all over Haiti. Many of the Haitian men and women carry heavy, large white bags of rice and salt on their heads, in wheelbarrows, and in large wooden carts. Several times I make the awkward mistake of getting in the path of this constant push across the bridge, and people don't hesitate to tell me to get out of the way. Almost all are glazed with sweat as they trudge their way forward.

The colonel walks through the crowd, through the murmur of people speaking Kreyol, to the border point where the U.N. soldiers from Uruguay are positioned with their blue hats. The U.N. military presence in Haiti started in 2004 to "restore a secure and stable environment"[2] after the United States helped to orchestrate a coup d'état that ousted then-president Jean-Bertrand Aristide, one event in a long history of U.S. meddling in Haitian affairs. And now this controversial U.N. presence has stuck, long after the 2010 earthquake. One of the Uruguayan soldiers holds a video-recorder in his hand and pans back and forth in an ambitious attempt to monitor the flow of people walking by. When Colonel Cruz arrives at the point where the blue-hats are standing, he abruptly stops without setting foot in Haiti, as if he were the only one on the bridge respecting the boundary line. Just as abruptly, he turns around and walks back through the wheelbarrows and carts, past a woman balancing five blue barrels on her head.

Colonel Cruz occasionally stops to talk to somebody. Maybe he is interrogating, I'm not sure. I am sitting on the Dominican side of the two-lane bridge that spans the 100-yard width of the river. I sit in a shaded area next to a man in a bright yellow shirt from the Haitian consulate in Dajabón. We watch the constant movement of people under the blue sky that is beginning to build up clouds. I ask the guy from the consulate what he is doing, and he tells me he is there to make sure there isn't any abuse. I look at him for further explanation. He smiles and tells me that sometimes the military takes money from Haitians. "I try to make sure it doesn't happen," he says. The look on his face says that abuses have been going on for a long time. His look also says that some of the abuses have been much worse. As we sit directly above the Massacre River, we can see Haitian kids splashing in the water.

The river is named after the slaughter that imposed the Dominican-Haitian border. In one week in 1937, Dominican forces killed approximately 20,000 people, mostly Haitian, on the orders of U.S.-backed dictator Rafael Trujillo, in what National Public Radio termed the "twentieth century's least-remembered act of genocide."[3]

Before 1936, there was no mutually recognized border between the Dominican Republic and Haiti. In places like Dajabón, there was no clear, defining line separating the two countries. It was true borderlands, a zone where two countries simply smudged into each another.

There were many *rayanos*,[4] people of mixed Dominican and Haitian heritage. Haitians were more and more often filling the area in search of work. Trujillo was worried about a land grab, that these Haitian workers would claim what he increasingly saw as disputed land. Trujillo also was actively repopulating the area with lighter-skinned people from Eastern Europe and Japan, a racist program as poorly disguised as the dictator's practice of bleaching his skin. Although the "boundary agreement"[5] of 1936 finally demarcated a clear international divide, this wasn't enough. The expulsion of Haitians and the massacre—which mostly targeted Haitians but also included dark-skinned Dominicans—were the acts that imposed the Dominican-Haiti border. In a place where there was once uncertainty regarding territory and even social boundaries, now there was not a doubt.

According to Father Regino Martínez, director of the Jesuit organization Solidaridad Fronteriza (Border Solidarity, based in Dajabón), it was at a party in Dajabón on an October evening in 1937 that Trujillo declared, "*Está nublado*" (it's cloudy), referring to the precise moment when clouds are their blackest before unloading a torrent of rain. "We have to clear this up," Trujillo reportedly said at the party, held in a house that has since been converted into a funeral parlor.

In his Pulitzer Prize–winning novel, *The Brief Wondrous Life of Oscar Wao*, Dominican American writer Junot Díaz describes Trujillo as a "portly, sadistic, pig-eyed mulato who bleached his skin, wore platform shoes, and had a fondness for Napoleon-era haberdashery."[6] The era of Trujillo (1930–1961) was bookended by two U.S. military interventions and occupations. Trujillo remained in power with U.S. support because he was exactly the type of pliant dictator that the United States knew would protect its "backyard" interests. The Dominican Republic was a place where Washington's influence was so dominant and thorough that in 1915, President Woodrow Wilson insisted that U.S. citizens be appointed to all high posts in the Dominican government's cabinet. When Trujillo took power, he became the Dominican face of a U.S. empire that was expanding throughout Latin America and the Caribbean at a rapid rate.

Like most borders in the world, the borderline between Haiti and the Dominican Republic was not simply drawn by friendly geographers. In the slaughter of October 1937, Dominican soldiers and civilians armed with bayonets, rifles, and machetes scoured the borderlands in search of black people who could not speak Spanish. If people could say the Spanish word for parsley—*perejil*—with its difficult-to-pronounce "r" and the "j"—they lived.

Amabelle—one of the main characters in Haitian American novelist Edwidge Danticat's beautiful novel *Farming of the Bones*—could not pronounce the word when asked by a soldier. She was a servant to rich Dominicans, one of thousands of Haitians in the Dominican Republic's borderlands in 1937. Only a few blocks from where I sat on the bridge, she was beaten to the edge of death in the center square of Dajabón. Dominican soldiers pried her jaws open and stuffed parsley into her mouth. "My eyes watering, I chewed and swallowed as quickly as I could," explained Amabelle, "but not nearly as fast as they were forcing the handfulls into my mouth."[7] Then the crowd attacked. Someone kicked her in the back. Another person smashed her face with a fist-size stone. She crumpled to the ground.

Danticat described Amabelle's limp, almost lifeless body when the "air vibrated with a twenty-one gun salute."[8] People stomped their feet, applauded, and hurled rocks at the crumpled, injured bodies of Haitians strewn throughout the plaza while the Dominican national anthem thundered. Shocking as it may seem, this kind of violence often accompanies the imposition of new borders. What happened in 1937 could've been anywhere. It could have been the tens of thousands of dead and wounded during the Mexican-American War, strewn in what is now the U.S.-Mexico borderlands with the blood of Manifest Destiny. It could have been the slaughter of 5,000 during the War of 1812, establishing only a small portion of the international boundary between the United States and Canada and the imposition of U.S. territorial claim on Iroquois land.

Geographer James Anderson and sociologist Liam O'Dowd call this the "paradox of origins."[9] Throughout the world, in the creation of borders there is a "legacy of undemocratic and often violent origins—whether in national conflict, political revolution or the slaughter of native populations." In these border areas it's as if only the twenty-one-gun salute matters, not the broken bodies and shattered bones.

But the key is that the brutality and violence must then be obliterated from memory. Anderson and O'Dowd call it the "politics of forgetting."[10] The violent imposition "needs to be played down or concealed for territorial democracy to perform its legitimizing functions."

In Haiti, however, as in many places, the violent origins of a border cannot be forgotten. It is a "live issue." The history is in the colonel clenching the umbrella, walking back and forth along the bridge, who still enforces the results of this slaughter. The history here, like the Massacre River that runs below us, is alive.

The Present and the Past

It is an hour later when I walk onto CESFRONT's Dajabón base, a few blocks from my spot on the bridge. I approach the base while walking along the actual border line, behind the metal protest barricades placed as a type of border wall on the Dominican side of the Massacre River. CESFRONT border soldiers with long assault rifles between their legs slouch at their posts, ready to confront the "Haitian threat." I tell one of the guys that I am searching for Colonel Cruz. He says "sure" and points to the base. A group of people are standing in the patio area outside the base under a large, shady tree. I see Colonel Cruz without his umbrella. He's in the middle of everyone. Around the colonel is a mix of people, some in civilian clothing, some border guard soldiers with their rifles. The desert camouflage seems a little out of place, almost as though they were in a Middle East war zone, not staring across the Massacre River into Haiti. The station was painted the same way—sand-toned desert camouflage. Though it might slightly mix with the grassy savannahs in the north, it sticks out in the lush central mountain chain.

CESFRONT did not exist before 2006. That year, according to a report by the online newspaper *Dominican Today*, a group of "U.S. experts" reported that there was "a series of weaknesses that will lead to all kinds of illicit activities"[11] on the Haitian-Dominican border. Up to this point the Dominican military did patrol the area, but the "study revealed the lack of and in many cases bad shape of the Dominican Army's facilities, the lack of training, logistics, weapons, vehicles, garments, as well as low wages and bad nutrition."

In the report, which was never presented publicly but was leaked to the press, the U.S. team recommended that "there should be helicopters deployed in the region and [that] there be a creation of a Border Guard." Whether the report was the direct cause of what happened next might be debatable, but it shows, at the very least, Washington's persistent interest in the Dominican Republic starting to patrol its border. A month after this report appeared, Dominican president Leonel Fernández issued a presidential decree creating CESFRONT. Suddenly the Dominican Republic, like the United States, had its own border patrol.

The U.S. government has been involved with the formation of the Dominican border guard since the get-go. In 2008, the consul-general from the U.S. consulate, Michael Schimmel, told a group from the Columbia University Law Clinic that the U.S. military had given CESFRONT training in "professionalism."[12]

Schimmel went on to explain that the training of CESFRONT was part of U.S. policy to promote "strong borders"[13] abroad as part of the global war on terror.

Indeed, Schimmel was articulating something very new, not only in post-9/11 United States, but also in the rest of the world. His words echoed the *9-11 Commission Report*, which said, "9/11 has taught us that terrorism against American interests 'over there' should be regarded just as we regard terrorism against Americans 'over here.' In this same sense the American homeland is the planet."[14] This is a new, intense, yet overlooked manifestation of U.S. foreign policy and empire. In Haiti and the Dominican Republic, it is the newest of many faces of foreign empire—from the United States, France, and Spain—that has wielded its power in the island of Hispaniola since the time of Columbus.

Entering the Dajabón station is nothing like entering a U.S. Border Patrol station, where normally you can't get past the parking lot booth or the reception area without special permission. As I approach, I hear the booming voice of the colonel rising above the moaning of another man who is sitting on a metal bench. The man who is moaning wears a basketball shirt that says STARBURY in orange letters. He is moaning so loudly that I wonder if it is a bad time and consider not proceeding any further. But now all eyes are on me. I don't have a choice. A young boy sits next to the moaning man with a blank look on his face. Behind them is a brown CESFRONT truck, a symbol of the agency on the side door. As I approach, everyone stops talking. They look at me. There is an awkward silence. The man lets out a long, shrill moan, but nobody is paying attention to him anymore. When I explain myself, Colonel Cruz says: "Yes, of course, I will be happy to show you around."

Almost on cue, a shiny red SUV pulls up to the entrance gate of the CESFRONT base. A blonde woman gets out of the passenger side, and a man who looks Dominican steps down from the driver's seat. They look like tourists. The man yells to the colonel to see if it's okay for them to see the old international bridge, located on the other side of the station. "Yes, of course," says the colonel. He waves his hand for me to follow them too. The colonel tells me, as we follow the couple through the passageway to the old bridge, that this CESFRONT base was the old customs office. On the other side of the passageway, past the Massacre River, is Haiti. We can see people bathing in the river, kids splashing, women clustered in a small group on the other side of the river washing clothes in the rocks. Every once in a while the women break into a song that I imagine to be in Kreyol. Their voices are so sorrowful, brimming with emotion, that the songs send chills down the back of my neck.

The couple is now leaning on the railing of the bridge, looking down into the river and off into the distance, in the direction of the other bridge, where we can see hundreds of people hauling sugar and flour and crossing back and forth to the market. The man from the red SUV turns around from the railing and says to the colonel in Dominican-accented Spanish: "I really appreciate what you are doing, what the *militares* of the Dominican Republic are doing."

There is a pause.

"I mean," the man says, "look at that." He points to Haiti. He points to the people in the river, on the edges of the river. He signals to a point farther up on the bank where you can see the motorcycles in Haiti rumbling toward the river as if they might miraculously ride across the water and threaten his country and his loved ones. He points beyond that to where a cluster of off-color white tents have been pitched for a festival located at the edge of Ouanaminthe. Fifty-four percent of Haitians earn less than one dollar a day, 78 percent under two dollars. The man extends his arm and opens his hand as if he were blocking the idea of Haiti coming across and consuming the Dominican Republic. The dramatic hand gesture of this patriot implies that CESFRONT is indeed the first line of defense, Schimmel's example of a "strong border." But it is not terrorism that his hand mimics fending off, but rather the everyday crushing poverty endured by millions of black Haitans.

From where we stand, if we look the other way, we can see the CESFRONT agents on the Dominican side. They are sitting at their assigned posts, behind metal protest barricades, placed one after the other and that look like a row of crooked teeth, the rudimentary beginnings of a border wall. The agents look across the river with bored eyes, cradling their rifles.

When the couple and the colonel return to the front of the station, I stay. On the bridge itself, the international boundary is controlled by a metal gate, solid on the bottom and with rusty bars on top. It takes about one minute for two Haitian boys to prop themselves up so that their faces appear between the bars. One of the kids doesn't speak much Spanish but tries anyhow. He waves me over.

"*Dominicanos*," he says. I nod.

"*Haitianos*," he says. I nod again. He makes the figure of a gun with his fingers. He acts like he is shooting himself with his finger.

The Dominican Republic's new border guards have committed plenty of abuses against Haitians on the border, including killings. Earlier that day Father Regino Martínez of Solidaridad Fronteriza showed me a photograph of a dead Haitian child who had a bandage taped to his chest where a bullet had hit. According to the Catholic priest, this was just one incident in a long history of violence by the border guard against Haitians, including abuse such as threats, physical violence, illegal detention, and sexual harassment. CESFRONT shot the child on the brown banks of the Massacre River, where I stood with these two kids.

But, the thing is, the kids could be also referring to the slaughter of 1937, as vividly depicted to them by their families and relatives. Or maybe they are mixing them together. Maybe the present is but a logical continuation of the past.

Boundaries of Empire

In Santo Domingo, a balding, polite colonel named Orlando Jerez, in many ways a contrast to Cruz with his calm demeanor, receives a Dominican journalist and me in the CESFRONT headquarters. The office is in a swankier

part of Santo Domingo, far away from the historic center "founded" by Christopher Columbus's brother Bar-
tholomew in 1498. All around us are apartment buildings
and bungalows for the country's small but powerful upper class in this city of almost three million people. It is
likely that these buildings, including maybe even the CES-
FRONT office itself, were built by undocumented Haitian
people who do the majority of the grunt work in Santo Domingo's construction industry. Estimates of the number of
undocumented Haitians living in the Dominican Republic
vary from 700,000 to two million.

The white-skinned colonel is on the phone and mo-
tions for us to sit down in the chairs in front of his desk.
The first thing I see on the corner of his desk, much to my
astonishment, is a shiny box that contains a U.S. Border
Patrol model car, a replica of the car used on the NAS-
CAR circuit from 2006 to 2008. Next to the Border Patrol
symbol it says NOW HIRING. Along the side of the box is the
mission statement: "We are the guardians of the nation's
borders, we are America's frontlines." At first it is like seeing something familiar but out of context. The slick package and messaging seem corporate, almost like some sort
of U.S. fast-food icon such as McDonald's outside the confines of the United States. In such a case, even if you were
in an area you had never been to previously, you would
know that the place will be exactly the same, the same color
tile, the same countertops, the same greasy smell of fast-
food vats. Border security is messier, but there are striking
similarities to international corporate franchising.

When Jerez gets off the phone his talk is calm, friendly, and calculated. He sounds very public relations. He
only has a little time, but he will do his best. He tells us
that the Dominican Republic is a humanitarian country,

and by extension so is CESFRONT humanitarian, as if to preempt any accusations of abuse that we might have. The proof of the humanitarian mission is that they allow the binational market in Dajabón to happen. On those days, in a carefully controlled scenario, Haitians are allowed to cross without *papeles* (papers), he explains. He talks about the human rights training CESFRONT received, because they have to deal with "a lot of women and children" crossing the borderline. Jerez lets out a long, honest laugh when I asked if CESFRONT could cover the entire international boundary.

"Do they have technology?" I ask. He hesitates.

"No," he says.

"How many CESFRONT soldiers are there?" I ask.

This is when Jerez temporarily cuts off the conversation. He slices his hand through the air. He states that he had gone as far as he could go. To find out how many actual soldiers there were I have to ask the general, and the general is not there. He is talking about CESFRONT's chief, General Santo Domingo Guerrero Clase. Jerez points to the general's office to his right—with an empty chair, an empty desk, and an idyllic painting of the Dominican countryside on the wall. There is another U.S. Border Patrol NASCAR model car on his desk.

Do you have a relationship with the U.S. Border Patrol? I ask, with hesitance.

"Of course!" Jerez says. "They have an office in the U.S. embassy. In fact, on Monday they are going to have a three-day seminar with the U.S. Border Patrol in Santo Domingo."

"Can we go?" The Dominican journalist asks quickly.

"No," Jerez says, "it is a closed session."

Customs and Border Protection, it turned out, was

not as forthright about its relationship with CESFRONT. When the Columbia Law Clinic submitted a Freedom of Information Act request in 2009, the Department of State sent thirty pages of information for CBP to review. Of those thirty pages, nine were partially released, including two pages of email correspondence that are almost completely blacked out.

Phrases such as "We received the request letter from CESFRONT" and "We completed a cover memo to accompany the CESFRONT equipment request" peek out of the redacted text like clues to the mystery of why strong borders between the Dominican Republic and the hemisphere's poorest country might somehow, in someone's mind, have something to do with the war on terror, per Schimmel's earlier comment to the Columbia University students. Later emails reveal that Border Patrol agents came to the Dominican Republic to assist in the development of its "training curriculum and basic academy program" in 2009.

This sort of U.S. meddling in the Dominican Republic is not new. The United States has been focused on the Dominican Republic (as well as the surrounding Caribbean basin and Latin America) for a long time. In 1844—a mere year after the Dominican Republic's creation—a U.S. emissary declared that the Samana Bay, in the northeast, was "capable of providing protection to all the navies of the world."[15] This articulated a dream of European colonial domination that held sway on the island since the arrival of Columbus. The 1917–1925 U.S. military occupation of the Dominican Republic, under President Wilson, not only created a new national police but rewrote the laws regulating communal landholdings. This opened the floodgates for U.S. business interests. By 1925, twenty-one sugar companies controlled a quarter of the Dominican Republic's arable land, and more than 80 percent of this belonged to twelve U.S. companies, a historic and sharp example of "American interests 'over there,' " in the words of the 9/11 report.

It wasn't until after the Trujillo dictatorship, in 1965, that massive numbers of people from the Dominican Republic began migrating to the United States, often across the Mona Strait to Puerto Rico, according to Juan Gonzalez in his book *Harvest of Empire*. The year also marked the second U.S. military occupation of the Dominican Republic, when Washington stymied the minimal land reform agenda of Juan Bosch, which apparently didn't fit with U.S. plans for a region under the threat of "Communist tyranny."[16] As with today's Iraq or Afghanistan, the United States sent in 23,000 marines to "stabilize," as the common newspeak went, the country due to the presence of Bosch, a liberal progressive who claimed he was following the footsteps of U.S. president John F. Kennedy. Bosch's brief presidency in 1963 had ended in a military coup.

In 1965 there was "turmoil" because Bosch supporters wished to reinstate him, riling the Dominican military and spurring the U.S. invasion and occupation. "At stake are the lives of thousands, the liberty of a nation," said President Lyndon Johnson as justification of the invasion to the U.S. public in his May 1965 speech, "and the principles and the values of all the American Republics."[17] At first Johnson stressed that he had sent U.S. troops in to protect the thousands of U.S. citizens living in the Dominican Republic who were possibly going to "die in the streets," but then he got to what was really on his mind, and the minds of much of the elite, six years after the Cuban revolution: "The American nations cannot, must not, and will not permit the establishment of another Communist government in the Western Hemisphere."[18]

Noam Chomsky and Edward Herman note that "the invasion of 1965 reestablished a firm U.S. grip on the island."[19] U.S.-approved Joaquín Balaguer, one of Trujillo's most cherished public aides, took over the reins of the Dominican Republic from 1966 to 1978 (and again from 1990 to 1994). His iron-fisted rule protected expanding U.S. interests. In 1968, an Investment Incentives bill passed, encouraging foreign investment. U.S. companies swarmed into the Dominican Republic looking to cash in on the country's agriculture, food processing, mining, banking, and hotel and resort complexes. Union organizing was summarily crushed, as can be seen in this typical story from the *Wall Street Journal* in 1972: "When a union attempted to organize construction workers at a foreign-owned ferronickel mill project last year, Mr. Balaguer sent in the army to help straighten things out. While the soldiers kept order, the contractors fired 32 allegedly leftist leaders. . . . The strike was broken in eight days."[20]

In 1975, ten years after the U.S. invasion, the Dominican president Bosch described his country in these words: "This country is not pro-American, it is United States property."

Juan Gonzalez says that this sort of "U.S. economic and political domination," not only in the Dominican Republic but across the Western Hemisphere, has spurred a "torrent" of migration from places that "our soldiers and businessmen had already penetrated, cowed, and transformed." Gonzalez writes, "Most of us are uncomfortable thinking of our nation as an empire, even if Wall Street speculators and investment banks have repeatedly shown their ability to wreck entire economies halfway around the globe in a matter of hours—a power far greater than the Roman or Ottoman empires ever wielded."[21]

From Mexico there have been increasing levels of migration into the United States throughout the twentieth century, reaching historic levels, almost an exodus, after the investor-friendly North American Free Trade Agreement (NAFTA) was implemented in 1994. The harvest also comes from the great Puerto Rican migration of the 1950s, Cubans and Dominicans in the 1960s, Colombians in the 1970s. Central Americans, especially those fleeing U.S.-backed militaries in Guatemala and El Salvador, came to the United States by the thousands in the 1980s. Gonzalez writes that across the world migrants invariably "gravitated to the metropolises of their former colonial masters."[22]

Not only is all the world a battlefield, as many have said in the context of the U.S. global war on terror, it is also a place with many front lines, and thus many borders that need to be enforced. Dajabón is one of these places.

In his 2005 article "Where's the US Border?" Michael Flynn describes this post-9/11 dissection of the world and expansion of U.S. border enforcement efforts as almost a new form of military power. He argues that "U.S. border control efforts have undergone a dramatic metamorphosis in recent years as the United States has attempted to implement practices aimed at stopping migrants long before they reach U.S. shores."[23] Flynn claims that although since the early 1990s "the U.S. border has been hardened in a number of ways—most dramatically by building actual walls—it is misleading to think that the country's efforts stop there."

"Rather," Flynn writes, "the U.S. border in an age dominated by a global war on terrorism and the effects of economic globalization has become a flexible point of contention whose real presence can be both everywhere and nowhere at the same time—just like the migrants, terrorists, and smugglers at whom U.S. border controls are aimed."[24] In other words, the U.S. borders that now need protecting extend far beyond its national land-based boundaries to the virtual borders of its "national interests" and the edges of its ever-expanding military-surveillance grid—including cyberspace, the atmosphere, orbiting satellites and outer space.

The New World Border

U.S. response to Haiti's January 2010 earthquake provides a startling example of how quickly this new virtual border, and its associated fears of massive immigration or unrest, can mobilize. A large U.S. Air Force cargo plane flew one of the first U.S. aid missions. The plane circled over the devastated country for five hours. Over and over again it broadcasted the loud, prerecorded voice of Raymond Joseph, Haiti's ambassador to the United States in Kreyol:

"Listen, don't rush on boats to leave the country. If you do that, we'll all have even worse problems. Because I'll be honest with you: if you think you will reach the U.S. and all the doors will be wide open to you, that's not at all the case. And they will intercept you right on the water and send you back home where you came from."[25]

The disembodied voice from the sky was addressing Haitians still stunned and scrambling in the wake of an earthquake that killed approximately 316,000 people and left one million more homeless. U.S. State Department Deputy Spokesman Gordon Duguid explained the daily flights to CNN by saying, "we are sending public service messages . . . to save lives."[26] The announcements also contained messages about hygiene and information on where victims could go for food and other assistance.

Even DHS Secretary Janet Napolitano addressed the Haitian people in a televised broadcast from the Homestead Reserve base south of Miami. She underscored that traveling to the United States was a "dangerous crossing." She said: "Please do not have us divert our necessary rescue and relief efforts that are going into Haiti by trying to leave at this point."[27] The threatened diversion of resources soon happened. It included a bulky air force plane as well as sixteen Coast Guard cutters roaming Haitian waters. Authorities from the Department of Homeland Security also cleared space in a 600-bed immigration detention center in Miami and at the infamous U.S. base at Guantánamo Bay, Cuba, a detention center which was privately owned by the company Geo Group.

While the roots of such initiatives are very deep—U.S. efforts to police unwanted migration of people beyond the country's shores go back to the 1800s—the post-9/11 era represents a new level of intensity that has never been seen before. The modern blueprint for such policing took place in 1993 when the Clinton administration issued a policy directive shortly after the *Golden Venture*, filled with unauthorized Chinese nationals, ran ashore in Queens, New York. The Immigration and Naturalization Service's Operation Global Reach held to the spirit of the directive when it proclaimed that U.S. officials would "deal with the problem [of 'alien smuggling'] at its source, in transit, at our borders, and within the United States. We will attempt to interdict and hold smuggled aliens as far as possible from the U.S. border and to repatriate them when appropriate."[28] Before the homeland was called the homeland, it was already expanding.

This global boundary building expansion and promotion of "strong borders" show that this international border-building has reached new levels. More than 15,000 foreign participants in more than 100 countries have taken part in CBP training sessions since October 2002. For example, the Central America Regional Security Initiative, the $496 million U.S. counter-drug plan that has been in effect since 2008, identifies "border security deficiencies"[29] between different Central American countries as a key problem. U.S. Border Patrol agents with BORTAC, the Border Patrol's Tactical Special Forces Unit, have been sent to Guatemala and Honduras to train border guards. Since 2006, U.S. Customs and Border Protection has sent agents, dressed in brown jumpsuits, to the Iraqi borderlands to assist Iraqis in the creation of an enforcement apparatus and policing of their international boundaries. U.S. boundary-building efforts began even earlier in 2004 with an operation labeled "Phantom Linebacker" in which 15,000 border guards were trained to patrol—as the name of the operation indicates—in the spirit of American football. There are CBP attachés detailed to U.S. embassies in Brazil, Mexico, Kenya, South Africa, Italy, Canada, and many more countries.

In the May 2004 edition of the DHS magazine *Customs and Border Protection Today*, an article titled "CBP Attachés: Extending the Zone of Security" describes "our country's border" as "the armor of the body politic; it protects the systems and infrastructures that function within. Knives pierce armor and can jeopardize the body—so we sheath them; keep them at bay; and demand accountability from those who use them."[30] CBP commissioner Robert Bonner explained it as "extending our zone of security, where we can do so, beyond our physical borders—so that American borders are the last line of defense, not the first line of defense."[31] Now the Office of International Affairs has programs and initiatives focusing on "antiterrorism" and "global border security," among other things, worldwide. "Influencing policy throughout the world,"[32] says CBP, is what they are doing.

America's borders are being stretched in all sorts of complex ways. For example, as Michael Schmidt wrote in the *New York Times* in 2012, "An ocean away from the United States, travelers flying out of the international airport here on the west coast of Ireland are confronting one of the newest lines of defense in the war on terrorism: the United States border."[33] There, at Shannon International Airport, Department of Homeland Security officials set up the equivalent of a prescreening border checkpoint for air travelers.

Whether it is in your local airport or, as in Haiti's case, in the international waters around your country, the U.S. border is on its way to make sure that you are not a threat to the "homeland." If you are not suspicion-free in Washington's eyes, you will be stopped, forcibly if necessary, from entering the United States; in many cases you may even been prevented from traveling anywhere at all.

Perhaps this is why few here batted an eye when, in 2012, assistant secretary of international affairs and chief diplomatic officer for the Department of Homeland Security Alan Bersin flatly declared, "The Guatemalan border with Chiapas is now our southern border."[34]

The First Line of Defense

Against the Haitian threat to the "body politic" stands Colonel Juan Cruz, and in a very significant way he is the front line of U.S. defense. While he sits on the metal bench at the CESFRONT Dajabón base, he examines the identification papers of a robust Haitian woman who is wearing a white shirt and blue jeans. Cruz tells me that the man who had been moaning was caught transporting the young boy with the orange-striped shirt. Now the mother and the father of the boy have arrived to pick him up. The mother watches the colonel inspect her papers. It is her *matrícula*, a laminated residency card for the Dominican Republic. She tells Cruz that she has lived in Santo Domingo for eighteen years.

The colonel has a dark spot under his eye that looks like a bruise, as if he had recently been in some sort of bar fight in which he pissed off the wrong person. The colonel studies her residency card for one full minute. When Colonel Cruz talks he does so in a loud, declarative tone. When he talks, nobody else talks. He lifts up the card with his right hand and declares: "*Falso!*"

Everyone else stops talking. He doesn't say why he's determined it's counterfeit. The Haitian woman backs away from the colonel. She suddenly has a look that is tired and defeated. She is one of thousands of Haitians who live in Santo Domingo. The child's father steps forward. He pulls out a larger set of papers with several purple notarized stamps.

The colonel declares "*Falso!*" again. I am positioned in front of him just as he is raising the card. I snap a picture of Dajabón's CESFRONT commander. He explodes up from the metal bench and roars at me: "You can never, ever, take my photo."

There is a pause when everyone looks at me. The woman's husband then approaches the colonel again with the purple notarized papers to prove their residency in the Dominican Republic. "Don't talk to me," the colonel says dryly, "talk to the investigators." He points to people who, up to that point, I thought were random individuals on the patio, who were not in uniform, although one of them had been trying to soothe the moaning man earlier.

It doesn't take the colonel long to forget my picture-taking faux pas. He looks over at me. I am on the other side of the "investigations unit" official who is talking with the man. He points at the Haitian woman, who is still standing in front of the colonel.

"She says she's been living in Santo Domingo for eighteen years, but she doesn't speak Spanish," he shouts smiling across the patio, trying to explain to me the context. The woman hears everything he is saying and looks at me. Cruz says to her: "The Dominican Republic doesn't allow people into the country who don't speak Spanish." The woman stands there, saying nothing. I know what he says is untrue. They let monolingual gringos in all the time.

"*¿Cuantos años tiene aquí?*" The colonel asks her: "How long have you lived here?"

"*Dieciocho*," she responds in Spanish: eighteen.

"So now you *do* speak Spanish?" the colonel asks with a tone of fake astonishment. The woman walks away and sits on a cement border around a tree. She has a look that suggests she has been through this before, like so many other Haitians, and like so many Dominicans in Puerto Rico and the United States. It is starting to seem like a ritual of bombastic humiliation that the colonel is relishing. The father is still speaking earnestly with investigations. The man who was moaning before is now quietly watching the scene with a look of anticipation. The woman puts her face into her hands.

Then an idea occurs to the colonel. He declares what will be the ultimate proof, what will resolve the situation. If the child in the orange-striped shirt walks over and joins his mom, that will prove what they are saying is true. The colonel looks to the child and says, "If you are really her child go over and sit next to your mom." The kid looks at the colonel with a blank look. "If she is your mother, then go to her." The kid continues to stare. One of the men from the investigative unit catches wind of what is happening. He translates it to Kreyol. He leans to the kid, who now has a scared look on his face. He speaks softly to the kid, much more softly than the colonel. The kid doesn't budge. The colonel looks to me.

"You see," he says across a group of people, "she says that this is her son, but he won't go and join her." I look at the kid, but he isn't moving.

Another couple approaches the colonel. They whisper something in his ear. He is temporarily distracted. The Haitian mother drops her face into her hands. The couple is trying to convince Cruz of something, but I can't hear what they are saying. Suddenly he stops listening. He declares out loud that 80 percent of the sugar produced in the Dominican Republic is exported to the United States.

Since Cruz has now moved on to global economic affairs and how they affect the Dominican Republic, he doesn't see the child walk to his mother. The childs sits next to her on the cement border. He leans his head on her thigh as if it were a pillow.

After witnessing this, I ask Cruz if he would give me permission to talk with some of the CESFRONT border guards. I walk along the borderline where the Dominican Republic's border patrol agents are sitting, staring at Haiti. I approach an agent who is sitting on one of the stone monuments that officialy demarcates the boundary between the Dominican Republic and Haiti. I tell Díaz (according to his name patch) what I am doing, that I am a journalist, but he doesn't seem to want to talk. So I walk twenty feet away to the protest barricades that serve as the border wall and look at the clouds building over the Haitian-Dominican borderlands. When his partner, another CESFRONT guy but without a name patch, comes over carrying a long assault rifle, Díaz approaches me and we begin to chat.

As if I were a tourist, the first thing that they tell me is that I'm at the wrong place on the Haitian-Dominican border. They tell me I should go to Pedernales, another border town. They tell me that it is absolutely beautiful, well known for its waterfalls. They ask me about U.S. politics, especially news about upcoming elections. I ask them about how they like Dajabón.

Díaz tells me that their shift is from 6:00 p.m. to 12:00 a.m. He tells me that they live in the barracks and that they are stationed here temporarily. He tells me that people rarely cross here. He tells me that CESFRONT is not allowed to cross into Haiti. He asks me how the U.S.-Mexico border looks. I tell Díaz and his partner about the fencing, the sensors, the cameras, the agents everywhere you look. I tell them about the drones. I ask them if they have met agents of the U.S. Border Patrol. "Of course!" they say. "There have been trainings."

I ask him about terrorism, if terrorists were crossing this border, because that is the reason that the U.S. consulate gives for supporting the creation of CESFRONT, to promote strong borders.

Díaz gives me a look like I'm nuts. He holds this for a long moment, before saying emphatically: "No!"

My question was a rhetorical one. CESFRONT isn't really about terrorism. It is all about Haiti. It is about Central America and it is about Ecuador. It is even about the Dominican Republic. It is about the potential of mass movements of people anywhere. Mass movements of hungry people, usually desperate people, in a place that always has been considered the backyard of the United States of America. It is the manifestation of a new vision of global geopolitics in which human beings in need are corralled, their free movement criminalized, and their labor exploited.

Hunger

As I talk to the CESFRONT guys, the wind picks up and we can hear the rumbling thunder of an oncoming storm. I rush back to the Dajabón base and arrive just as the sky opens up. There is a passageway under the CESFRONT station and Colonel Cruz waves me in, gesturing to an empty space next to him. I look for the woman, the man with the notarized papers, the child with the orange shirt, the moaning man. But they are now gone, and the colonel is on to the next thing. I ask about them, but he points to some Haitian men who are sitting in a row across from us and are being detained. They are young—maybe seventeen, eighteen, nineteen. Their expressions range from forlorn to distressed to resigned. All are soaked from the downpour.

When I ask the colonel about the woman and the child, he points at the young men and says "*ilegales*," leaving his index finger hovering in the air like a micro-drone. I look at the young men. The word *ilegales* doesn't sit well with one of the teenagers. He looks at the colonel and says: "We came because of hunger." His Spanish is good, compared to the rest of the group's, as if he's been to the Dominican Republic before. There is also defiance in his voice, and desperation.

"You have resources there," the colonel declares to the kid. I am surprised that the Dajabón commander has decided to engage. He says this without any anger in his voice, as if he were relishing a great debate. "I have friends there," the colonel says. "They have resources. There are many who are not hungry."

The teenager gives the colonel a look of disbelief. The look says, *you don't know what you are talking about.* The look barely conceals that he is boiling inside. He lets it out, as if he no longer cares what the new Dominican border patrol thinks. "There is hunger in Haiti. There is poverty in Haiti." There is no way the colonel could not see that. "You are," he tells the colonel, "right on the border."

The kid looks at me, maybe for a sympathetic ear. And I think of what happened the day before at the restaurant when I arrived in Dajabón. I think back to Díaz's emphatic *no* when I asked about terrorists coming across. I think about Schimmel's statement that "strong borders" were a part of the global war on terror. The 9/11 report claiming that threats to U.S. interests were everywhere, and that terrorism was what threatened U.S. interests, that the U.S. homeland was the planet. However, the boundary-building on the Haiti border, and the post-earthquake confinement of Haiti, speak of a much broader understanding among U.S. policy makers and Homeland Security about what Haiti represents and what this young man tries to express to the colonel in raw, direct terms. Hunger makes people do extraordinary things.

"I know people with resources there," the colonel says, interrupting the teenager. The colonel is still enjoying the debate, even if it seems that he is losing and he is repeating the same thing.

"Very few," the teenager says, "very few have resources there." Even the way the teenager looks speaks to the bigger picture. He is pissed. He has seen enough. He has nothing left to lose. From the perspective of Washington, he is dangerous, a picture of the threat that lurks at the edges—and is a product—of the U.S. empire. In 2010, President Bill Clinton even apologized for Washington's free market agricultural policy toward Haiti during his presidency, which, according to Clinton, "has not worked." He told journalist Kim Ives, "We made this devil's bargain on rice. And it wasn't the right thing to do. We should have continued to work to help them be self-sufficient in agriculture."[35] Indeed, the highly subsidized U.S. rice, often known as "Miami rice," undermined three million farmers in the hemisphere's poorest country and cost hundreds of thousands of jobs. Again, aggressive economic empire-building spurred Haitians to unprecedented internal and international migration.

But the colonel thinks there are other motives. He looks at me as though he wants to share something personal. It is still raining; we can see the drops bouncing off the cement outside the passageway. The sky continues to growl with hunger. "And then there is the fertility rate," he says. I look at him, wondering what on earth he is going to say next. "They are going to come to my country and have seven to ten children." He gives the estimate in a tone of complete authority, as if he were going to pull a report out and show me instead of pulling loaded statistics from thin air. The tone of his words also seems to assert justification for the Dominican Republic's 2013 denationalization program—a ruling by its constitutional court to terminate the citizenship of more than 300,000 Dominican citizens of Haitian descent.

I look back at the kid, and he says, "We are coming because of hunger, plain and simple." I have heard people say the same thing across "America's backyard." I have heard people in Mexico say it, I have heard it said in Guatemala and Honduras. And I will hear a Dominican man say it to me in Santo Domingo two days later. This happens when I am watching a military parade near the *malecon*, a pathway that runs along the Caribbean shore in Santo Domingo. The vast blue sea backdrops the parade of military vehicles as the newly inaugurated president looks on. It is a hot but gorgeous late afternoon in one of the first settlements of the "New World." I begin to chat with a man standing next to me named Francisco, who is as captivated with the military parade as I am. We watch the CESFRONT contingent, the border guards, and it is much bigger than I thought. The first row of soldiers, although in their typical brown uniforms, have their faces painted the blue, red, and white of the Dominican flag. Other CESFRONT patrolmen sit in the back of long trucks with desert-camouflage combat helmets and stare stone-faced at the large crowds grouped along the avenue.

Francisco works cleaning the sewage system of the city. "A nasty job," he tells me, smiling. As we talk he tells me that he makes about 180 U.S. dollars per month. We eat, he says, but barely. He says he knows how difficult it is, and he has had friends who have traveled across the heavily policed Mona Strait (policed, of course, by the U.S. Border Patrol) to Puerto Rico, but he is going to try to go to the United States mainland.

PART III

THE WAR WITHIN

Total surveillance is increasingly the general condition of society as a whole. The prison begins well before its doors. It begins as soon as you leave your house—and even before.

—*Michel Foucault*

A shocking headline from South Carolina in 2011 seemed to say it all: the state was going to form its own "border patrol." The message was about something that has been going on for quite a while; border control has extended deep into the interior of the country and continues to expand at a rapid rate in what geographer Mathew Coleman calls the most significant post-9/11 fallout. More and more local police, and even more federal forces, are in one way or another becoming de facto border patrol agents. At the same time, more and more civilians are being indoctrinated to police each other in an ever more controlled "if you see something, say something" society.

Individual states such as Arizona, Alabama, and South Carolina that have passed anti-immigrant laws are often described as rogue by the media and the federal government. However, these laws would not exist without being empowered and sustained by the most advanced federal deportation and incarceration regime in U.S. history. Never before have so many people been expelled from the country. Never before have so many people been incarcerated while not being punished for a crime. And never before

Two Tucson Police Department officers keep reporters and public at a distance as protester Gabriel Schivone is cut out of the lock boxes holding him to a bus carrying nearly seventy recently arrested migrants to Operation Streamline. More than twenty people were involved in the act of civil disobedience that successfully shut down the controversial federal district court program on October 11, 2013. Photo by Murphy Woodhouse.

has the private prison industry in the United States reaped so much money.

Communities in vast swaths of the country now find themselves living in an intolerant and authoritarian border world where martial law, rather than civic authority, increasingly reigns. In this climate, municipal police, such as Maricopa County Sheriff Joe Arpaio and his armed posses in Arizona, assume a paramilitary quality as similar groups extend farther, and into more and more places, in the country. Patrols, both private and public, track and hunt people in ways that evoke the infamy of slave trackers. Some U.S. citizens, such as North Carolina–born Mark Lyttle, who was deported and spent more than 125 days wandering Mexico and

Central America, are expelled as if they were "foreign aliens" in the eyes of the state.

The art of surveillance, profiling, and monitoring of specific groups of people has reached a new level of militancy at the U.S. borderlands and other points of entry, but is no longer practiced there alone. Today, U.S. society as a whole is becoming a virtual border zone where the entire population is being monitored, evaluated, and categorized based on ever-changing threat levels assigned to ethnic, social, and political associations. Shutting down the government and impacting the work of hundreds of thousands of Americans is okay if you are a politician, but if you are among those who use your right to free speech to critique state or corporate power, you may find yourself in handcuffs, as have the more than 7,000 U.S. citizens jailed as a result of exercising their right to free speech at gatherings organized by the Occupy movement.[1]

Billions of dollars are flowing into this world of police and the policed, while the most basic of public interest programs and social services continue to be sequestered and cut: education, housing, food programs, environmental protection, national parks. Economically ravaged places like Detroit and Niagara Falls look like enemy attacks have already been carried out there, but we are told that they are key points to guard—not rebuild—in order to secure the "homeland."

Many argue that the militarization of police and the mass surveillance of the population undermine social conditions necessary for freedom, democracy, and an open society. They argue that these social conditions must be secured and defended as strongly as our borders are. In the absence of a federal initiative to do just that, increasing numbers of people are organizing and resisting the destructive ways of the wall and the drone and the prison and the gun, and imagining a much more humanistic, community-centered world for future generations.

chapter eight

FEEDING THE MONSTER

It is 6:00 a.m., and there is a loud pounding on the door. Gerardo looks to Luz, who is also suddenly jarred awake, and both get up quickly. He is in shorts and an undershirt. It is a cold March morning in Tucson, Arizona. Across the bedroom is a bunk bed. Somehow Adrián and Sammy are sleeping through the loud pounding. Adrián is twelve and Sammy is ten, and both, it seems, can sleep through a war. Gerardo looks out the window. There are armed men out there.

"Okay," he tells Luz, "they are coming for me."

Gerardo opens the door. Outside there are six agents from Immigration and Customs Enforcement (ICE)—a division of the Department of Homeland Security like the Border Patrol, but with a focus on internal enforcement. Minutes earlier, Gerardo and Luz were sound asleep in their bedroom. Now they are both disoriented, somewhere between awake and asleep. It is so early that there isn't even a hint of the sunrise. Luz listens with her heart racing. The men outside are just shapes with flashlights and guns.

Similar to military operations, predawn house raids have become a routine tactic for ICE. It's a time when people are at their most vulnerable: at home and likely asleep and defenseless.

While post-9/11 immigration geopolitics has mostly focused on the Mexico-U.S. border, writes geographer Mat Coleman, "perhaps the most significant yet largely ignored immigration-related fallout of the so-called war on terrorism has been the extension of interior immigration policing practices away from the southwest border."[1] Immigration raids have been going on for decades, but the current political climate has created a new scope and intensity for ICE, an agency that, like CBP, has seen an unprecedented flood of resources and funding. These resources are behind not only enforcement operations such as the one at Gerardo's house—programs with thousands of police and jails nationwide—but also the creation of the largest detention and deportation regime in the history of the United States.

Before 1986, the number of annual deportations in the United States rarely exceeded 2,000. It was that year, with the passage of the Immigration Reform and Control Act (IRCA), that the seeds for big changes were planted. IRCA was the first bill to define some crimes as deportable offenses. Perhaps this change seemed like a small addition to the law—more popularly known as a reform bill that brought legalization to hundreds of thousands of unauthorized people in the United States—but it wasn't. It provided the legal blueprint for a deportation regime that would only become more massive. The 1996 Illegal Immigrant Reform and Immigrant Responsibility Act considerably expanded the number of crimes considered deportable, launching a new system of banishment that would impact millions of people. By the late 1990s, the U.S. government was deporting more than 40,000 people annually, still only a fraction of what we see today. By the early 2010s Homeland Security was expelling well over 400,000 people per year from the United States. "One of history's most open societies," according to historian Daniel Kanstroom, "has developed a huge, costly, harsh and often arbitrary system of expulsion."[2]

The U.S. deportation regime is an efficient and finely tuned governmental monster that seems never to be satisfied but is always hungry for more human fodder. Blurring the boundaries between the militaristic and the bureaucratic, it is a coercive force that rules from above with discretion, violence, and military-style tactics, as seen with the ICE raid on Luz and Gerardo's home. It is also a "political-economic power" that is "anchored by relatively steadfast legal and administrative practice," as Mat Coleman told me in an email. In other words, according to Coleman, "there's no hard boundaries here between infrastructural and despotic powers, even though there may be important differences." The monster is a legitimized army of bureaucrats and "soldiers" in a promiscuous relationship.

Disoriented, twelve-year-old Adrián wakes up and looks into the jaws of this monster. There is a window by the bunk bed. He looks out and sees his father, Gerardo, surrounded by uniformed agents in the parking area outside their Tucson apartment. What happens next is an image Adrián will never again be able to shake from his mind. He sees an ICE agent telling his father to turn around. He sees an ICE agent handcuffing his father. It is still dark out. He sees his father being forced into a white van. His crime: using a false Social Security card in order to work.

"Mom," Adrián yells in the dark, "it's a white van." He yells it as if his father is being kidnapped. Luz rushes to the window, looks out, and sees the ICE vehicle backing out fast. Adrián looks at her intently as if they could track the van down and get his father back. There is still a chance. They can still hear the vehicle. When he sees his mother's shocked, panicked, and saddened face he explodes into tears. Neither of them has any idea about what might happen next.

Hidden in Plain Sight

The west Manhattan neighborhood of Chelsea is known for its vibrant arts scene, its gourmet food, and its high-end residences. It is also famed for the long-abandoned elevated train line that city officials have converted into a one-mile park, the High Line, that slots through a canyon of buildings containing blue-chip condos, art galleries, and expensive office spaces. As I walk around, it's hard to imagine that ICE would be concealed amidst all this high-end chic.

The epicenter of this neighborhood is the bustling Chelsea Market, located in a refurbished five-story brick building where the New York Biscuit Company invented the Oreo in the 1950s. Three stories above Chelsea Market is the office of the U.S. Marshals Fugitive Task Force, the workplace of A&E reality TV star and ICE Enforcement and Removal Operations supervisor Tommy Kilbride. The office's rise to reality television stardom is no surprise, given its location in the heart of the New York media empire.

Kilbride himself was a Border Patrol agent for four and a half years in San Diego before joining the Immigration and Naturalization Service in 1995. He says he is an early riser, and makes sure he gets to the office before anyone else, because he wants "to make the world a safer place to live."[3] Kilbride's role as a star in *Manhunters: Fugitive Task Force*, he asserts, has brought the "valuable" work of ICE to the national imagination.

Kilbride has a no-nonsense tone, underscored by a Brooklyn accent. In one of the show's episodes the agents go after a Jamaica-born man who "snuck back into the country," according to Kilbride, "an illegal re-entry."[4] Kilbride lets viewers know that it is not acceptable that this "seven-time convicted felon"[5] is roaming the streets of his native Brooklyn.

The episode opens with a panoramic shot of the Manhattan skyline under a dark cloudy sky, setting the scene for the predawn raid. It is 6:15 a.m. when the six-person task force arrives at the entrance of a brick apartment building in Brooklyn. Snow is slowly falling, giving a graceful look to this quiet part of the morning. The tranquility quickly dissolves when they enter the building. The music gets dramatic, tense, and anxious. In the background you can hear a heart thumping. The camera pans onto a solitary black door and slowly zooms in. One of the ICE agents silently mouths to the rest of the group: "Somebody is at the door."[6] The camera focuses on the hand of an agent clutching the handle of his holstered gun.

Although the impression is that the worst criminals in the world lurk on the other side, the officers politely knock on the door, as if they were visiting an old friend at midday. However, according to findings of a 2009 report, *Constitution on ICE*, by the Cardozo Immigration Justice Clinic, this detail is inaccurate. ICE agents rarely knock on the door. They pound, and they pound hard. [7] The authors analyzed hundreds of cases of house raids in New York City and the surrounding area. If a person voluntarily opens the door, even just a crack, agents force their way into the person's residence, most times with no judicial warrant.

In one case on Long Island, agents like Kilbride entered the bedroom of a sleeping woman, pulled the covers off the bed, and shined their flashlights onto her face and the face of her child, who immediately began wailing with terror. In another case on Staten Island, armed ICE agents entered the private bedroom of a man, forced him into a hall, and made him stand in his underwear before his brother, his sister-in-law, and their children while they searched the residence. Around the same time in Massachusetts, ICE agents burst into a three-family apartment building by kicking through the front door, leaving splintered wooden fragments on the floor. As in a war, they commanded everyone to lie down and stay still. They shined bright lights directly into each person's terrified face. They forced open more doors as well as a safe. They left the safe open, its contents and papers strewn around.

There were other cases of agents standing above people while they are still in their beds and barking things at them like "Fuck you!" and "You're a piece of shit!"[8] In response to such abuses, immigration judge Noel Brennan said: "It is hard for me to fathom a country or a place in which . . . the government can barge into one's house without authority from the third branch."[9]

In the episode of *Manhunters*, however, Kilbride and his crew have a made-for-TV judicial warrant to search the home of the Jamaican man's wife. When they capture him in Queens, Kilbride turns to the camera and says, "This is Lloyd [the Jamaican man's name]. He's done."[10] Kilbride says this with the confidence that they are right to remove this man from the country, as well as the other 400,000 people they will deport. To the public, they are fulfilling their mission of promoting "homeland security and public safety."

When walking through the Chelsea market—through its gourmet food stalls and high-end coffee shops—you don't even know that such a national security effort is constantly in progress right above you. Across the street from the Marshals Fugitive Task Force office are the restaurants of two of New York City's most prized chefs, who also have their own reality TV shows. Mario Batali stars in ABC's daytime show *The Chew*, and Tom Colicchio tops the bill in Bravo's reality cooking series *Top Chef*. Above their restaurants—Batali's Del Posto, where a seven-course meal goes for $145, and Colicchio & Sons, where a white asparagus salad is priced at $23—is another one of ICE's unmarked offices, this one for a counterterror joint task force. ICE is everywhere, and who would ever know?

This is just one of 186 unmarked ICE facilities as of 2009 that political scientist Jacqueline Stevens highlights in an article in *The Nation*. These secret locations exist in addition to ICE's listed field offices and detention sites. Some are located in strip malls and office complexes, places that seem so normal to everyday life in the United States that one wouldn't suspect they are government sites where armed federal authorities detain and interrogate people. It could be the Chelsea High Line. Stevens quotes Natalie Jeremijenko, a professor of visual arts at New York University, who called it "twisted genius" to hide federal agents here, in the "worldwide center of visuality and public space."[11] But it also could be in a suburban strip mall crammed in between neon-lit fast-food restaurants and retail outlets. Expansive as a retail chain with the budget of a large corporation, a national security necessity to some, a large monster to others, yet hidden in plain sight.

Through the good deeds of Tommy Kilbride in *Manhunters* and similar "reality" television programs such as National Geographic Channel's *Border Wars* (which profiles the U.S. Border Patrol), the public can be assured that

ICE and the Border Patrol are on the case, and that with the increasing militarization of immigration enforcement, the homeland is protected. The enemy—the ominous "criminal alien"—is presented, cultivated, and sustained in the public imagination. This makes the call for more resources all the easier; without a doubt there are many enemies who are out to get us.

The Feeders

From 2005 to 2012, ICE's detention operation budget more than doubled, rising from $864 million to $2 billion. The agency's detention facilities went from an 18,000-bed capacity in 2003 to a 34,000-bed total in 2011. Five hundred twenty-five of those beds are located in Batavia, New York, at the Buffalo Federal Detention Facility where I meet with ICE Supervisory Detention and Deportation officer Todd Tryon.

Tryon, a former U.S. Border Patrol agent, has a thick brown book on immigration law placed smack in the middle of his desk. Tryon tells me that the Buffalo Federal Detention Facility is "accredited by the American Correctional Association," as if it were a resort or hotel, or some feature you'd see in a guidebook for tourists.

Tryon wears a white button-down shirt and a blue-striped tie. He is balding and has a mustache. The Elmira, New York, native speaks with a Buffalo accent. He leans back in his chair and talks about "feeders," as if the Batavia detention facility were a large, hungry predator. The feeders, those who send people who have been arrested to the Batavia facility, are the Border Patrol, he says, the bridge authorities (CBP officials stationed at the bridges crossing the international border from Canada), and the ICE detainers. The people that CBP arrests are indeed filling immigration detention centers across the country. The ICE detainers underscore a whole new mission. Instead of just keeping people out of the United States, since 1996 they've been deporting people who are already here.

"ICE places detainers on aliens arrested on criminal charges to ensure that dangerous criminals are not released from prison/jails into our communities," ICE spokesperson Nicole Navas explains in an article. "Even though some aliens may be arrested on minor criminal charges, they may also have more serious criminal backgrounds, which disguise their danger to society."[12]

Navas might as well be next to Tommy Kilbride on *Manhunter* as she describes the "criminal alien" to the greater public, showing how easy it is to fill ICE facilities such as Batavia with violators. It doesn't matter if these non-citizens are unauthorized or legal permanent residents, they are the targets of U.S. government "criminal alien" enforcement programs, which began in the 1990s but are now led by Secure Communities, a high-tech information-sharing program linking ICE, the Department of Justice, and local law enforcement. In 2008, Secure Communities piloted in sixteen locales, but in five short years spread across the United States into more than 3,074 jurisdictions, covering 97 percent of the country.

Of all ICE's internal enforcement programs, Secure Communities is creating the most detainees for places like Batavia. In 2010, for example, ICE issued more than 65,000 detainers. It works like this: if police in any of those jurisdictions book a person, for whatever reason—including loitering, driving with an expired license, a broken taillight, or not carrying identification—their biometric data goes to the FBI and is checked against DHS databases. FBI forwards any potential "matches" to ICE officers at the Law Enforcement Support Center who look at the person's record for past immigration violations and criminal history.

Several things could trigger a detainer for a non-citizen, and with the significant expansion of what constitutes an "aggravated felony"—a category of offenses that could make one deportable—it became even easier for officials to expel people from the country. The term "aggravated felony" originally referred to three crimes: murder, weapons trafficking, and drug trafficking. The 1996 Illegal Immigration Reform and Immigration Responsibility Act significantly expanded this definition by adding two long subsections that could be applied retroactively. This has created an ever-widening list of crimes that can be considered aggravated felonies, such as a theft offense with a sentence of a year or more—even if the sentence is suspended. Many aggravated felonies have been interpreted by federal courts to include misdemeanors, and many are nonviolent offenses, underscoring the sensationalistic nature of the term, which is construed to apply to non-citizens only, and often applied to those holding green cards.

Widening the enforcement and deportation web even further is the category of "crimes of moral turpitude"—which include charges of fraud, forgery, and controlled substance violations—and the stage was set for today's deportation regime. According to the Florence Immigrant and Refugee Rights Project, which has provided legal services to thousands of detained immigrants in Arizona, DHS charges many undocumented people with crimes under these categories, such as using false documents or minor drug offenses (even possessing a pipe), and this makes it very difficult to qualify for any form of relief or bond. The fundamental legal parameters defining who is a criminal are expanding. With the post-9/11 security bonanza came more resources than the lawmakers of the 1980s and 1990s could ever have imagined. There are now more people to deport than ever before.

Secure Communities is the shining star of this deportation machine. If ICE determines that a person is a "criminal" or "removable alien," this information is sent to one of the twenty-four field offices that ICE has in all major U.S. cities. The field office will then examine each case, and if it wants to expel someone and initiate the prerequisite removal proceeding, ICE will issue a detainer.

Tryon tells me that when detainers are issued, "jails will hold people for up to seventy-two hours for us." ICE officers will pick them up at the jail and transport them to where we are sitting in the Batavia facility.

With approximately 34,000 beds at their disposal nationwide, Tryon says, ICE has the budget and resources to expel 400,000 people from the country per year. He says this without emotion or embellishment. He says it as if the detention facility were a factory. According to National Public Radio, that's exactly what it is: Congress has given "U.S. Immigration and Customs Enforcement . . . a policy known as the "detention bed mandate.""[13] They must keep those 34,000 beds full each day.

Tryon doesn't mention that the United States has never before deported so many people.

Even so, the glass is half empty. There are most likely more than 11.5 million people in the United States who do not have the proper paperwork necessary to live and work here legally, Tryon tells me, "and you have to take your resources and go after the criminals. If we catch someone and find out that they are a farmer without correct papers," he says, "we will release them."

Batavia is located right between Rochester and Buffalo on Interstate 90. Although the ICE facility is huge, it is still easily missed and completely out of view from the throughway around this town known for horse racing and Batavia Downs. Unlike Manhattan's Chelsea office, the detention center here is clearly marked, one of the nine such facilities that ICE actually owns in the United States. The other 300 or so sites are contracted out, more than half to private prison companies and the rest to cities, towns, and counties.

Club Fed

Sometimes the Batavia Police Department calls ICE when officers pull over a person who speaks only Spanish. When ICE agents interpret, Tryon explains, they must ask, by virtue of the subject only speaking Spanish, if they have documentation to be in the country. But he insists that the ICE officers are also humanitarian. He insists that "if the Batavia police call us over because they have pulled over a Spanish-speaking woman who is nursing, we will let them go on their own recognizance."

This is Tryon's tone—a sort of jagged humanitarian benevolence—as he explains things to me during our tour of the innards of the detention-deportation apparatus. Yes, there are the coils and coils of razor wire. Yes, there are the motion sensors placed all around the detention center. Yes, there are the dark control rooms where guards look into dim monitors twenty-four hours a day, 365 days a year. And, yes, he would say, this is what is needed in the world to keep people like Tryon, me, and other law-abiding U.S. citizens safe.

There are also good things—such as taco night on Tuesdays. Everyone loves taco night. But even taco night has its drawbacks, because it's a fire hazard, Tryon explains. "That's when they put the tacos in the toaster." When we enter the industrial kitchen, Tryon exclaims with a broad smile that this is the "best-smelling place in the facility." It gets its food from Sysco, the same company that delivers food products to restaurants all over western New York. In other words, "delicious and nourishing," Tryon gushes.

True, he concedes, a few of the "bigger guys" sometimes complain. He explains that some people may think they need more than 3,200 calories, which is the "correct amount."

Tryon shows us the basketball court that also serves as a chapel and a mosque. He tells us that they even removed the Buffalo sports teams' logos that had been painted on the wall, because the incarcerated Muslims complained that the logos were inappropriate for a space being used for religious worship. Not only are the detainees' spiritual needs satisfied, so are their intellectual and artistic pursuits. There are two small libraries next to the basketball court, and one is a law library—much needed, since many of the detainees have no lawyer and only limited, if any, legal support.

And there is the "public art." We see this when we are walking down a hallway that extends—for what looks like a good mile—from the medical unit to the processing room, past the kitchen and laundry room to where the detainees are caged. In a section of the hallway there are dozens and dozens of flags of countries drawn in perfect rows on the wall by, Tryon tells us, done by a feisty Jamaican who had disciplinary problems but was an excellent artist. We stop there for a moment to appreciate the flags, as if Tryon were a restaurateur showing off the diverse international backgrounds of this Batavia resort's visitors. Tryon says that there have been people from every single one of these countries, his hand sweeping the landscape of colors and flags. I see red-striped Peru and Iceland and Honduras.

"Except for one," he says. "Can you guess which one?"

"The United States?"

"No."

"Canada?"

"No," his voice is restless with this one, Canada being so close.

"Iceland?"

"No, no, no."

"I'm giving you a hint," he says, "I am standing right in front of it." He is standing in front of North Korea.

In the processing room Tryon finally boasts, "They call it Club Fed." He pauses, then says: "Both the detainees and the staff." He continues to talk about how well the prisoners are treated. I am looking at a group of men, all wearing white ICE T-shirts, joking behind the counter. One of them stands out: he has a blond flattop and a red face that looks as if he had too much sun on the Fourth of July. I wonder if it is difficult or easy for these men to explain their jobs to people outside their world.

Indeed, what Tryon is describing with colorful and comfortable language is the Batavia facility as a perfect, micromanaged, "Border Patrolled" territory in which everything is under control and everyone is under surveillance, even in the shower. The person who designed their phone system, for example, should be "awarded a medal," Tryon says. He can listen in on phone calls, all of them, past and present. "Good intel," he says, tapping his head. It is a place where everyone is properly classified in red, orange, and blue uniforms according to their criminal records.

Despite all this, the only reason anyone is in the facility is that they are non-citizens who are in the United States without the proper paperwork, like a visa or green card. If they were U.S. citizens, they should not be there, although citizens have been detained and deported before, as will be discussed later. If they have committed a crime, and the majority have not, they would have already been released by the criminal justice system. This civil detention is considered administrative; its purpose is to hold detainees in place so they cannot skip out on their hearings. They are not here to be punished. "Detention centers are not legal punishment," said Jacqueline Stevens. "They are for people who are trying to pursue their civil right to remain in the country."[14] The idea that that these detainees are "criminals" is a dangerous myth that even penetrates the halls of Congress.

But you would never know this when we visit Bravo One on the final leg of the Batavia tour. It is an area divided into three separate sections. We go up the stairs to a control room. It is like climbing up one of the Border Patrol's desert surveillance towers. Like the central control room, it is dark inside and has lots of switchboards. There is no need for monitors, since the large windows overlook the three areas. Through the window we are watching the "reds," the worst criminal offenders, finish their lunch. Though the number constantly fluctuates, says Tryon, on any given day there might be a 100 or so "reds" in detention. These are the "aggravated felons," Tryon explains, taken from the street. Although he uses this term that is specific to immigration law, and which could also be derived from a previous misdemeanor, he doesn't explain further.

One of the reds is a black man with short dreadlocks. He has on a blue medical mask and holds a spray can in his hand. He is wiping the tables and cleaning up after lunch.

Another man who looks as though he may be of Asian ancestry is the only person who continues to eat. He is eating slowly. Maybe he doesn't want to go back to his cell where he is locked down for fifteen hours a day in administrative detention.

I ask Tryon again about the number of beds. He says the inmate population will go up "when harvesting season comes." When he says the word "harvesting" his voice cracks, and he pauses awkwardly. Earlier in the conversation he said that they didn't go after people who work on the farms. Then he says, "Sometimes Mexicans want to get picked up after harvesting season to get a free ride home."

Through the window we can see some of the "reds" returning to their rooms. We can't see the bunk beds from where we stand, but Tryon says that they are welded to the wall. Tryon explains that the men we see below us are "dangers to society," even though it is civil detention.

We turn around and look out another window. This time it's the "oranges." "Oranges" might have committed some minor crime in their past. They aren't completely in the clear, like the "blues," but they are not locked down, like the "reds." Most men are crowded downstairs, some sitting at white tables surrounded by blue chairs, some mingling around, only a few upstairs where there are no separate rooms. There is bunk bed after bunk bed after bunk bed. I can see an "orange" sleeping on one of the beds. He has on a white T-shirt and orange pants, and his arm hangs over the side.

"We have to make gut-wrenching decisions sometimes," Tryon says about the large number of removals ICE executes each year, "but I don't let my personal feelings get in the way." Tryon pauses, looking down at several men grouped around the phones, many attempting to make calls to loved ones. "I'm here to enforce the law. If they don't like the law, why don't they dialogue with Congress and change that law?" He continues talking as if the very presence of the men in front of him were a critique of his work.

"I have four children of my own," Tryon says. "It's gut-wrenching, but the law is the law."

Most of the detainees are people of color. The men employed to guard them sit behind a countertopped island in the middle of the detention area in a sea of orange jumpsuits.

People stay anywhere from two weeks to seven years, Tryon tells me. "These guys appeal, appeal, and appeal until they finally get tired of appealing and say they can't do it anymore. They hold the key to their own jail cell." They also hold the key to their permanent banishment from the United States.

However, Lauren Dasse, executive director of the Florence Immigrant and Refugee Rights Project says: "Many times, detained immigrants must make the extremely difficult choice of whether they stay in detention and fight their case, or take a deportation and be sent back to a country that in some cases doesn't feel like home, because they have been in the United States for so long, or they may have a fear of persecution if they are an asylum seeker. Both options include being separated from their loved ones." Dasse refers to something that Tryon doesn't mention: many of the people who Homeland Security detains are established in the United States and have families. Dasse explained to me that the vast majority of detained people are represented pro se—by themselves—in immigration court because neither they nor their families have the resources to hire an attorney. The Florence Project (which is located in Arizona), like many other organizations across the country, provides assistance to people who are forced to represent themselves in court.

"We have to act for the greater good," Tryon continues, "and take out the greater risk to society. It's been proven by John Hopkins or someone, I can't remember who," he says, waving his hand in the air in annoyance at his own inability to remember, "for every aggravated felon we take off the streets, five less crimes are committed in the country." When I search for the study Tryon wishes to cite, I can't find it.

"You do the math," he says, "400,000 times five." He pauses to allow us to attempt the complicated mathematical feat. With this, Tryon describes a ravenous monster that is kept in line with bureaucracy and budgets.

An article by Nina Bernstein in the *New York Times* quotes another term used by many for the massive growth in the number of people—non-citizens—being detained by the United States: "the immigration gold rush."[15] Now towns from New Mexico to New Jersey, from the Pacific Northwest to the Deep South, are in hot pursuit of these prisons and jobs, and the rivers of federal money gushing into them.

The *Times* article describes a detention center in Central Falls, Rhode Island, one of many town and city governments with an ICE contract to set aside jail "beds" for people being detained due to their residency status. In cash-starved Central Falls, where the prison is located just beyond a Little League baseball field, the federal government paid $101.76 per day for each bed, a bit lower than the national average of $122 per day. This "rare growth industry"[16] (during the recession, the *Times* stresses) has helped private companies such as Corrections Corporation of America (CCA), whose contracts with the Department of Homeland Security have more than doubled. In 2005, Corrections Corporation of America made $95 million. By 2011, it was making $208 million per year. Its stock prices have risen right along with it, as has its lobbying budget. Since 2003, CCA has spent on average $1.8 million per year to lobby Washington officials. They want detainees, more and more detainees.

Since the 1980s, jails have been a good "investment," with new strict laws that led to the mass incarceration of drug offenders. The immigration "payoff came after 9/11 in an accelerating stream of new detainees: foreigners swept up by the nation's rising furor over illegal immigrants," according to Bernstein's article in the *Times*.

Like Central Falls, western New York is a place where incarceration rates help boost a struggling economy. The Batavia ICE facility, Tryon says, is one of the biggest job providers in the region. He says this knowing that Buffalo, the second-poorest city of its size in the United States, is a place starving for good jobs.

"There are 270 contracted employees at work 24/7, including a medical unit, guards, and health services. The guards," he says, "make $30 an hour."

"They make more than me!" Tryon exclaims, with a controlled law enforcement smile. "They're not gonna get another one like that around here." Besides keeping the world safer, his smile seemed to say that immigration detention creates jobs, and even makes careers.

Border Patrol Court
Every single weekday in the Tucson Federal Courthouse, dozens of people face a judge as a result of their residency status. Pérez Méndez is among those dozens. While he in-

sists that he is twenty-one years old, he has the soft facial features of a child of fourteen or younger, which makes the interaction between him and U.S. magistrate judge Jacqueline Marshall even more painful to watch. Pérez Méndez's crime occurred four days before, when he crossed the U.S.-Mexico border without authorization. The U.S. Border Patrol arrested him in the Arizona desert. And now he is in the courthouse—shackled at the wrists and ankles, and chained around his waist—along with sixty other people convicted for "illegal entry" into the United States.

The judge has singled Pérez Méndez out, and unlike the others, who approach her in groups of five, this kid, obviously frightened, is the last one to shuffle up to the stand. He does it alone.

"I don't believe you are twenty-one," says the judge. "We don't lie in this court. That isn't how we proceed." She explains that this is why she singled him out.

Pérez Méndez doesn't respond.

"Do you have any relatives? Parents? Brothers? Cousins traveling with you?"

"No," he says. The judge looks at him suspiciously, trying to discover, I imagine, the motivation for his assumed lie.

The judge tells him that she has no other choice but to place him under oath. She explains to him what that means—if he were to lie, then it would be perjury. Perjury is a criminal offense carrying prison time. "Is that what you want?"

Up to this point the Operation Streamline proceedings—a zero-tolerance border enforcement program that criminally charges all people who cross the U.S.-Mexico border without authorization (not through an official port-of-entry)—have unfolded as they normally do. On this day in mid-March 2012, fifty-eight men and two women, all with brown skin reddened after days of walking under the blazing Arizona sun, have already approached the judge in groups of five with their heads bowed submissively, their bodies weighed down by metal shackles and chains. In Tucson alone, approximately 17,850 people will approach the judge this way in 2012. Some will go to prison, and everyone will be formally deported, all for being in the United States without the proper papers. They are wearing clothing dirtied and damaged by the desert. They contrast sharply with the much whiter judicial personnel, well dressed in pressed shirts, dress pants, and polished shoes, some milling about or checking their smartphones, others sitting at tables.

Programs like Operation Streamline, which is active every weekday in more and more places along the southern U.S. border, are a significant part of the U.S. Border Patrol's interior advance, and its 2012–2016 goal is explicitly stated in the title of the strategy paper "The Mission: Protect America."[17] Operation Streamline has been in existence since 2005, running in the Tucson sector since 2008, and now is a cornerstone program of the "Consequence Delivery System"[18] of the Border Patrol's strategic plan. In many targeted areas along the border, undocumented people from Mexico are no longer "voluntarily"[19] returned after arrest, as part of what Border Patrol termed the "catch and release"[20] protocol. Like the ever-hardening border, things have changed in the judicial apparatus. They now face a judge.

These types of multi-agency efforts (Streamline includes the U.S. magistrate, federal judiciary, U.S. Attorneys' Office, and the U.S. Marshals service among others) are paramount to the Border Patrol's quest to efficiently enact the "layered approach to national security"[21]—meaning more boundaries of all shapes, sizes, and purposes, well past the actual international divide.

U.S. Border Patrol chief Mike Fisher describes the strategy as a "multi-layered, risk-based approach" to "enhance the security of the border"[22] by more efficiently using the resources and personnel at Border Patrol's disposal, particularly after the massive post-9/11 resource buildup.

"This layered approach," Fisher explains, "extends our zone of security outward, ensuring that our physical border is not the first or last line of defense, but one of many."[23]

Operation Streamline joins ICE operations and programs such as Secure Communities in the execution of many more arrests, producing much more human fodder for the incarceration mill. All the men and women facing the judge on this day will be charged with the federal criminal charge of "illegal entry" since they were "caught in the act." The courtroom becomes the judicial extension of the U.S. international boundary line. And, as displayed so poignantly through Judge Marshall's interaction with Pérez Méndez, the judge becomes one of the many anointed border guards for a mushrooming judicial enforcement program. For example, the U.S. Senate's proposed immigration reform bill in June 2013 calls for an expansion of Operation Streamline in Tucson from 70 to 210 people prosecuted per day.

However, on another occasion, when a group of students asked Marshall about the effectiveness of Streamline, she responded by saying it was a waste of resources. When pressed by students from Vassar College as to why she even did it, she said she had to put her children through college. Magistrate Judge Bernardo P. Velasco continued Marshall's logic, telling a group of students that Operation Streamline is a "jobs bill" as recorded by student Elena Stein: "We have Border Patrol officers who are employed, prosecutors employed, marshals employed, courtroom deputies employed, prison guards employed. A lot of people are making good money to support their families."

In this context, it seems almost like absurd theater watching Pérez Méndez attempt to take the oath. He has to raise his right hand, but can barely do so because it is shackled and chained to his left hand. So he also has to raise his left hand almost up to his chin in order to be able to lift up his right hand too. This is sufficient for the judge, but incomplete, because his right hand is never entirely raised.

After the oath, the judge asks, "Do you want to consult your lawyer?"

His lawyer, referred to by the judge as "Washington," is a tall African American man who towers over Pérez Méndez. They talk for a few minutes off to the side.

Washington then approaches the stand again and tells the judge: "My client has maintained since the get-go that he is twenty-one years old. His birth certificate gives him a birthday in 1991."

"It could be fake," the judge says abruptly.

"Yes," Washington says reluctantly, "he has the mannerisms and look of a fourteen- or fifteen-year-old." It's true. Pérez Méndez looks younger than twenty-one. He looks like a teenager who should be starting high school, not shackled in front of a judge.

The judge looks at Pérez Méndez, who is now under oath.

"How old are you?" asks the judge.

The following pause is loud. To the right side of the judge sits the interpreter, who speaks her question into a microphone on his headset. Pérez Méndez's headset, with its curving band under his chin, almost looks like another fixture of the detainment apparatus that chains down his ears.

"Twenty-one years."

The judge looks up to the ceiling as if she were trying to see the sky.

"Where are you from?" she asks with a hint of exasperation.

"Chiapas."

"How far is Chiapas?"

"Three days."

"Did you walk?" the judge asks, but it is unclear if she means from the border or from Chiapas.

"Yes."

A bald, stocky man dressed in a fresh-pressed shirt and tie stands up and says: "I'm sorry, but the U.S. government does not believe that he is twenty-one years old."

The judge says that she both applauds and agrees with the U.S. government.

Then, surprisingly, she drops the charges against Pérez Méndez. But she isn't finished.

"Three days," Marshall says, dwelling on the number, "I imagine you came to find a job?"

The new question seems to startle Pérez Méndez. His story could be one of many. If he is under eighteen years of age, as the judge suspects, he might be trying to unite with other stateside family members who are also in the country without authorization.

"There aren't as many jobs as there used to be," Judge Marshall says. "Once you get back there," she says implying Chiapas, "don't come back."

"And those who hire illegal aliens are no longer going to do so," Marshall continues, adding, "they will be charged," as if the Department of Homeland Security were busting employers left and right throughout the country.

Perez Mendez stands there nodding to everything that she says, but the judge is just getting to her punch line: "If you do it again you will be charged. And do you know what will happen to a person who looks like you in prison?"

She pauses.

"They beat people who look like you in prison. That should scare you. Do you understand that?"

Pérez Méndez only nods.

I Have Got to Get Out of Here

After watching ICE take away his father in a white van, the normally talkative, yet extremely sensitive, twelve-year-old Adrián will not say another word for hours. He will not see his father, who will be incarcerated at the Corrections Corporation of America (CCA) facility in Eloy, Arizona, for another six months. Adrián's grades will plummet at school. His teacher will tell his mother, Luz, "His body is here, but his mind is not." He and his brother, Sammy, will be extremely aware of the police. Both of them will be sensitive to knocks on the door. Like many other children whose parents have been taken away by immigration authorities, any knocking will produce anxiety and they will try to hide their mother. Luz says that they tell her, "I don't want them to take you away."

They are not the only children left in the traumatic predicament of suddenly losing one or both of their parents. Between 2010 and 2012 this has happened 200,000 times. According to the Applied Research Center in its report "Shattered Families: The Perilous Intersection Between Immigration Enforcement and the Child Welfare System,"[24] there are so many obstacles between parents and their children that Child Protective Services has terminated parental rights in 5,100 of these cases.

When Gerardo and Luz came to the United States, Gerardo bought a fake Social Security card in order to be able to work. For eighteen years, Gerardo used this card to work for construction contractors and restaurants. He was first arrested in the Tucson restaurant where he had ascended from dishwasher to busboy to cook. Cooking, according to Luz, is Gerardo's passion. He has an excellent *sazón*, she says, an excellent chef's intuition, and the couple has dreamed of opening a restaurant together. Even in jail his chef's mind is always at work. He even learned how to make cheese from the cafeteria milk while in detention.

The first time the police came, he was chopping vegetables in the restaurant's kitchen. It was a joint police operation between the Tucson and Mesa Police Departments that arrived with a caravan of vehicles, both marked and unmarked, including several armored cars. The Social Security card he was using (and paying into) was that of a twenty-one-year-old from Phoenix. He spent five months at the Pima County jail. When he was released on bail, it was not his family but ICE that picked him up. He was charged with a crime of "moral turpitude"—being present without "lawful admission" to the country—and placed in removal proceedings. ICE transferred him to the CCA facility in Eloy. After several months there fighting his deportation, his family, with help from their community, posted bail. This was not identity theft. It was the equivalent of somebody getting busted with a fake ID.

He was out for a year when ICE arrived with the intensity of Navy SEALS going after Osama Bin Laden. Homeland Security had decided that letting Gerardo out on bail was a mistake. He was a "criminal alien" and should not be on the streets.

It was a cold and windy March day in southern Arizona when I traveled with Adrián and Sammy from Tucson to Eloy to see their dad. The latest news was that there was actually a white guy in there, a French guy. "The first one I've seen," Gerardo told the kids before we left.

Gerardo has been in the CCA facility in Eloy for one year. The kids have been going every two weeks for the last six months. They know the routine. They know we have to wait in the foyer with all the other families, most of whom only speak Spanish. They know that in the real waiting room there is a vending machine. It only sells junk food and candy, but getting some is a goal that the kids latch on to. I am here because the family has offered to give me a glimpse into their nightmare. When they finally allow us into the waiting room, Adrián and Sammy beeline it to the vending machine. Then they poke each other with pens for a bit and start playing I Spy. I walk to a plaque on the wall that shows a list of CCA's employees of the month. Then I watch a shift change. The guards come in carrying clear backpacks, their law enforcement belts over their shoulders.

To economically depressed Eloy and the surrounding area in central Arizona, the four CCA prisons have not only created jobs as the top employer, but also helped the small city of about 17,000 inhabitants upgrade its water lines and purchase new police cars as well as fund the construction of a "new town playground."[25] This is quite an improvement for a town that looks almost abandoned when you drive past it on Interstate 10 between Tucson and Phoenix, and where 32 percent of residents still live below the poverty line. CCA also pays Pinal County $2 per bed per night, which funds the county's now infamous sheriff's department.

When they announce Gerardo's name we all jump to attention. The two children run to their dad. There he is, standing in a dark green jumpsuit, the equivalent of an "orange" in Todd Tryon's world. They hug him at his waist, one kid on each side. Gerardo tenderly caresses their heads and faces. I look on awkwardly, not saying anything. I shake Gerardo's hand. His face is friendly but worn. His dark hair is parted on the side. We greet each other in Spanish.

In the visiting room emotional reunions are going on all around us. To my left a woman and a man sit across from each other, their hands clasped across the table. The woman wears a dark green jumpsuit like Gerardo's. They don't seem to be talking, this couple, just staring into each other's eyes. I watch them for a full fifteen seconds before the man whispers something across the table as if quietly fighting the clicking seconds.

Across from me, the two children place themselves on either side of their father. Gerardo tells Adrián to work harder at school because he's now failing five of his six classes. Gerardo's voice has a sad tone to it, as if he knows why Adrián hasn't been putting in the effort. Sammy places his chin on Gerardo's shoulder on the other side. The thick-eyebrowed Sammy is the quiet one, and he seems to be content with just Gerardo's physical presence.

From across the table Gerardo tells me about a job that he had hauling material to build a swimming pool. He hauled really heavy stuff, so much that when he got home he collapsed. "I was so exhausted," Gerardo says, "that I even said no to the kids when they asked if they could massage my back."

"I just don't want my kids to have to do the same thing," he tells me. He looks from side to side, from Adrián to Sammy, curled up on either arm. Gerardo then looks to Sammy. He asks about school, his life. He asks them both about Luz, their mother. Since he's been here they lost their apartment. Now they are living in someone else's house, a member of the community who offered them space in her home until they got through the crisis.

"I have got to get out of here," Gerardo says with a release of emotion. He says this knowing that he has to remain strong. He could leave if he signs the "voluntary" removal papers, as he almost did when his mother died. He almost did it. He came close. But he didn't.

"I have got to get out of here," he says once more, as if talking for the 400,000 people ICE will arrest and detain that year. It is such a large number, yet its horror is concealed and bureaucratized. It only reaches the national dialogue for brief moments before the next news item drowns it out. Gerardo seems to realize the futility of trying to stay in Arizona with family—you can hear it in his tone of voice.

Michelle Alexander, author of *The New Jim Crow: Mass Incarceration in the Age of Colorblindness,* closely captures the experience of Gerardo and so many others incarcerated in this deportation machine in a speech: "All of this, all of these systems of racial and social control, and this entire system of mass incarceration all rest on one core belief. And it is the same belief that's the same Jim Crow. It's the belief that some of us, some of us, are not worthy of genuine care, compassion, and concern. And when we effectively challenge that core belief, this whole system begins to fall right down the hill."[26]

In Eloy, as Gerardo continues to look longingly at his children, the gray-haired guard behind the desk, who seems friendly, loudly announces that visitors only have five minutes left.

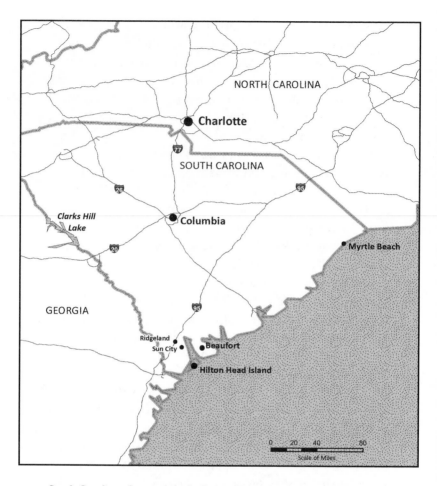

*South Carolina. Cartography by Louise Misztal. Data provided by ESRI,
The National Map.*

chapter nine

THE BORDER POLICE STATE

It's Sunday, so they don't think that the police will put up the checkpoint. María de los Angeles and Manuel discuss it, but the Ridgeland, South Carolina, police normally set up the checkpoint on Thursday, Friday, and Saturday. Not Sunday. The police always put the checkpoint at the entrance to the mobile home park where María and Manuel live. A road barely two lanes wide leads through the park with its approximately sixty gray, white, and beige mobile homes tightly concentrated in a two-block area. Just in case, María and Manuel check to make sure the shiny black police cars and orange cones aren't there. They decide to risk it and go to church.

Even though they are in South Carolina, María says the placement of the checkpoint makes it feel as if the U.S.-Mexico border were right at her doorstep. That's saying something. María, though originally from the Mexican state of Michoacán, grew up in Naco, Mexico, right on the border. Although police checkpoints are often used throughout the state of South Carolina to find people driving under the influence, they are also there to make sure a driver's residency status is in order.

"They put it in the entrance of the trailer park," María

tells me. "You *have* to go through the checkpoint." There isn't any other way to get in or out. The authorities at this particular checkpoint have already busted Manuel three times, each time for driving without a proper driver's license. And this checkpoint has caused serious havoc for María's neighbors, family, and coworkers, many of them non-citizens who have come into the area to work in the booming construction industry around the island of Hilton Head. Many are carpenters, landscapers, and construction workers who now live in the small town of Ridgeland. They are the people who have sculpted and landscaped gigantic gated communities built around golf courses and fake waterfalls. These modern subdivisions are now filled with mainly affluent white retirees, the majority from the Northeast and Midwest. Some places, like the 10,000-person town of Sun City, didn't even exist fifteen years ago.

In one way the checkpoint is another example of the type of hostile—if not outright racist—climate that immigration-rights advocates say that non-citizens face here. South Carolina is a place where Jeff Duncan, a member of the U.S. Congress who represents the so-called Palmetto State (a reference to the state tree), compared "illegal" immigrants to "animals and vagrants." It is a place where a series of emails sent between police officers in Horry County, home to Myrtle Beach, contained links to a game called "Border Patrol." In the game the player is a Border Patrol agent armed with a gun. In the crosshairs is a large woman called a "breeder" who carries her husband and children past a sign that has an arrow pointing to the "welfare office." South Carolina is also a place where Police Chief Richard Inman, on the other side of the state from Myrtle Beach, in the town of Williamston, resigned after posting a picture of a portable toilet with MEXICAN SPACESHIP scrawled on its side. Inman said he thought the post was funny and that it was not meant to be racially insensitive.

However, while these examples are particular to South Carolina, this sort of racism is a deep part of the national climate in which non-citizens, particularly those without legal authorization to be in the United States, are one of the most negatively stereotyped groups. Sociologist Douglas Massey writes that "undocumented immigrants are not perceived as fully human at the most fundamental neural level of cognition, thus opening a door to the harshest, most exploitive, and cruelest treatment that human beings are capable of inflicting on one another."[1]

Clearly, this national vindictiveness—if not outright bigotry—has driven immigration legislation since the Chinese Exclusion Acts in the nineteenth century, and it is also part of what María and Manuel experience that Sunday when they try to go home after church. If it were a weekday and they were returning home from work, they would check to see if the checkpoint was there. They would park at the post office, and then either María or Manuel would walk several blocks to check it out. But again, it's Sunday. They don't do this.

Going to the trailer park, it seems as though you are leaving Ridgeland. You go through a forested area where tall trees lean over the two-lane road, with Spanish moss hanging from low branches. The deep green grass goes right up to the road's edge. Then it clears, and to the right you can see the trailer park and the mobile homes side by side in the distance.

When they see the police checkpoint, their spirits drop to the floor. They know the police have seen them. They know they can't avoid the checkpoint. They know they can't turn around, or the police will chase them.

This is the border-policing apparatus advancing into the interior of the country, the "elastic border" that make places like Ridgeland, South Carolina, seem like the U.S.-Mexico divide. Criminologist Nancy A. Wonders says that in this new world, "border performances occur in locations that may be far from the actual geographic border" and the day-to-day decisions by government agents, police officers, airport workers, employers, and others "play a critical role in determining where, how, and on whose body a border"[2] will be imposed.

María has been living in South Carolina for eighteen years. But looking at the police yelling at them to stop the vehicle, she knows that she has had one too many clashes with this border-police state. She has two sons, one daughter, and several grandchildren living here. While through these years there have been many ups and downs, she has never felt so relentlessly targeted by police, so immobilized. What happens next at the checkpoint is a crucial decision. María decides to return to Naco, Sonora, Mexico.

The New Super State

María's ordeal takes place in June 2011, just before the time that the South Carolina legislature votes to pass a strict immigration law known as SB 20. With this, South Carolina joins the ranks of states such as Arizona, Alabama, Georgia, Utah, and Indiana, all of which have passed sweeping, draconian legislation obligating local or state police to enforce federal immigration law.

But South Carolina's state law has something completely new. As a state senator, Jake Knotts added a startling new provision to the law that sets it apart. The provision called for the state to form its own "border patrol,"[3] as a headline put it. This is a first. No other state has created its own "Immigration Enforcement Unit," as it is officially called. Not even Arizona's SB 1070, the father of all these laws, has such a provision.

When I arrive in South Carolina's capital, Columbia, I arrange a meeting with Knotts in his office, which is located behind the only statehouse in the United States to still fly a Confederate flag. Behind the statehouse and in front of the Gressette Building, one of many in the cluster of buildings where Knotts's office is located, stands a statue of South Carolina's most famous U.S. senator, Strom Thurmond, in his days an ardent supporter of Jim Crow. The monument portrays the notorious segregationist in a suit and tie walking urgently to what must be an important appointment. Thurmond switched from Democrat to Republican in 1964 due to his opposition to the Civil Rights Act. No other senator has ever reached the age of 100 in office.

I want to meet with Knotts because I want to ask him why he thought that South Carolina needed its Immigration Enforcement Unit. When the South Carolina legislature was debating the bill in May 2011, Knotts, who is known for saying whatever he thinks, exclaimed, "They are going to have to put their money where their mouth is," making the case that SB 20 was going to be an underfunded, and thus ineffective, mandate. He said that without the Immigration Enforcement Unit, the legislature "would have walked out of here today with a bill that would fool the public." I want to know why a cash-strapped state like South Carolina would put its resources toward such a unit.

Perhaps South Carolina, like many other states, was following Arizona's model legislation (and discourse) on the matter. For many, Arizona is heroic, an inspiring example to other states since passing SB 1070 in 2010. For example, when I enter Knotts's office, sweating from South Carolina's humid summer, I meet his receptionist. She is a white woman with short brown hair who greets me with an energetic smile. She asks if I want to talk with Senator Knotts about the "Voter ID issue," which was particularly hot at the time. When I explain to her why I've come, she tells me that as a retired teacher she knows all about the "illegal problem" and that "they" are a burden to South Carolina's school system. When I tell her I live in Arizona, she responds, "They've got a lot of people working really hard there."

When I ask her what she means, she asks back: "What's the governor's name?"

"Jan Brewer."

"Yes," she says, "they are really giving it to the federal government." The receptionist's perception of Arizona's defiance is common: Jan Brewer and America's toughest sheriff, Joe Arpaio, are heroes who, against all odds, are constantly defying the feds.

Another common impression is that Arizona, like South Carolina and other states in the Deep South, come from the wing-nut fringe and have nothing to do with the country at large, the federal government, and the much saner "blue states." However, as geographer Joseph Nevins points out, the "war" on the people who are undocumented in such states is very much related to what is taking place on the national level.

"Just as it was an error in the 1960s to analytically ghettoize U.S. institutionalized racism in the South,"[4] writes Nevins, "and effectively separate it from the larger national socio-political fabric which gave rise to, and sustained it, it is deeply mistaken (and politically dangerous)" to treat as exceptional what is happening in places such as

South Carolina, Arizona, and Alabama. What we have, Nevins asserts, is "fertile national soil"[5] for anti-immigration legislation and a culture of intolerance where people are encouraged to profile and police each other.

"So Sad That I Could Barely Move"

When María and Manuel pull up to the checkpoint, María has already been in a "deep state of depression" for quite a while. She has already lost her full-time job, and for a year she has been without a driver's license. Being without a driver's license means that she, and all the other undocumented people in Ridgeland, have to figure out the basics of mobility: how to get to work, how to get the groceries, how to get basic services.

Even if there isn't a checkpoint, you have to worry about getting pulled over. Esteban Velásquez, María's son, who lives in the mobile home next to hers, tells me that Mexicans are simply criminals in Ridgeland. If the police see you, they "get behind you," he tells me. "So before you even leave the house you have to make sure everything is perfect," he says: "no broken lights or blinkers. And if you are driving and they are behind you and you do one"—he pauses, then stresses—"*one* mistake, if you go on the white line, even if you barely touch the white line or yellow line, just something, and they pull you over."

Facing such a reality, people have formed a loose protection network: Those who have licenses drive people who do not. People without documentation know to transit at 6:00 a.m. and 6:00 p.m., the times when the local police work shift changes. If there is a checkpoint, people communicate quickly with each other and know to avoid certain areas.

What Esteban and María describe is something undocumented residents along the U.S.-Mexico border have lived with for a long time—a persistent feeling of being cornered, detained, rounded up, "trapped like cattle," according to researchers Guillermina Gina Núñez and Josiah Heyman. They describe the U.S.-Mexico borderlands as a "tightly interlocked" and heavily policed zone with "multiple trapping processes." "People who might solve one of them cannot resolve all of them at once and, as a result, suffer high degrees of anxiety and discouragement."[6] In their ethnographic study of locations around El Paso and southern New Mexico, they describe a world of confined mobility that would be unthinkable for the average documented white person, a world in which risks—even for the simplest of chores—must be constantly evaluated.

On top of this, local cops in the ten years since 9/11 have received $34 billion in Homeland Security grants dedicated to counterterrorism and have received equipment such as military-grade assault rifles, Kevlar helmets, and even armored trucks with rotating turrets. For those targeted in the entrapment areas, this creates ever more menacing-looking police forces now using "the sort of gear once reserved only for soldiers fighting foreign wars,"[7] according to journalist Andrew Becker. But others see this as good TV. In March 2011, actor Steven Seagal, for his television program *Lawman*, oversaw an operation for the Maricopa County Sheriff's Department in Arizona in which an armored assault vehicle that looked like a tank leveled a gate to the yard of sleeping, unarmed Jesús Llovera, and blew out two windows in his house. Seagal was accompanied by a SWAT team in full gear, several other armored vehicles, and a bomb-detecting robot in search of Llovera, who was the alleged ringleader of a cock-fighting operation—and who has since filed a lawsuit against Seagal and the police department.

In 2005, Mark Krikorian of the Center for Immigration Studies discussed how the use of entrapment as a border-policing tactic should be spread to the interior and complemented with a series of "virtual choke points."[8] Although the Center for Immigration Studies is known as a conservative organization, it describes itself as a non-partisan research group that provides "reliable information about the social, economic, environmental, security, and fiscal consequences of legal and illegal immigration into the United States."[9] Krikorian used the analogy of "computer firewalls" that people can pass through only if their legal status is verified. He said that these "firewalls" should be placed between people and the "events that are necessary for life in a modern society but are infrequent enough not to bog down everyone's daily business."[10] So if you want to get a job, a car loan, a mortgage, or a driver's license, or obtain a government service of any kind, there should be a firewall. In other words, he wants to live in a world where everyone employed by the government and certain key business sectors would constantly police for "illegals." A world of innumerable de facto Border Patrol agents.

Krikorian's world of perpetual firewalls—along with the constant "trapping processes" seen on the U.S.-Mexico border—had already arrived in Ridgeland before the Immigration Enforcement Unit and SB 20. A year before María's encounter with the checkpoint, she had a driver's license and was able to transit without problems. ("She got lucky," her son said, in the late 1990s.) She regularly gave rides to other undocumented people in the area, and even helped some get car insurance. One day, she went to the Department of Motor Vehicles after receiving a letter regarding the renewal of her license. When María came to the window, they called over the supervisor. "Let me see your license," the woman told her. María produced it with great reluctance, since a license is like gold in a place where almost no undocumented people had them. With her hand slightly trembling, she pulled it out of her wallet and showed it to the supervisor. She grabbed the license out of María's hand, saying: "You shouldn't have a license."

Astonished, María stood there a moment and then said the only thing that came into her head: "How am I going to get home?"

"Your problem," the supervisor said, without missing a beat.

It had also become policy in South Carolina, as it is in many other states, to show proof of U.S. citizenship in order to obtain or renew your driver's license.

This happened around the same time that María, reported to management by a coworker, lost her job at Boat and RV on Interstate 95, where she had worked for eight years. At the time María was vying for a management position. For the second time, she was taking classes to improve her English. The company quickly let her go after a coworker accused her of using false documents to get the job.

South Carolina's Immigration Enforcement Unit encourages such acts of civilians policing their coworkers or neighbors. A "citizen call" is now one of the three ways that the new agency can "make a case" through a state-level "if you see something, say something" policy. Cases are also initiated if the agency receives calls or complaints from ICE or local law enforcement.

"I give everything and I am nothing because I don't

have papers," María told me emphatically. Her face looked troubled with the memory of this.

María said: "I became so sad I could barely move." She lost her driver's license, then her job. It was a year of anguish leading up to the detainment at the checkpoint. At this point in the interview we had to break. María's voice was quavering. Her body began to convulse. She started to cry.

Defying D.C.

Knotts is a rotund man with thinning gray hair who looks you straight in the eye when he talks. He is a former police officer and navy man. He has been a state representative since 2002. When he leads me into his office, the first thing I see is a marble chessboard. I also see an intricately carved rooster lamp on his desk and a large Confederate flag draping behind his desk.

"Do you play chess?" I ask, to break the ice.

"No," he says adamantly, as if he were afraid I was going to challenge him to a game. "It's for my grandchildren." Somewhere in the Little League and soccer pictures next to his desk are his grandchildren, I imagine.

Senator Knotts lost his seat in the November 2012 election, but he is still a famous personality in South Carolina. Tammy Besherse of the Appleseed Center told me, "He definitely says what he wants; he doesn't hold back." State Senator Bradley Hutto, who vehemently opposed SB 20, told me earlier that day in his Orangeburg office that he was their Boss Hog. On a radio show, he called South Carolina governor Nikki Haley, who is a Republican of Indian descent, a "raghead" when she was running for office in 2010. "We have one in the White House, we don't need one in the governor's mansion,"[11] he said on a live radio broadcast. Feeling the heat of the aftermath, Knotts said: "Since my intended humorous context was lost in translation, I apologize. Ms. Haley is pretending to be someone she is not, much as Obama did, but I apologize to both for an unintended slur."[12]

When I sit down with Knotts and ask him why he thinks it is necessary to have a border patrol unit, I expect him to demonize the "illegals" in South Carolina. I wouldn't have been surprised if he echoed Rep. Lou Barletta (R-PA), who said that "any state with an international airport is a border state." He doesn't disappoint at first, but he will surprise me in some important ways later in the conversation. He gets to "federal government inaction" right away. He says there is "no border protection" on the U.S.-Mexico divide. He says even deportation is just a "revolving door" in which people are "back across the border before the ink's dried on the deportation papers." He says that in South Carolina these people are many of the farmworkers who pick tomatoes, strawberries, peaches, and vegetables out in the field.

Then he homes in on what he calls "another problem" that they have in South Carolina: "the illegal family." For him a family is "illegal" when "mother and father have children who are citizens and they are not." For Knotts, this is a big problem. Even though the children are U.S. citizens, he resents that they "are in the schools and we are required to educate them, we are required to give them medical treatment, we're required to give them certain services . . . we have to give them the same rights and privileges that every South Carolinian American citizen is entitled to."

Knotts speaks slowly, deliberately, and with conviction. He uses his own citizenship as an example. "I'm a South Carolinian. I was born here. I've got proper paperwork. I've got a driver's license. I've got a photo ID. I've got a voter registration card. I've got the proper paperwork to show who I am." And this, for Knotts, is the main point of SB 20, and of his amendment to include creation of the state's Immigration Enforcement Unit: "to make sure that in South Carolina . . . you can prove the fact that you are here legally. And that law enforcement has the ability to stop you on suspicion or probable cause that you are not a legal citizen or resident of the United States."

The seven-person-strong Immigration Enforcement Unit went into action in July 2012 under the command of Lieutenant E. C. Johnson. By May 2013, the unit had more than three dozen cases and had made seventeen arrests. "Some have been referred to federal authorities for deportation,"[13] the Associated Press reports.

South Carolina Department of Public Safety director Leroy Smith proudly states: "We built this immigration unit from the ground up; there was no map."[14] The unit has its own insignia and its own dark gray uniform. The insignia includes South Carolina's state motto, "Dum Spiro Spero," which means "while I breathe, I hope." On one side of the insignia a beautiful robed woman walks along a beach littered with weapons. On the other side is a palmetto tree standing over the fallen tree of British imperialism. "Animis Opibusque Parati" appears beneath the tree—Latin for "prepared in mind and resources." Underneath that: IMMIGRATION ENFORCEMENT UNIT.

The excitement about South Carolina's "border patrol" has spread to the upper echelons of South Carolina's political class. The state's governor, Nikki Haley, declared in an October 2012 press conference that with the creation of the Immigration Enforcement Unit South Carolina had "defied D.C."[15]

In the very next sentence Haley uttered, she contradicted herself in an important way: "It is the only statewide jurisdiction that we know of in the country that is actually working with Immigration and Customs Enforcement (ICE) and making cases."[16] In other words, ICE, which is part of the Department of Homeland Security, is enabling the enforcement unit, which could not make cases without federal assistance. The police unit that is "focused on stopping human smuggling and trafficking, gang violence, and drug smuggling"[17] becomes another auxiliary, and a significant force multiplier, of the Department of Homeland Security.

For SB 20, South Carolina originally made several attempts to establish a 287(g), a type of agreement with ICE that would formalize the relationship between the Immigration Enforcement Unit, Homeland Security, and the broader detention and deportation regime. Section 287(g) of the Immigration and Nationality Act allows the federal government to establish agreements with local law enforcement agencies to enforce immigration law. However, South Carolina's Department of Public Safety spokesperson, Sherri Iacobelli, tells me, "South Carolina, along with thirty other law enforcement agencies nationwide, were denied this training" (through a 287(g) agreement)—which allows for the deputization (and "border-patrolization") of non-federal police officers—"by the federal government."

Nevertheless, although it is not named a 287(g), Iacobelli says that South Carolina's Department of Public Safety still received "extensive training" through ICE for the Immigration Enforcement Unit, and that ICE and the IEU have a collaboration agreement. The IEU will also carry out immigration enforcement training programs for local law enforcement agencies throughout South Carolina in the "proper implementation, management and enforcement of applicable immigration laws," including the SB 20 "show me your papers" mandate.

"The local officers will not be able to arrest undocumented people, that is our job, but the immigration unit can investigate people who commit state crimes and we can help them,"[18] says ICE spokesman Vincent Picard, underscoring again that none of these state laws would work—not in Arizona, Georgia, Alabama, and beyond—without the personnel, institutions, incarceration apparatus, and infrastructure of the Department of Homeland Security. What are characterized as rogue states, states that in some cases the feds desperately try to distance themselves from, are actually the result of federal policy to a very significant degree. In 2002, for example, Attorney General John Ashcroft asserted the "inherent authority"[19] of state and local police to enforce civil and criminal violations of immigration law. (Ashcroft's statement was not released until years later.) Monica Varsanyi, in the book *Taking Local Control: Immigration Policy Activism in U.S. Cities and States*, writes that the Ashcroft memo "opened the door to the devolution of immigration policing powers,"[20] ushering in an era that blurred the distinction between unauthorized migrants and terrorists. The 287(g) agreement, although written into the 1996 immigration law, is a key part of post-9/11 dynamic. Steven Seagal driving through Phoenix in an assault vehicle might not be as far-fetched as we think.

For María, Manuel, and Esteban (María's son) in the low country of South Carolina, it is just one more way to get nailed in an ever-widening immigration web, involving more and more actors and institutions throughout the interior of the country. This type of entrapment, once a tactic used only on the border, has now come to them. Esteban has been so routinely hounded by police across a landscape of several surrounding counties—each with distinct ICE programs such as 287(g) and Secure Communities—that he didn't even realize that a new state law had been passed. But it isn't a surprise to him that there is another "border patrol" unit on the prowl for "illegals." "You mean, like Arpaio?" he asks.

Self-Deportation

When María and Manuel pull into the police checkpoint located at the entrance of the trailer park, the two officers are agitated before they even arrive at the orange cone. Even though Manuel is already putting on the brakes, one officer yells: "Stay right there!" When they stop, the officer says: "Don't move. Don't touch anything." When they are satisfied that María and Manuel are not going to pull out a weapon, they ask for the papers. Manuel produces his Mexican driver's license, the registration, and insurance.

The police look at the papers and ask, "Whose car is this?"

"It's mine," María says.

"So why is he driving?" ask the police.

María thinks about how to answer that one.

"In Mexico the men always drive," she says.

"And where is your license?"

"They took it away," María says.

"Okay, get out of the car, both of you." The police handcuff them right in the entrance of the mobile home park.

Later María tells me: "They treated us like criminals." They say they are going to tow the car, as they always do. This is the fourth time that they have arrested Manuel.

The total costs of getting both Manuel out of jail and re-covering the car will be about $1,000 again.

Looming over this is the threat of deportation. In Ridgeland, it is usually just the fine, the brief incarceration, the towing fee, as if police were squeezing the un-documented population for a quick buck in a cash-strapped county. Esteban guesses this might be the case. He says that in Ridgeland, which is in Jasper County, maybe "one out of every twenty" people gets deported. However, in 2010 ICE implemented Secure Communities in Jasper County. If you get booked, as the police are about to do to Manuel, ICE could begin your expulsion process and put a detainer on you. While this wasn't happening with any regularity yet in Ridgeland, Esteban told me they were "deporting people left and right in Beaufort County," down the road from Ridgeland, near the South Carolina coastal resorts where many of Ridgeland's residents work. Equipped with a 287(g) agreement, Beaufort has a task force of deputized police officers who can enforce immigration law. But the differences in deportations might have more to do with unevenness of enforcement, since both counties have pro-grams with ICE. And now both work under SB 20.

"From 2005 to 2010, nearly a thousand laws were passed by state legislatures addressing illegal immigration," writes Sonia Nazario, the author of *Enrique's Journey: The Story of a Boy's Dangerous Odyssey to Reunite with his Mother*. "In 2008, the federal government told all police depart-ments to turn over any unlawful migrants they arrested to federal immigration authorities, a program called Secure Communities. A result: deportations nearly doubled be-tween fiscal 2006 and 2012 to more than 409,000 a year."[21]

Criminologists Meghan McDowell and Nancy Won-ders see Arizona's Sheriff Joe Arpaio as the embodiment of this countrywide advance of border policing. They argue that Arpaio is a local version of the harsh global disciplining strategies meant to keep people in their proper place. This means that he, like any police in any part of the United States with similar practices, represents a "mobile, elastic border."[22] This internal policing underscores people's "illegality" and "deportability" if they are in the United States without the right papers. And out of sheer fear of brushing up against the state or its surveillance technology, there is a process of self-segregation of undocumented people. This has an effect of "cleansing" or "purifying" the body politic to ensure that "public space—parks, libraries, streets, and hospitals—will be largely reserved for those privileged by citizenship, wealth, and, most important, whiteness."[23]

For María, constant reminders of her "illegality" begin the second she leaves her trailer park. Now she pleads with the police not to tow the car; someone with a license will come to pick it up, she tells them. But the police response is a blunt no. "We're towing the car," they say. It is at this moment, handcuffed, María says, that she thinks it will be best to return to Mexico. "I was imprisoned and I couldn't go out even to buy food." She repeats again: "It is as if they are at my front door. They are at the front of your house and you can't even enter."

María's decision to leave after eighteen years is what Kansas secretary of state Kris Kobach would call a more humanitarian mode of deportation, in which conditions deteriorate so much that they become unbearable, and people decide on their own to leave. María's story is a textbook example. Kobach said people like María "should go home on their own volition, under their own will, pick their own day, get their things in order and leave. That's a more humane way."[24] Along with Arizona state senator Russell Pearce, Kobach was the architect of SB 1070. He also served as an informal adviser to 2012 Republican presidential candidate Mitt Romney during his campaign. Not surprisingly, Romney advocated for the "self-deportation" philosophy prominent in this model legislation, although "self-deportation"[25] is a term that goes back to California governor Pete Wilson in the early 1990s, and Proposition 187, the state's anti-immigrant legislation. Prop. 187, which had provisions to deny social services to undocumented people and was approved by California voters in 1994, never went into effect.

However, the first clear impact of these "self-deportation" policies are the "self-segregation"[26] tendencies. Public places become unsafe for a large sector of the population, and people react in a multitude of ways, including forming protection networks—and other forms of mutual aid within the targeted community—and learning creative ways to avoid the barriers put in place by the State. María's son Esteban Velásquez tells me that he hadn't left the "trailer park" for one year. Another guy, he says, hasn't left for two years. At first I think he might be exaggerating. I will also think this later, when he guarantees that police will tail me after I leave his mobile home.

Everything in Its Correct Place

For Senator Jake Knotts, the original sin happens when a person enters the United States without proper documentation. It's a criminal act, according to Knotts, and is therefore similar to other crimes. "You don't get a second bite of the apple when you rob a bank," he reasons. "You don't get a second bite of the apple when you steal a car." To Knotts, it's about maintaining that divide between law and lawlessness, it's about the kind of border enforcement that imposes lines one can't even trespass in the social terrain.

Up to this point it might seem as though Knotts is calling for the total elimination of South Carolina's undocumented population. Indeed, the mastermind behind the Immigration Enforcement Unit is advocating for a deeper criminalization of the immigrant population in his state. But he is also, more significantly, articulating a new vision as to how the state of South Carolina, and perhaps even the entire United States, should be divided internally. Knotts clearly understands the work that this huge population offers his state, and especially in the area of South Carolina he represents, Lexington.

When I pose to Knotts the argument of many immigration rights organizations, that people from other countries who are working here without papers are doing jobs that U.S. citizens don't want to do, he agrees.

"They are not taking jobs from Americans," says Knotts. "Because Americans won't work in the fields like it's needed to be done. I mean, you go to Clayton Farms, you go to Rawl Farms, you go to Sease Farms, you go to any of the peach orchards, you got to run them out of the fields when it's thundering and lightening. You got to go out there and say, listen, y'all got to get out of the field, we don't want you hurt. And they work day and night, seven days a week."

Then Knotts talks about taxes. There are "a lot of taxes" taken out on "them," he tells me. "Because they are illegal, they never file for income tax return." Knotts confides that he knows that many are using other people's Social Security numbers, and paying Social Security taxes. "And they get no benefits from that."

Knotts tells me that his "sources tell him" that "Hispanic children have an eagerness to learn and they are very mannerable and polite kids, unlike some of the kids we have that are American citizens." He tells me that the Hispanic community holds to "family values and they are trying to achieve things like a home or a car, the basics that Americans are accustomed to having automatically."

In between, he tells me how much he despises E-verify, a federal system mandated for employers across the state of South Carolina (and many other states) that verifies the current residency status of a person applying for a job. He says that this system becomes offensive when it is used on his family, which is "South Carolinian through and through."

And then Knotts tells me the very thing many say is the primary reason why anti-immigrant laws across the country are fundamentally bad. He says he has been told that "in communities where illegals reside that they don't use law enforcement services . . . like regular American citizens do."

Through all this, the brains behind the Immigration Enforcement Unit is arriving to his crucial point: "We have a need for legal farmworkers." He imagines them getting a visa for six months, and then there is some sort of enforcement to make sure that they don't overstay. He doesn't want a South Carolina devoid of people migrating from Latin America; he simply wants them bound in what he sees as their proper role and place. He wants them to pick South Carolina's fruits and vegetables, and then go back to their countries of origin. He wants their labor.

Many of the people working in the Lexington, South Carolina, peach orchards are foreign nationals who hold temporary work visas. In the Titan Farms orchard I visited, the Mexican workforce—mainly people from the small state of Tlaxcala, just south of Mexico City—lived on the orchard in trailers supplied by the farm. When I was there, the workers were at the tail end of a six-month stay, and their living space almost had the feel of a small community in the Mexican countryside. I remembered fondly a town I had visited in Tlaxcala called Vicente Guerrero. For its sustainable, local agricultural practices, Vicente Guerrero has become a grassroots model community known throughout Southern Mexico and Central America.

Vicente Guerrero's agricultural practices contrast deeply with those of the large, for-profit orchards in South Carolina where I found workers scattered all over the place, chatting on cell phones with family in Mexico, as a gorgeous August South Carolina dusk set in. Although the harvest was almost over, the humid air still smelled faintly of peaches, a fruit that came to South Carolina with the Spanish Conquest. Old school buses were scattered around the compound, even though there was little or no contact between the workers and the surrounding community. They came in, did the job for low wages (hovering around and sometimes below minimum wage), and left. This was Knotts's vision of South Carolina.

The Sun City–Mexico Border

When retiree George Kanuck, a former U.S. Customs agent, called the security guard of his gated community in Sun City, South Carolina (near Ridgeland), to alert him that Eric Esquivel would be coming to his house, the security guard asked if this was his "domestic help." "No," he replied. Kanuck is the cochair of the Lowland Immigration Rights Coalition. Although the question from the security guard was irritating to Kanuck, he knew it was logical. He is the self-described "gringo cochair" of the coalition, and the other cochair is Esquivel. Rarely, if ever, did anyone with a Spanish-sounding surname come to Kanuck's predominantly white community to just visit. In only ten years, primarily Latin American migrant workers such as Esteban Velásquez had constructed the 8,000 houses, landscaped the yards, the three golf courses, the twenty-acre lake. They built the fitness center, the performing arts center, the indoor pools, the outdoor pools, the cushion-floored aerobic studio. They constructed this "active adult playground," the ten clay tennis courts, the softball field, the dog park, the outdoor party pavilion. They constructed the villa-style town homes with expansive living rooms and "entertaining kitchens, with ample living space outside."

"We built everything," Esteban told me in his mobile home next to where his mom used to live—"*everything.*" This was one of the main reasons for the 88 percent increase of primarily Latin American migrants in South Carolina between 2000 and 2010.

Most residents of Sun City (which bears the same name as a boycotted resort town in apartheid South Africa) are also migrants, but they come from elsewhere within the United States—from the North or the Midwest. Almost all have a good amount of money. Almost none have southern accents. And, I am told time and time again, it is in this area, in Beaufort County and Ridgeland's Jasper County, that some of the worst rights violations are perpetrated against undocumented people in the entire state. In resistance to the full-fledged arrival of the border police state, Colombian American Esquivel and Kanuck of the Lowland Immigration Coalition have filed a lawsuit against the state of South Carolina and SB 20.

In a meeting in Sun City, Kanuck describes to me their difficult situation and discusses their participation in the push for comprehensive immigration reform, with heavy emphasis on a path to legalization so that unauthorized workers can regulate their status. Kanuck tells me that such immigrant workers put "$250 billion into Social Security and will never collect a dime. They are subsidizing these old people across the road," he says, pointing to one of the endless subdivisions, "who hate the immigrants."

After my meeting with Kanuck I drive twenty miles up I-95 to Ridgeland. I drive through the exact location of the checkpoint where María decided to go back to Mexico. I visit Esteban in his mobile home. María's three grandchildren, whom she longs for but cannot see, are sitting on the couch playing games.

Esteban says his mother told him she was leaving on a Friday, shortly after that incident with the checkpoint. And then, the following Monday, after eighteen years of living in South Carolina, she was gone. They have not seen her since.

"She said she wanted to stay," Esteban tells me. "She wanted to keep us all together."

"Do you miss her?" I ask.

"I call her every day."

As I am leaving, I tell the kids that their grandmother sends her love. María had asked me do this when I saw her in Mexico several months earlier. For the first time, the kids pay attention to me. They stop what they are doing. They keep looking at me as if I'm going to say more about their grandmother.

Outside, I stand with Esteban between his mobile home and the mobile home where his mother used to live. He tells me that if the cops caught wind that I—a white guy—was here, they'd probably pull me over.

I give him a look.

"You think I'm exaggerating?"

I drive slowly through Ridgeland trying to absorb the small town. After ten minutes I see one of Ridgeland's police cars waiting on a side street. The black vehicle turns and accelerates until it's behind me. I slow down a little to let it pass. But no, it comes right up to my tail. It stays there. My heart starts to pump. Esteban was right; I am going to get pulled over just because I went to the trailer park. I keep looking in my rearview mirror, and there it is. The last time this happened I was followed for a good mile by a Border Patrol agent near Nogales, Arizona. I expect the same thing to happen: the lights to flare up, the siren to wail. But then, just as abruptly, the police car turns off on a side street.

I tell María about this when I next meet with her in Naco, Mexico. She is utterly unsurprised to hear that the police tailed me; it is a non-story in her eyes. María and I are sitting in the central plaza, a mere two blocks from the border wall with the United States. When I ask her what she thinks about the wall and the lights and the Border Patrol agents, she says, "You have to respect the divisions."

Then she corrects herself.

"They are unjust," she says.

Then she begins to mix up the U.S.-Mexico border and the checkpoints in Ridgeland. She talks at length about the checkpoints as if she were reliving the horrors over again. Then I realize that she isn't mixing anything up. For her there is little difference between the checkpoints at the U.S.-Mexico international boundary and the ones in Ridgeland.

chapter ten

U.S. CITIZENS IN NAME ONLY

The first time it happens it takes Egyptian American Abdallah Matthews by surprise. It is a freezing cold day in late December 2010, and Matthews, a newly minted lawyer, is sitting in the passenger side of the car as he and three friends cross the Blue Water Bridge from Sarnia, Ontario, to the old industrial town of Port Huron, Michigan. They are returning from the Reviving the Islamic Spirit Conference in Toronto. They are chatting and glad to be almost home when a blue-uniformed U.S. Customs and Border Protection agent approaches their car. What is about to happen is the furthest thing from Matthews's mind. He is a U.S. citizen from Port Huron, the home of Thomas Edison, and has crossed this border "a million times before."

After scanning the passports and looking into a computer screen for a moment, the Homeland Security officer directs the driver to turn off the vehicle, hand him the key, and step out of the car.

Matthews hears the snap of handcuffs going around his friend's wrists. Disoriented, he turns around and sees uniformed men poised, kneeling behind their car, their guns drawn.

"To my disbelief, situated behind us are agents, pointing their guns."

The CBP team instructs Matthews and the remaining passengers to get out of the car and escorts them to a waiting room. Thirty minutes later, Matthews is handcuffed and in a cell. Forty-five minutes after that, CBP brings him into a room with no chairs. The agent tells him he can sit down, but all he sees is a countertop. "Can I just stand?" he asks. Matthews says that he stands there for what feels like an eternity. The door to the interrogation room is wide open, and Matthews attempts to smile at CBP agents who pass by.

"I'm trying to be nice," he says.

Once they get to a third room the interrogation finally begins. Although they question Matthews about his religious beliefs and different Islamic issues, the two agents are "nice." They ask him: "Where were you? Where'd you go? What kind of law do you practice?" He tells them that his law professor was presenting at the conference whose purpose was to "revive Islamic traditions of education, tolerance, and introspection." They ask Matthews if he has received military training abroad.

This, he tells me, "stood out as one of their more bizarre questions."

Lena Masri of the Council of American Islamic Relations–Michigan (CAIR-MI) says that what Matthews is experiencing is becoming "chillingly" commonplace for Michigan's large Arab and Muslim community. The city of Dearborn has the country's highest concentration of Arab Americans—40,000 in a city of 100,000 people. In 2012, CAIR-MI was receiving five to seven complaints per week. There is a pattern. All the people filing the complaints to CAIR are Arab American, all are male, and all have been interrogated about the details of their religion, their mosque, their imam, and their prayers. According to CAIR-MI, Customs and Border Protection uses hand-cuffs, often brandishes weapons, conducts "invasive,"[1] often sexually humiliating body searches, and detains people from two to twelve hours. As a result of these practices, some U.S. citizens have lost jobs that require cross-border travel, some have lost educational opportunities in Canada, and many are now afraid to cross the border to see their families. Based on four exemplary cases CAIR-MI, has filed a lawsuit against CBP and other federal agencies. And similar cases arise at Buffalo's border crossing.

This should come as no surprise in a United States where civil rights complaints by Muslims have increased since September 11, 2001. Anti-Muslim hate crimes spiked in the year after 9/11, and continue at high levels to this day. These crimes typically include physical attacks and threats on mosques, clergy, and people who are perceived to be Muslim. In addition to these serious offenses people have made complaints about rights abuses by the U.S. government, including systematic profiling derived from heavy surveillance. However, by far the most numerous civil right complaints from the Muslim community, according to CAIR, are immigration issues with government agencies. It's as if governmental agencies adopted the popular notion that Muslims, whether citizens or non-citizens, have a hidden agenda and should be treated as foreigners.

Following the attack on Pearl Harbor in 1941, Franklin Delano Roosevelt also worried that people of Japanese descent in the United States might have a "hidden agenda" to subvert the country. It didn't matter if they were "citizens" or "non-citizens"; they were the "alien enemy."[2] By creating an exclusion zone on the U.S. West Coast, what

Roosevelt put in place was a form of martial law in which constitutional rights were suspended for the "public good," but in this case it applied only to people specifically identified by their Japanese nationality or descent. U.S. soldiers with bayoneted rifles were deployed to cities such as Los Angeles and San Francisco and ordered to round up people of Japanese descent and ship them to internment camps far away from their homes. Of the 110,000 swept up in the dragnet, 62 percent were U.S. citizens. The camps—several of which were operated by the U.S. Border Patrol—utilized barbed wire, armed guards, and towers to deny freedom and prevent escape. "Our crime was looking like the people who bombed Pearl Harbor," wrote former internee George Takei, the actor of *Star Trek* fame, in 2012 in the British newspaper *The Guardian*. The experience, he said, "left scars that today remain unhealed, even after the government later apologized and issued reparations."[3]

We don't have internment camps today, but we do have the Department of Homeland Security and a massive federal detention system for foreign nationals. Since 9/11, the U.S. government has spent $791 billion on a budget that very much targets people like Matthews, whose families once originated from "special interest countries." "To give you a sense of just how big that [amount of money] is," write Mattea Kramer and Chris Hellman of the National Priorities Project in *TomDispatch*, "Washington spent an inflation-adjusted $500 billion on the entire New Deal."[4]

The price tag is even higher when you contemplate the entirety of the post-2001 "top-secret world" of counterterrorism, a terrain so vast that it is an "alternative geography"[5] of the United States, according to *Washington Post* reporters Dana Priest and William Arkin. This alternative geography has grown at such a fast pace that it almost defies credibility; its network of high-tech operational head-quarters spans the country with 10,000 distinct locations, almost as ubiquitous as Starbucks coffee shops. Priest and Arkin report that as of 2010 that there were 1,271 government organizations and 1,931 private companies working on programs related to counterterrorism, intelligence, and national security.

Months later, Abdallah Matthews had yet another run-in with the national security monolith. Even though he thought that there could be no way he would be subjected to such indignities again, upon returning home from another trip to Canada, he was yet again arrested and interrogated by Customs and Border Protection at the Port Huron checkpoint. At the time he still did not realize that his hometown had become part of the front line to protect the "homeland." He had become a casualty in a new war not only against actual enemy combatants and criminal predators, but also against people like himself who are associated with an ever-changing list of political groups and ethno-religious communities deemed to be undesirable or suspicious. In other words, the targeted group goes far beyond known criminals and terrorists to include ordinary people who may be associated with certain political positions, religious practices, community activities, and even some areas of study. If U.S. citizens can be treated as if they were hostile "aliens," then they are citizens in name only.

Citizen Deported

In December 2008, ICE deports Mark Lyttle, an English-speaking U.S. citizen born in Rowan County, North Carolina, to the Mexican border in Reynosa. He has three dollars in his pocket. He is mentally ill. Before his deportation it was well known that he was mentally ill. U.S. officials knew it when ICE detained him at a Corrections Corporation of America facility in Georgia. An ICE agent wrote in a document that Lyttle, who is of Puerto Rican descent, is a Mexican citizen. He wrote that they thought that his real name, Mark Lyttle, was an "alias." He said that the man's real name is "Jose Thomas."[6] That was the rationale for deporting him to a foreign country—Mexico.

For eight days Lyttle begs for money. He sleeps in the streets of Reynosa. He tries to cross back into the United States, but CBP detains him. They interrogate Lyttle in Spanish. He doesn't understand Spanish. He doesn't answer. The U.S. officials hand him back to Mexican officials.

For the next 115 days, Lyttle is literally stateless. Since he is unable to prove his Mexican citizenship, Mexico deports the monolingual English speaker to Honduras. Since Lyttle is not a citizen of Honduras, Honduran immigration officials immediately arrest him. They put him in an immigration detainment camp where he suffers "severe physical and mental abuse,"[7] according to the ACLU. He is stuck there for months. When they release him, he goes to Nicaragua, where he is unable to prove his citizenship and is incarcerated again.

Lyttle's case may seem bizarre, but he is far from the only U.S. citizen to be treated as an "alien" and deported or detained by the immigration enforcement regime. Northwestern University's Jacqueline Stevens did an extensive study on this, with a detailed examination of 8,000 federal immigration records. Stevens found that approximately 4,000 of the 400,000 people detained by ICE in 2010 were actually U.S. citizens.

When expressed as statistics, says Stevens, it's as if the wrongful expulsion of U.S. citizens might fit into a simple and understandable margin of error that could be acceptable to Congress and the American people. "However, if we think about the magnitude of our deportation process, that means that thousands of U.S. citizens each year and tens of thousands in the course of a decade will be detained for substantial periods of time in absolute violation of the law and their civil rights,"[8] she says.

People caught up in cases of detainment or deportation are, like Lyttle, people whose citizenship status is in quotes because of their ancestry, level of English fluency, skin color, and/or physical features. U.S. citizens from Puerto Rico often fall prey to this, a constant reminder that they are treated as sub-citizens on the mainland, even though they are as much U.S citizens as are people born in Boston. U.S. citizens from Puerto Rico arrested during a 2012 immigration operation in South Carolina—a state where the Department of Motor Vehicles rejects birth certificates from Puerto Rico—say that police told them they were going to send them "back to Mexico." ICE detained Eduardo Caraballo in Chicago for three days in 2010, even after the Puerto Rico-born man had showed them his U.S. birth certificate and repeatedly told authorities that he was a U.S. citizen. "I have Mexican features,"[9] he admitted, as if trying to rationalize ICE's behavior. ICE also held Anthony Clarke, a U.S. citizen of Jamaican descent from Minneapolis, for forty-three days in 2011. "It was really terrible," he told the *Minneapolis Star Tribune*. "Here I am, a citizen. . . . I didn't know what to think or why they would do this to me."[10]

Stevens says that in the cases she studied, the people were detained between one week and four years. One Mexican American man, a former U.S. Marine named George Ibarra, who was wounded in the first Gulf War, "voluntarily deported"[11] himself after ICE told him that he would get out of the Florence, Arizona, detention center much quicker by doing so." Ibarra was facing nine months' detention. When deported to Nogales, Mexico, he simply turned around, went through the port of entry, showed them his military ID and driver's license, and returned to Phoenix. When he got into trouble a second time and ended up in Florence again, he did the whole thing again.

For Mark Lyttle, the "foreignness" that taints his citizenship is not only his Puerto Rican heritage but also a diagnosis of mental illness. After 125 long days in expulsion, authorities at the U.S. embassy in Guatemala finally figure out that Lyttle is a U.S. citizen. They issue him a passport. They contact his family. But like Matthews he is stopped en route to the United States and transferred from the CBP port of entry to ICE. ICE again mistakenly thinks he is a Mexican citizen, as if they cannot help repeating over and over again the same bad song on a broken record. They detain him, interrogate him, and issue a removal order. Finally Lyttle's family's lawyer locates him, and ICE releases him. In October 2012 Lyttle wins his case against ICE and is awarded $175,000.

Be Careful about What You Study
On May 1, 2010, French American citizen Pascal Abidor arrives by Amtrak at the U.S. port of entry in Champlain, New York, on his way to visit family in New York City. His trip began in Montreal, Canada, where he goes to school at McGill University. At the Champlain checkpoint, a CBP agent named Officer Tulip boards Abidor's train car. She asks him where he lives and why. She asks him where he was the previous year. Abidor explains that he lives in Canada and that his major is Islamic Studies. He says that the previous year he lived briefly in Jordan and traveled

to Lebanon. Tulip tells Abidor to bring all his stuff to the café car that has become a mobile federal office filled with blue-uniformed CBP agents. Tulip removes Abidor's laptop from its case and fires it up. She asks for his password, and he types it in. She finds images of a Hamas rally and a Hezbollah rally. Without showing Abidor, she lifts up his laptop and shows it to other agents in the café car.

She asks Abidor why he has "this stuff." Abidor replies that it's for "research purposes," as he is "studying the modern history of the Shiites."[12]

His laptop has all kinds of personal information. CBP agents ask him about his girlfriend, where he has been living since 2006, and his plans for the future. They say they will have to take him in to the port. A male agent pats him down. He applies pressure at different angles around his groin and genitals. They handcuff him. "Standard procedure,"[13] they tell him.

They walk him to the CBP building at the port of entry and lead him to a cell with cement walls and a small window. The cell is approximately five feet by ten feet. Tulip and the other officers continue the questioning. They say he has a lot of "symbolic materials"[14] in his possession, and he needs to explain why he has them. They ask him about his parents, his Ph.D. research topic, his travel plans, his thoughts on the Middle East.

When he is released five hours later, to his disbelief CBP tells him that they will not return his laptop or his external hard drive. Abidor insists that he needs the devices for his doctoral research. Without his laptop, he boards a bus to New York City. He is frightened and disturbed, and he can't stop thinking about what just happened.

Between October 2008 and June 2010, CBP searched the computers, phones, cameras, flash drives, and other electronic devices of more than 6,500 people, more than half of them U.S. citizens. CBP regularly goes through other personal records, including notebooks, journals, and credit card receipts. Constitutional lawyer and columnist Glenn Greenwald says that "one of the more extreme government abuses of the post-9/11 era targets U.S. citizens re-entering their own country, and it has received far too little attention."[15]

Along the border, DHS has plenary power. Its agents don't need a search warrant. There is little constraint about who they target or why. There is little oversight. Greenwald says that this makes a mockery of the U.S. Constitution, particularly the Fourth Amendment, which mandates that the government must first convince a court of reasonable suspicion before obtaining a search warrant to invade the privacy of an American citizen. Now, Greenwald says, little or nothing is needed to justify such invasions—especially if you are a U.S. citizen involved in "sensitive journalism or activism," in which case the U.S. government, free of constitutional obstacles, "can just wait until you leave the country, and then, at will, search, seize and copy all of your electronic files on your return."[16]

Journalists, scholars, and activists increasingly seem to be in the crosshairs of the U.S. national security state. For example, filmmaker Laura Poitras has been detained multiple times at New Jersey's Newark Liberty International Airport since 2006—the year she released her documentary *My Country, My Country*, which critically examines the impact of the U.S. war and occupation of Iraq and which earned her a nomination for an Academy Award.

This has also been the experience of Jacob Appelbaum, a computer programmer from Seattle, Washington, who has done volunteer work for WikiLeaks, the not-for-profit organization that has been instrumental in distributing thousands of classified documents, including those from the U.S. government. CBP has interrogated Applebaum and taken away his electronic devices on numerous occasions. The only electronic device he now carries when he travels is a memory stick with an encrypted Bill of Rights. "I dread US Customs more than I dreaded walking across the border from Turkey to Iraq in 2005. That's something worth noting," Applebaum expressed on Twitter.[17]

Similar things have happened to David House of the Bradley Manning Network (now the Private Manning Network), the support group for the famous U.S. military whistle-blower. Bradley Manning, who has since changed her name to Chelsea, released thousands of pages of classified documents to WikiLeaks to expose U.S. military abuse in Iraq. CBP seized House's electronic devices when he returned to the United States from Mexico in November 2010. In a federal lawsuit House alleged that his First and Fourth Amendment rights were violated by "the prolonged seizure of his laptop computer and other electronic devices and the review, copying, retention, and dissemination of their contents"[18] about the Bradley Manning Network. CBP returned House's devices forty-nine days later. House asserts that DHS officials did not ask him about his immigration status or anything to do with the border crossing when they questioned him at Chicago O'Hare Airport. The focus of their interrogation was his connection to Manning and WikiLeaks. Indeed, released documents now show that a "look out" order had been placed on House since July 2010, and that he was "wanted for questioning re leak of classified material."[19]

Among those who have been harassed by the Department of Homeland Security, though, Laura Poitras is a veteran. DHS had subjected her to this so many times that in April 2012, at Newark Liberty International Airport, she pulled out her pen and started jotting notes when CBP detained her. She wrote down the date, the time, and the name of the officer detaining her—Wassum. She recorded their questions, the length of the interrogation, and what they did to her. Wassum ordered her to put away her pen. She didn't do it, but continued to jot down her notes. He gave the order again. "Put away your pen,"[20] he barked, but she kept writing. Wassum threatened to handcuff her. Her pen could be used as a weapon, he told her. She put away her pen. She asked to see a supervisor. She told the supervisor that she was a journalist and that her legal counsel had told her to take notes. The supervisor told her that she was prohibited from taking notes.

Poitras tells Greenwald that it is "very traumatizing to come home to your own country and have to go through this every time." She says it is "infuriating," "horrible," and "intimidating."[21] These are emotions shared by Pascal Abidor and Jacob Applebaum, who have also significantly altered their behavior. Applebaum no longer travels with electronics. Poitras is editing her new film on surveillance in Europe and will not cross the border into the United States with her work. In January 2013, Poitras was approached by the renowned whistle-blower Edward Snowden—former employee of the National Security Agency (NSA)—who would leak thousands of classified documents to her and Glenn Greenwald, precipitating the ongoing controversy over the extent and expanse of the U.S. government's surveillance practices in the United States and across the world. It turns out, according to journalist Peter Maass, "Snowden had read Greenwald's article about Poitras's troubles at U.S. airports"[22] with CBP. International borders and places of entry, as zones where fundamental constitutional protections can be stripped away, have become a key element in the U.S. surveillance state's ever-expanding strategy.

Abidor no longer takes the train.

After eleven days, CBP returns Abidor's computer. Homeland Security agents have gone through everything—his chats with his girlfriend, private photos, email, class notes, journal articles, tax returns, graduate school transcript, and his résumé. When finally returned, his laptop is clearly damaged by CBP's intrusion. And his ordeal has not ended. Two months later, at John F. Kennedy Airport in New York City, Abidor is directed to secondary inspection. CBP asks him what he will do once he receives his Ph.D, how he pays for his travels, and details about his girlfriend. They ask him if he is a Muslim.

A few months after that, crossing the U.S.-Canada border once again, agents make Abidor empty his pockets and seize his two cell phones. They search his wallet. While scrutinizing everything he has, they ask him about his career plans, whether he has experienced anti-American sentiment abroad, and why he travels with a French passport.

The Watcher and the Watched

"There is a continuum between those who express dissent and those who do a terrorist act," then-FBI-director Robert Mueller said in a 2002 speech. "Somewhere along that continuum we have to begin to investigate. If we do not, we are not doing our jobs."[23] Today, as a result of Snowden's revelations, we know that the U.S. government conducts surveillance on a majority of the population, whether or not a person is simply exercising his or her First Amendment rights.

The firestorm of debate resulting from Snowden's whistle-blowing on clandestine government spying has rocked the world, and its full ramifications will take years to fully evaluate. In response, the United States has defended its actions as necessary to protect the population from attacks. In February 2013, the DHS Office on Civil Rights and Liberties asserted that DHS could search the contents of all electronic devices "for any reason whatsoever."[24]

But there are serious consequences to all this, warns *Philadelphia Inquirer* journalist and author Stephan Salisbury. He says that "the surveillance net in the name of security" today is much bigger than in other eras known for intense surveillance. And he underscores that "surveillance has multiple uses, not the least of which is to sow mistrust, which in turn eats at the cohesion of families, social and political movements, and ultimately the fabric of the community itself."[25]

To understand the vast amount of information covertly acquired, one need only look at the NSA's newest data center, a million-square-foot palace located in Bluffdale, Utah, and five times the size of the U.S. Capitol building. James Bamford writes in *Wired* that this place will house all kinds of information, "including the complete contents of private emails, cell phone calls, and Google searches, as well as all sorts of personal data trails—parking receipts, travel itineraries, bookstore purchases, and other digital 'pocket litter.' "[26]

"Large as it is," writes national security analyst Tom Engelhardt, "that mega-project in Utah is just one of many sprouting like mushrooms in the U.S. intelligence world."[27] Maybe this was the future that the House Un-American Activities Committee foresaw for the United States when it was first established in 1938. This committee was a government group tasked with identifying "anti-American" or "pro-communist" activities, one that conducted infamous witch hunts into the 1950s. However, what we see today, as further corroborated by Snowden's revelations, would have been an unattainable dream for those involved with twentieth-century McCarthyism. The "20 trillion"[28] domestic transactions sourced from private email, texts, chats, phone calls, and other electronic transactions since 9/11—that former NSA employee William Binney estimates that the security agency has recorded—would have been McCarthy's dream come true.

"During a single day last year, the NSA's Special Source Operations branch collected 444,743 e-mail address books from Yahoo, 105,068 from Hotmail, 82,857 from Facebook, 33,697 from Gmail and 22,881 from unspecified other providers," write Barton Gellman and Ashkan Soltani in an October 2013 article in the *Washington Post*. "Those figures, described as a typical daily intake in the document, correspond to a rate of more than 250 million a year."[29]

More and more cities such as Oakland, California, which the federal government awarded a $7 million grant to "help thwart terrorist attacks," are becoming intense surveillance hubs. "The police can monitor a fire hose of social media posts to look for evidence of criminal activities," writes Somini Sengupta in the *New York Times*, and "transportation agencies can track commuters' toll payments when drivers use an electronic pass."[30] The surveillance system of the New York City Police Department connects 3,000 cameras with terrorist suspect lists, criminal databases, radiation sensors, and license plate readers, the kind of products peddled at border-security trade fairs across the country.

Anthropologist Josiah Heyman might have been describing this post-9/11 United States when he wrote about "the birth and development of a new locus and means of domination, born of the mating between moral panics about foreigners and drugs, and a well-funded and expert bureaucracy."[31] But he was writing in 1999, and exclusively about the "militarized border society" on the U.S.-Mexico frontier. Heyman wrote that we have created a world where "more and more people either work for the watchers, or are watched by the state."[32] He said it was tragic "to witness the distorted development of the US-Mexico borderlands into a society comprised substantially of 'police and thieves.' "[33] In other words, the domestic surveillance regime the country is now experiencing as a whole, more and more, has long been the experience of people in the U.S.-Mexico borderlands. The borderlands showed us the future. And we are now becoming a country of those who watch and those who are watched, of those who are police and those who are accused of being thieves. We live in an "if you see something, say something" world, a Homeland Security dream world, where we are taught to be suspicious of one another, and thus, in effect, police each other. This is the country we have become.

The international boundary, with its exclusionary mechanisms, also has long attempted to keep out "undesirables," identifying, in effect, those whom the state targets with policing and surveillance. The 1882 Chinese Exclusion Act was the first instance in which the federal government "codified in immigration law the elision of racist and nationalist discourse" by excluding those of Chinese nationality from entering the United States. The Immigration Act of 1917 excluded those who were "morally undesirable"[34]—including anarchists, idiots, and beggars—and required that people take a literacy test upon entry into the United States. The 1952 McCarran-Walter Act underscored this sort of discrimination, calling for the exclusion of homosexuals and ideological leftists. Throughout the 1980s, various surveillance operations infiltrated organizations working on behalf of Central Americans, including the Sanctuary Movement—a church-born network that offered refuge to Central Americans fleeing U.S.-supported wars in their countries, most often El Salvador and Guatemala.

According to Heyman, it was along the U.S.-Mexico border in the 1990s that the U.S. government's "modern expertise of creating and tracking a marked population"[35] was practiced and developed. In effect, the militarized U.S.-Mexico borderlands with its surveillance technology, databases, and army of federal forces created the scaffolding of today's surveillance state. The range of suspicious activity has become so wide and deep that the NSA now monitors virtually everyone. What was once just a border reality is now a national reality.

The anything-goes borderlands still remain an ideal testing place for the U.S. surveillance state to energize and reinforce itself, as we know from the "deception detection" technology, integrated fixed towers, and microdrones created and evaluated at the University of Arizona and its tech park. It was a cold night in March when I camped with Tohono O'odham David Garcia on his family's land, three miles from the U.S.-Mexico border. We were so far from any city that the stars were bright, clear, and layered. But then came the strange blinking lights in silent swarms, for hours, from the west. It was almost like an episode from *Welcome to Night Vale*, the popular storytelling podcast that depicts a dystopian world constantly monitored by the "secret police." Garcia and I looked up at them but could not, for the life of us, figure out what they were. You begin to wonder if you are seeing things. Occasionally, one would first glow like the back end of a firefly, then it would cast a spotlight down onto the desert. It was as though a strange science fiction movie had been imposed on us from above. Although neither Garcia nor I had any idea what they were or what their purpose may have been, there was an eerie feeling that we were seeing the testing of a new technology—a regular occurrence in the borderlands—and that we were witnessing the future that the national security state has imagined for us. As the U.S. Homeland Security grid consolidates itself with more than 10,000 locales and hundreds of thousands of employees, it will be increasingly difficult to challenge the militant influence of its armed and aggressive presence, policies, and practices.

Who knows where those blinking lights came from or what they were? ("They must be drones," a national security expert told me from Washington.) They are all on guard for people who are "undesirable" in Mueller's continuum. People like Abdallah Matthews or Mark Lyttle or Pascal Abidor or Laura Poitras.

Close to Home

The next time Abdallah Matthews crosses the international boundary, the same nightmare begins again. He is arrested, led away, and while he is in handcuffs a familiar face begins interrogating him with the standard questions: Where did you go in Canada? What was the purpose of your trip? He can't believe this is happening *again*.

The CBP agent stops the string of standard questions and then pauses and asks: "Do you remember me?"

Matthews looks at him, trying to remember. "Yes," he says, "I played soccer with you." Matthews is a year younger and hasn't seen his acquaintance since high school. They reminisce.

There they are. Two friends who grew up together along the St. Clair River before the government put all the expensive surveillance towers with infrared cameras and radar on the river. This was before CBP's Operation Integration Center was inaugurated at nearby Selfridge Base, a $30 million endeavor whose prized toy is a video wall where all the info from a network of remote surveillance cameras is streamed live.

Although Matthews and the CBP agent were friendly in high school, although they grew up in the same small town, there is now a human-constructed boundary between them: on one side the watcher, and the other side the watched, regardless of their common U.S. citizenship. Matthews struggles against this divide. He pleads with his friend, "You know who I am. I grew up here. I've been over this border a million times."

But his friend has to do his job. He guides him to the same room with the counter where three interrogators are now waiting for him. He will not see his old acquaintance again. They tell him to spread his legs. Even though his hands are cuffed behind his back, they command him to take off his shoes himself. Interrogators are in front of him and behind, yelling orders and interrogating him.

The guy behind him: "Take off your shoes."

The guy in front: "What were you doing in Canada?"

The guy behind him kicks his shoes. He kicks them hard. Shoes finally off, he searches Matthews's belt area.

When they are done, Matthews asks the agents what they would do if he circles around, reenters Canada, and crosses the border again. The agents respond that they would have to do the same exact thing—handcuff, detain, and interrogate him—as if the first time never happened.

chapter eleven

REIMAGINING THE NIAGARA FRONTIER

When I meet with retired Border Patrol agent John Attanasio, we sit at a picnic table in a small park in Lewiston, New York—about fifteen minutes downriver from Niagara Falls. Behind Attanasio is the natural Canada-U.S. border, the beautiful Niagara River, beyond it the forested banks of the province of Ontario. It is a view unencumbered by the types of barriers and militarized policing props now deployed along the Mexico-U.S. borderlands. On the boat landing 150 feet below, where a bunch of fishermen cast their lines into the river, two Border Patrol agents on bikes are chatting with their superior officer, who is inside an unmarked vehicle. To the right of our splintery picnic table is the Freedom Crossing Monument, celebrating the participation of Lewiston, a suburb of Niagara Falls, in the Underground Railroad. It is a reminder that this border was once a threshold crossed to escape from the United States and its population of legally protected enslavers and human traffickers. And in the distance, behind the trees on the Canadian side, I can see Brock's Monument, a historical marker dedicated to the Canadian general who helped stop the United States from annexing Ontario during the War of 1812. It is one more reminder that the shape of the United States could have been radically different, and that the origins of the international border, in this case located in the lands of the Iroquois Confederacy, was one of violence and ultimately the imposition of a foreign nation onto diverse communities of people who were already there.

Attanasio is a balding white man with kind eyes. He is worried about his sick dog. At first, I am interested in talking to Attanasio because he was a Border Patrol agent in the Niagara Falls region when I was growing up in the area. No matter how much I strain my brain, I cannot ever remember seeing the "men in green," even though at one point my family lived three blocks from the Border Patrol station in Niagara Falls, a small industrial city just north of Buffalo. Attanasio tells me what it was like to be an agent here from the late 1970s to the early 2000s, doing the rounds in the region, right up to the mouth of the Niagara River in Youngstown, where you can see the skyline of Toronto across Lake Ontario. He talks about the people who came across smuggling cigarettes, and the migrants from China they once caught close to where we sit, and one man from Yugoslavia who was a "tough son-of-a-bitch." The man ran straight across the border at the Whirlpool Bridge, Attanasio says, as if he was going to singlehandedly tear apart the international boundary and its layers of administrative bureaucracy. But Attanasio stepped up like a football player; he put his head down and smashed straight into the charging "invader," bringing the two of them to the ground.

As Attanasio talks, it occurs to me that I am experiencing two distinct things that are difficult to reconcile. On the one hand he gives me the information I am seeking from his perspective. He explains not only his job as a Border Patrol agent during the time I was growing up in the region but also its significant expansion well after I moved away from my hometown, especially in the aftermath of 9/11. He talks about the increasing number of agents and level of surveillance technology now evident in so many places throughout the country. He tells me that he thinks that there are now forty agents at the Niagara Falls station, up from seven when he was on duty, and that they are looking for more. "I am not sure what they will do," he tells me.

On the other hand, when he mentions the rusty Whirlpool International Bridge, Lewiston's Art Park, or Old Fort Niagara, I know each of these places intimately, each location woven with many personal childhood memories, both good and bad. I am spellbound by the way he talks about the place where I grew up, the Buffalo–Niagara Falls region, and even Lewiston itself where my family lived for many years, through the prism of the border surveillance apparatus. Our conversation is very personal, and at the same time it is so much a product of our current national condition. I haven't lived here since the early 1990s and some places have become almost unrecognizable, like the deindustrialized city of Niagara Falls, which looks nothing like the bustling city I knew as a child and teenager. While Attanasio talks, I am trying to reconcile the collapse of my hometown with the nationwide expansion of the Homeland Security state.

The Honeymoon Capital of the World
With its majestic and breathtaking cascades of rushing water, Niagara Falls has to be one of the world's most naturally dramatic, ferocious, and beautiful international borders.

Approaching the falls, even from miles away, you can see the white mist floating up from the natural wonder that was once known as the Honeymoon Capital of the World, a place filled with hotels featuring heart-shaped jacuzzis as well as a place known for daredevils doing death-defying feats. You can see the Skylon Tower with its needle in Niagara Falls, Ontario, and the tall hotels built up along the gorge on the Canadian side where most tourists go. There has been growth in both the population and the economy on the Canadian side. But on the U.S. side, many of the hotels have closed, and some are boarded up, only the beginning indications of an economy gone bad. Places I loved as a kid—and places where I worked as a teenager—have crumbled into ruins: the Wintergarden, a Cesar Pellini–designed indoor arboretum, is now derelict and half torn down; the Rainbow Centre, the outlet mall that was all the hype in the 1980s, has a tall fence surrounding its now mostly vacant 50,000 square feet (though the Niagara Falls Culinary Institute currently occupies a small portion of it).

A couple days before I meet with Attanasio, I go to Goat Island, located on the brink of the three waterfalls that make up Niagara Falls—Horseshoe, Bridal Veil, and American Falls. Goat Island is where you go to get a great up-close view of 150,000 gallons of water gushing over the brink every second. For decades, much of that flow has been diverted to generate the hydroelectric power that spawned Niagara Falls's metallurgical and chemical industry, which would eventually employ my father in the 1970s. In the early twentieth century, Niagara Falls, New York, placed its bets on industry, not tourism, and then developed and declined in a pattern similar to Detroit's.

Goat Island has always been a place of refuge for me, one of my favorite places in the world. I used to take long naps on the cool grass upriver after working a graveyard shift at a nearby hotel, and I would listen to the frothing rapids rush by before falling asleep. This time, as I cross the two-lane bridge that connects the forested island to the mainland, I see a green-striped Border Patrol SUV parked off to the side of the road next to a Park Police vehicle. Both vehicles are idling, and the Border Patrol agent appears to be chatting with the other officer. This is the first time I have seen in Niagara Falls the precise type of SUV that I always see where I live now in Arizona. It isn't just that the Border Patrol vehicle strongly reminds me of the Southwest border that creates a surreal moment, it is also that I've just driven through the environmental and economic catastrophe of Niagara Falls, a city that struggles to provide even the most basic services to its residents.

I purposely took a nostalgic journey to reach Goat Island. I drove through the shuttered factories on Buffalo Avenue, an industrial corridor that once employed most of the city, including my dad, who worked for a company that made rust preventive for cars. This is the avenue that always had a strange smell of chemical concoctions. It was home to dozens of factories like Occidental (formerly Hooker Chemical), the company behind one of the worst environmental tragedies in the United States, the Love Canal Disaster. Occidental put so much toxic sludge into the Hooker Ditch (as the canal was also called), including waste from Cold War biochemical and nuclear weapons experiments, that President Jimmy Carter deemed it a federal disaster area in 1979 and initiated a mass evacuation. This was after a school was built on top of the toxic waste. So were homes. Poisonous chemicals could leach into basements, their fumes evaporating into people's homes. One baby was born with two sets of teeth, another with three ears. One of my first memories was when a family, evacuated from a Love Canal neighborhood, moved in next door. It was during this time that plants like Hooker were at such high levels of productivity that, according to former Hooker employee Paul Gromosiak, as cited by Ginger Strand in her book *Inventing Niagara: Beauty, Power, and Lies*, everyone in Niagara Falls "would go outside every morning and wipe a layer of sooty, greasy scum from the railing of the family's front porch." But no one minded, he said, because "those plants employed the town's workers,"[1] which included, of course, my father.

But it is not Love Canal I think of, necessarily, when I see the Border Patrol vehicle. I think more of that hill—or is it a mountain?—on the west side of Interstate 190, which cuts through Niagara Falls. In the winter the snow on this hill is so pristine and untouched that you could want to run up it with a sled. That is until you notice that there is a fence around it. And until you see the strange tubes coming out of the ground that look much like the cordoned-off area of the nearby Love Canal. These 385 acres of tumorous growth are a series of landfills, one of ten Superfund sites in the Niagara Falls region with God knows what festering underneath. I have watched the toxic hill grow from nothing to something so spectacular in size, and so prominently visible in the middle of the city, that it almost overshadows the majestic falls itself. There is constant musing about what is inside. Some have sarcastically speculated that it might also be the final resting place for the poisonous remains of animals injected with radioactive plutonium for experimentation and medical waste from humans exposed to plutonium in other experiments, such as the material that was buried near my high school (which still needs to be decontaminated) about ten miles away.

It's too bad, to put it mildly, that the rivers of resources and expensive technology that flow into Border Patrol can't be used to protect the city of Niagara Falls from the real and imminent threats posed to people's physical security by corporate contamination, waste, and other "Love Canals" in the area. Surely, from up above in the Border Patrol helicopters or drones, they have cameras that can zoom in on the sign on Buffalo Avenue that warns of a BUMPY RIDE due to potholes. Big, gaping potholes are found throughout the city, but they are especially prevalent on this ghostly avenue of empty or barely functioning factories, unlike its profile in the 1940s, when the "fumes of industry"[2] wafted up from factories about to boom with World War II. Munitions, metals, lubricants, and petroleum were needed by the government for the war machine that Eisenhower would eventually cite with deep concern in his 1961 farewell speech about the military-industrial complex. One example of many, the culprit behind the Love Canal, Hooker Chemical, opened a subsidiary plant during this time named the Niagara Falls Chemical Warfare Plant.

Homeland Security cannot bring back or protect the economic security of the tens of thousands of people who lost their jobs when companies began closing. In 2000 came the final blow to my father's workplace: the plant closed, and fifty-five workers were laid off. The Cataract City—so named due to the waterfalls—was a place beloved by Marilyn Monroe and used to be one of the biggest cities in the state of New York. Now it is bleeding people like Detroit, Cleveland, and other derelict industrial cities in the northern borderlands Rust Belt.

Now Niagara Falls is simply trying to "survive as a city,"[3] as its community development director Seth Piccirillo puts it, and he means that in the literal sense. Since its population peak of more than 100,000 people in the 1960s, the population of the Cataract City has plummeted, and according to the 2010 census there are now only 50,100 people, just above the critical threshold. If the city dips below 50,000 before the 2020 census, the U.S. federal government will cease to consider Niagara Falls a city, and it will cut off crucial subsidies for housing. The federal government has already insisted that cities like Niagara Falls make "hard choices"[4] with housing, such as cutting off grants to first-time homeowners and terminating programs for the elderly and disabled. By promising to pay off their school loans, the Honeymoon Capital is now trying to lure college graduates into a city with no jobs, a Herculean attempt to stop the population from continuing to plummet.

Right before my moment seeing the Border Patrol SUV on Goat Island, I visit the neighborhood where I lived in the early 1990s. I guess I shouldn't be surprised that the stocky brick building where I once lived has a sign on the front door that says CONDEMNED, but I am. I pull over to the side of the street where I used to park. I look at the weeds and grass crawling up through the cracks in the sidewalk. I look at the empty parking lot of the once modern-looking Whitney Apartments, across from my former home. The empty lot used to be full of cars. I look up to the smashed windows in the apartment complex, and then I realize it really is dead. The place is thoroughly gutted. The shattered windows look like eyes that no longer have life behind them. I look down Eighteenth Street and see the sign for the laundromat I used to go to, thinking that at least that's still running. I walk to it. No. It's boarded up. The little store across the street? Boarded up. Every single store around here is boarded up. My favorite Italian deli? Boarded up. And down the street? The only words that remain on the outer facade of a church are: THE GRACIOUS LORD OUR GOD. Behind the facade, not even the foundation of the church still exists. There are small trees, flowers, and weeds crawling back into life. According to one estimate, there are 5,000 such derelict buildings in the city. When I moved away in the early 1990s, things were indeed starting to look dire, but I never imagined that there would be such an acute level of collapse.

A walk through the neighborhoods of Niagara Falls make its official poverty rate, which hovers at around 35 percent, look conservative. In many ways the frail city looks like a city of refugees, as though the war has already happened, as though thirty-ton bombs have already been dropped and the increasing federal, state, and local law enforcement presence in the city—including the U.S. Border Patrol—is meant to "manage" the toxic aftermath. One embodiment of the crisis that I see on this gorgeous summer day as I drive away from my condemned apartment, and seemingly everywhere I look, are people walking down the middle of the streets. Not on the sidewalk, but right in the middle of these cracked, potholed streets. Sometimes the people are carrying plastic bags. Sometimes they have nothing at all. They are almost always alone. I see them as I make my way from Eighteenth to Fifteenth, down toward the library, the old YMCA, and my favorite diner, The Why. The people always seem to be walking slowly, in no hurry at all. The officially named "street walkers"[5] are everywhere. They are an ever-growing group of people to whom law enforcement authorities are paying increasing attention.

"People seem to have the idea that they have the right

of way over traffic. That's not the case,"[6] Niagara Falls police superintendent John Chella said in 2012 after an incident involving a young red-haired man who walked slowly, in the middle of the road, in front of the police vehicle that Chella himself was driving. At first officers tried to issue warning tickets. But according to traffic division captain Salvatore Pino, "that did absolutely no good, because people just kept walking in the streets,"[7] as if walking in the streets were the obvious, logical expression of objection to a city gutted of resources, a city that has abandoned them, a city that really doesn't exist anymore in any meaningful way. "So now," Pino said, "we're going to start to give them real tickets." Street walkers are now charged with the following offense: "'Pedestrian Failed to Use the Sidewalk When One Is Provided."[8] The street walkers are people of all races, genders, and ages. Almost all are living in poverty. The population of Niagara Falls is more than 50 percent white, mostly of Italian ancestry, and it also has a significant African American population.

The street walkers seemed to epitomize what Niagara Falls has become, but it is in the city's so-called redevelopment zone—an area thoroughly eviscerated, square miles of grasslands with abandoned, collapsing homes—that I begin to mourn the place of my first memories. For it is dying. It is here, standing alone in an empty urban prairie, hearing the piercing buzz of locusts, that I realize that the Niagara Falls of my childhood is long gone. If it weren't for the silver casino of the Seneca Nation in the background, it would seem like a massive Superfund site, an ecological killing field. The city can't afford to put any money into the Memorial Medical Center (where my mom once worked), the only hospital in Niagara Falls that miraculously survives without dedicated government funding.

They are cutting funding to the city library. They are cutting funding to the Niagara Arts and Cultural Center. In 2013, Niagara Falls public schools continued to crumble, with $315,000 removed from its already shrunken budget. (Buffalo lost $2.5 million that year.)

In 2013, the city of Niagara Falls implemented a new series of cuts and layoffs in what the mayor named the "disaster budget."[9] There were fewer city workers to collect trash, to plow the streets in one of the snowiest regions in the country, and to cut grass in a city that already looks as though it has been left to the dogs. Seasonal street pavers, so needed in this place of so many potholes, were cut. There were no summer hires for youth recreation workers and lifeguards. "I'm losing twenty-seven people, okay," Ferris Anthony of the United Steel Workers local 9434 (the union for the city workers) said. "Not one fireman and not one policeman are being touched. I'm not afraid to say it."[10] Niagara Falls feels similar to a lot of low-income towns in the U.S-Mexico borderlands. As money for other services gets cut, more resources are concentrated in law enforcement and first responders.

When I cross the two-lane bridge onto Goat Island, I momentarily forget about the Border Patrol. I am now more just looking to get away, to escape from this Niagara Falls reality I have just experienced. Goat Island was always the place where I could escape, get away from it all, if just for a few hours. It wouldn't make sense for the Border Patrol to be here—the rushing water and falls renders a border crossing impossible. But there is the green-striped vehicle, idling its engine and polluting the air we breathe, doing nothing productive really, but serving as a symbol of what we are becoming: a Border Patrol Nation.

They've Got Everything

When I go to meet seventy-three-year-old Norma Higgs at the Tim Horton's Donut Shop in downtown Niagara Falls, I am expecting her to repeat what she expressed in the two columns she wrote for the *Niagara Gazette* about the U.S. Border Patrol. Higgs, born and raised in Niagara Falls, generally writes columns profiling the Cataract City's rich history. But she has just finished a Citizen Academy program at the local Border Patrol station. A Citizens Academy is like an Explorer program for adults. Before we met I was expecting her to talk about the "long green line,"[11] her way of introducing to the readership the U.S. Border Patrol's enhanced presence in the area. I was expecting the words of a true believer, who after explaining the Border Patrol's surveillance capabilities wrote that "not much can get past these guys."[12] I was expecting her to talk about one of the overall goals of the academy, to encourage the people of Niagara Falls to be the Patrol's "eyes and ears,"[13] and to repeat the oft-said Homeland Security motto: "If you see something, say something." But the energetic Higgs, in charge of her neighborhood watch committee (or "block club," as it is known in Niagara Falls) is purely and refreshingly "Niagara Falls" with her accent and her sass.

The first thing she says is: "Do you know what time we had to meet for the Citizens Academy?" She looks at me and answers her own question: "Friday, six p.m." She pauses to let me take in the ridiculousness of it.

"I mean," Higgs says, "don't they go to happy hour? Or a fish fry?" In Niagara Falls Friday evening means fish fry; everybody knows it, except, apparently, the Border Patrol. The fish fry is what Higgs would miss six times. The way she repeats that to me with emotion makes me think she is still astonished by the Border Patrol's gaffe.

However, Higgs makes sure I know that she thinks they are good guys and gals ("and yes," she tells me, "I met a few gals.") For example, they were respectful of the seventy-three-year-old when she said she didn't want to shoot a gun because she wasn't a "gun person." On that day they learned a lot of tactics used to protect the homeland, such as applying painful pressure to joints, handcuffing, and "field interviewing"—a nice way of saying interrogation. They held other weapons besides guns: a Taser and the Border Patrol's pepper-ball launching device. They discussed vehicle stops. Her classmates, including other neighborhood watch people, did rather well, she says. They hit their targets regularly, and even tackled the agent who mock-threatened them with a baton.

Another time, the Border Patrol showed the group what Higgs calls a "monster truck"—a vehicle rigged with surveillance cameras attached to a "long series of pipe-like sections" that rise out of it "like E.T." An agent inside the truck controls all of the tech with a laptop. This "peek and seek"[14] technology, they say, is great for the terrain around the gorge or the banks of the Niagara River. Higgs describes a trip to Buffalo Sector Headquarters on Grand Island, ten minutes from Niagara Falls by car, where a large wall of video monitors provides real-time information on "any activity" registered by surveillance devices located on the Niagara River and along the riverfront in Buffalo.

Higgs pauses to let me soak it in, then says: "Big Brother."

This Big Brother technology has also assisted the Niagara Falls Police Department. The U.S. Border Patrol has given the NFPD "active shooter"[15] and hostage-situation trainings in abandoned buildings throughout the city. They patrol with the NFPD in roving anti-crime units as part of the Operation Stonegarden collaboration, in which DHS funds the police department for overtime in its border enforcement operations. "I can't say enough about the Border Patrol and what they've done for us," Police Chief John Chella said in a 2012 interview with the *Niagara Gazette*. "They have accompanied us on drug raids and have backed up our officers when they've needed help. They have really stepped up their involvement in the community."[16]

In the 2009 Operation Blood Clot, for example, the Border Patrol gave air surveillance support for the most massive law enforcement operation in the history of the Honeymoon Capital. A Border Patrol helicopter flew circles over neighborhoods of abandoned homes, like my old neighborhood, as a caravan of fourteen SWAT trucks, twenty-four K-9 units, and other marked vehicles charged into the area. "It may have looked a little bit like an invasion," wrote Rick Pfeiffer in the *Niagara Gazette*, and "in a way, it was."[17] Police hurled concussion grenades that exploded with bright bursts and stunning decibels of sound. They used battering rams to smash doors from their hinges, and pulled people, primarily African Americans, out of their homes in their quest to bust the "Bloods" gang. The *Gazette*, getting into the adrenaline rush of the whole thing, describes a makeshift central headquarters as a "war room"[18] humming with federal investigators and prosecutors who sat around a large conference table looking into laptops.

Operation Blood Clot and the later 2011 operation named Wild Nation are examples of the Border Patrol's expansion in Niagara Falls, a reality John Attanasio alluded to as we talked. The agency is looking to move out of the brown wooden station—a building that looks like a

National Park Service station—next to a dilapidated apartment complex, just down the road from the Niagara River. Since the 1920s—when the agents were after smugglers and migrants trying to circumvent the restrictions associated with the Chinese Exclusion Laws—they have been located in this station. But now the dreams are bigger. With more agents they need more space, at least 25,000 square feet, a secure indoor garage, sixty outdoor parking spaces, and a helipad. U.S. Representative Louise Slaughter, a Democrat and the local congressperson, says, "It is an efficient use of federal resources . . . and it takes advantage of the incredible workforce of Niagara County and Western New York."[19]

As block club captain in her neighborhood, Higgs stresses to me that she wants a safe community. She tells me she was mugged in her own home, and that got her started in the neighborhood watch group. At the same time, she wonders why the Border Patrol is expanding while almost everything else in Niagara Falls is falling apart.

"They've got everything," Higgs tells me.

"They have helicopters, boats, planes, bikes, and mopeds. After 9/11 they threw all the money to Border Patrol and not to the people," she says. "We used to get all kinds of money to give classes, workshops for our firefighters. And now that is all dried up."

Higgs is talking about programs for the block club, but she could be talking about many other things. In Niagara Falls, instead of funds for repairing potholes, they get motion sensors. Instead of housing, they get surveillance towers. Instead of public transportation, they get video walls and radar. Instead of strong public schools, they get FLIR cameras and thermal imagery. Instead of cleaning up the city's brownfields and environmental catastrophes, they get more Border Patrol agents on the lookout for "terrorists" slipping across the swift-moving Niagara River. Instead of basic services, they get the expensive immigrant detention facility in nearby Batavia. Instead of a police force concerned with community well-being, they get a police force fueled by federal grants, more focused on "defending the homeland." Perhaps the most striking example of the rise of the Homeland Security state in this iconic city of profound natural beauty is the shiny, expensive, multi-use law enforcement center built on the once-bustling Main Street, now a wasteland of boarded-up storefronts and street walkers. As with many other cities across the nation, the solution to Niagara Falls's social ills is, indeed, ever more Homeland Security—more guns, more uniforms, more surveillance, more arrests, and a homeland of a very particular sort.

Seven Generations

While talking to ex-Border Patrol agent John Attanasio, it isn't difficult to imagine how this landscape looked before the international boundary existed. Although there are Border Patrol agents below us on the landing, surveillance cameras upriver on the Niagara River, and agents supposedly stationed miles away in Grand Island watching the video wall for all suspicious movement, from where we sit the river looks peaceful, the Canadian shore friendly. There was a time when the Canada-U.S. border did not exist at all, and Iroquois-speaking indigenous communities inhabited the land. While the Iroquois had loosely defined, highly porous borders defining their territories, it was absolutely nothing like the hardened, intensely patrolled divisions of today, whose sanctity, rationale, and militaristic institutions are rarely questioned.

How radically different is this world of divisions to what the world was even 150 years ago, let alone more than 500 years ago when Deganawidah, Peacemaker, one of the founders of the Iroquois Confederacy, said: "Be strong of mind, O chiefs: Carry no anger and hold no grudges. Think not forever of yourselves, O chiefs, nor of your own generation. Think of continuing generations of our families, think of our grandchildren and of those yet unborn, whose faces are coming from beneath the ground."[20]

While Attanasio tells me a story of a detail he had on an anti-drug task force in the city of Niagara Falls, I look across to Canada and realize that, growing up here, I had never imagined it being anything other than a border. It occurs to me that I probably lived closer to teenagers my age in Canada than to some of those who went to my high school. Yet I never met my Canadian neighbors and peers, I know nothing about them, and somehow this was all unquestioned, all natural.

As with many Border Patrol agents I've interviewed, I could tell Attanasio was not completely comfortable with his job. He tells me a story in which Border Patrol partnered with this drug task force with the NFPD, just in case a non-citizen like a "Dominican" or a "Cuban" was involved. He didn't like it that the police would go into a supermarket and slam people—usually people of color—against the wall. If they raided a house, the police would do it with "black boots and jackets" and the Border Patrol would follow, looking for foreigners. "I only did it for six months," Attanasio tells me, though the detail was for one year. I tell him that I think what he did—quitting that detail—was courageous. He shrugged and said "I just told my boss that I just couldn't do it."

Like so many of the other Border Patrol agents that

I talked with while researching this book, Attanasio opens up to me, knowing full well that I might be critical of the agency that once employed him. Border Patrol agents have told me that they feel vilified by everyone across the political spectrum, left, right, and center. Many have expressed to me that within the agency they have created an insular world that even has its own language, in which only other agents understand one another. Being as visible as they are, when something goes wrong at the border they are the easiest to blame. They are the uniformed face of the Department of Homeland Security. In many important ways the agents of the U.S. Border Patrol too are dehumanized, unable to say anything or explain their work to the public outside of the chain of command. They are either glorified heroes "securing" the border, or uniformed thugs trampling human rights.

I have met with so many Border Patrol agents who, like Attanasio, took time out of their day to speak with me, and who on several occasions bought me dinner or lunch. The daughter of one agent in Douglas, Arizona, drew me a picture and gave it to me. Agents met with me multiple times and told me story after story, sometimes gruesome tales that expanded my picture of their world. One agent, imagining a simpler life for a moment, told me he sometimes wished that he could give it all away—meaning his expensive suburban house and all the things supported by his Border Patrol salary. He longed to quit his job and move to a place where he could do everything necessary with just a bicycle.

The humanization of the Border Patrol agent is essential to understanding the bigger picture. I don't mean that we need to more fully understand the agency's mission, which is anti-human since it imposes and enforces militarized divisions between human beings, communities, cultures, and their relationships and freedom. I mean that we need to lift the veil, to see the bigger world behind the Border Patrol agent and behind the growing "homeland security" grid. The U.S. Border Patrol is not just the "men in green," it is a much larger, complex, industrial world that encompasses robotics, engineers, salespeople, detention centers, and the incoming generation of children in its Explorer programs. The clamor of politicians from both the major political parties fuels this world by always insisting that we need "more boots on the ground." This world has a high-powered lobbying machine working for the border-policing technology industry and its incarceration apparatus, projected to mushroom for decades to come. "If You Draw the Line, We'll Help You Secure It," DRS Technologies advertised at the Border Security Expo in 2012. It is a Border Patrol world that needs its architects, engineers, and construction workers, as any city would. It is the world in which we now live, where eradicating border violations is given higher priority than eradicating malnutrition, poverty, homelessness, illiteracy, unemployment, and all other serious needs of communities in so many places like Niagara Falls. It is a world, as Norma Higgs suggests, brimming with money and resources.

The Super Bowl security apparatus is the shining star of this industrial complex, spawned by a multibillion-dollar DHS budget and able to be mobilized quickly, efficiently, and expensively. In come the fixed-wing jets, the Blackhawk helicopters, the Special Forces units. In come agents like Lazaro Guzman and his team, who scour the bus and train stations looking for "suspicious" people. This is the intense collusion between the federal government, private industry, and law enforcement, with Border Patrol leading the charge. This is a Border Patrol Nation that can be installed anywhere in the country, or the world, to monitor and thwart an ever-changing group people who may be— or become—a threat. It is the ability of the government, as in Boston in April 2013, to lock down an entire region, impose virtual martial law, and execute a house-to-house manhunt, all at breakneck speed.

And the result is always the same: all this expensive gear and resources and surveillance equipment and drones and one of the only arrests is, as shown on the National Geographic Channel at the Super Bowl, the Nicaraguan woman with her face dehumanized by pixelation as she is taken off a Greyhound bus in handcuffs, as if she were an imminent threat to the homeland. You don't learn her name. You don't learn anything about her. She has been made into something less than a human being. She could be María in Ridgeland, South Carolina, or someone in the row of hungry young Haitian men in Dajabón, Dominican Republic. She could be Gabriela in Sodus, New York, or Gerardo in Tucson, Arizona. This nameless woman from Nicaragua represents tens of thousands of other faceless people who are constantly up against this daunting apparatus, and whose human life and dignity are presented through media as something so worthless and disposable that we are expected not to give a shit about her.

At the Drones and Aerial Robots Conference in New York University in October 2013, a philosophy professor from the University of Massachusetts, Lowell, asked participants to find a partner and "look him or her in the eyes for just five seconds," according to Matt Flegenheimer in the *New York Times*. Most, at first, refused. The professor insisted. Never had five seconds seemed like such an eternity. One attendee couldn't hack it and after three seconds looked down and tapped something into a smartphone.

"You feel that little quiver in your stomach?" the professor John Kaag asked. "It's called a sign of being human. Drones don't feel that."

And perhaps we're not supposed to either, not if we're to quietly accept everything that separates us and makes us suspicious of each other: the walls, checkpoints, weapons, surveillance towers, and federal forces. The United States has embarked upon an ever-changing yet permanent witch hunt for "foreign aliens" and other "existential threats." What might have been an improbable scenario out of a science fiction flick not too long ago, now has legitimacy and power.

As we go from a relatively open and civilian society centered on principles of democracy and accountability to a closed society very much enforced by the authority of the gun, we stand to lose much more than contact with our government. We stand to lose community: the ability to look into each others' eyes and live and relate as equals, as Kaag so brilliantly demonstrated. The Border Patrol creeps into a community's most intimate relationships and deeply affects the way we perceive and even treat one another. It can impact and skew basic human emotions such as empathy and kindness. It can make us suspicious of people, stilting the natural impulse to cultivate rich friendships with others regardless of whether those connections cross national, racial, or class boundaries. It can stilt one of the most powerful forces in the world: cross-border solidarity.

However, people are fighting back. In 2011, a Border Patrol agent approached Ofelia Rivas when she was with a student group from the Earlham Border Studies Program as they stood on the borderline on the Tohono O'odham

Nation. The Border Patrol agent was speaking codes, numbers, and military-style jargon into his crackling radio. He looked at Rivas and explained to her the exact statute her group members were violating by being where they were, with another long bureaucratic-sounding code. He told Rivas that they were not supposed to be there.

Rivas responded calmly in the Tohono O'odham language.

In O'odham, Rivas reminded the agent that he is a guest on her land. In O'odham, Rivas told him that it didn't seem he had a good grasp of the laws if he didn't know that this was her people's land and that she could invite friends there if she wished. She kept speaking for about a minute until the agent interrupted:

"Do you speak English?"

"Yes, I do," Rivas responded.

"Can you speak English?" he responded, "I don't understand O'odham."

"I don't understand your language either," Rivas replied. She repeated back the military jargon the agent was spitting into this radio and said, "I don't understand that." She repeated the exact statute that the agent had cited to say that they were in violation of the law, saying, "And I don't understand that." She translated what she had told the agent in O'odham. She reminded the agent that he was a guest on their land. The agent became apologetic, as if capitulating to ancient force, as if knowing that this force, like the Iroquois Great Law, was much more powerful than anything that Homeland Security could ever muster.

"Resistance is my language and I survive in living the Him'dag," Rivas has said, referring to the ancient, subtle, and sustaining resistance that has made people like her unafraid and unintimidated. Resistance is in the O'odham traditions of hospitality, generosity, and kindness towards others—practices which, in the Border Patrol worldview, could be construed as radical, if not illegal acts.

In February 2013, when Raul Alcaraz Ochoa was biking in Tucson, Arizona, he saw a man who had been pulled over by three police vehicles. René Meza Huerta was pleading with police not to arrest him; he had six children to take care of, several of whom were in his car. In Tucson, a rather typical scenario followed. The police called the Border Patrol, one of tens of thousands of such consultations that happen each year. Alcaraz Ochoa saw the future generation in the car: "They were scared; they were startled; they were crying."[21] Then something in him snapped. Now off his bike, he took out his notebook and started writing everything down, the officers' badge numbers and their vehicle numbers. A Border Patrol vehicle arrived, with one agent. Alcaraz Ochoa only had a green card, so what he would do next would be at great risk to his legal status. He went on pure instinct. When it was clear that Huerta was going to be arrested by the Border Patrol, the activist did what has never been done before in this context. He lay down under the Border Patrol vehicle to attempt to impede the arrest. He said he wasn't going to move. The Border Patrol agent barked that he would get a felony for impeding the work of a federal officer. He didn't move. They took pictures of him, and Alcaraz Ochoa took pictures back. They threatened to pepper-spray him. He didn't move. Then they did pepper-spray the young activist and dragged him out from underneath the vehicle.

The thing is, Rivas and Alcaraz Ochoa are not alone. There are people around the country—citizens and non-citizens—organizing, networking, and advancing a long history of resistance in the United States. Sometimes it is underground, clandestine; often it is ignored by the media. Alcaraz Ochoa is part of a protection network, one of several in Tucson, called Corazón de Tucson. The semi-underground networks (including Fortín and Tierra y Libertad Organization) are designed so that if one of their members gets detained by Border Patrol or police, it triggers a wave of phone calls, text messages, and emails. People are mobilized. The network helps provide a variety of resources and support, from legal counsel to fight any pending deportation to child care if a parent is separated from her or his children. The cumulative effect of the small actions by these community-based networks is providing the basis for something much grander. Yet this is done at great risk. Never before have acts of solidarity, hospitality, and even friendship been so criminalized as they have in the U.S. borderlands. This has created an increasingly volatile—and sometimes explosive—climate of tension.

In October 2013, Tucson police pulled over two members of Corazón de Tucson because the light above their license plate was not working. The police called Border Patrol when they suspected that the occupants of the car, two leaders from the protection network, were undocumented. At the same time, the community members in the car called in their situation to Corazón de Tucson, and the network went into action, unleashing a chain of communications and social media posts informing people of what was going on.

The quick and extraordinary mobilization that happened next is a testament to how communities of conscience are pushing back against the Border Patrol Nation. In no time roughly 100 people surrounded the Border Patrol vehicle, where the leaders sat caged in the back. Instead of just Alcaraz Ochoa in the earlier incident, now hundreds were saying *you are not going to leave*. People made two circles around the Border Patrol vehicle so it could not move, one inner circle and one outer. Enclosed by two human walls, the Homeland Security vehicle growled, driving back and forth as though it might force through or over the people encircling it. Then two beefy Border Patrol agents (among about fifteen total who showed up to the scene) burst through the outer circle and shoved people aggressively out of the way to create a path for the Border Patrol vehicle. They trampled people and threw them to the ground. Tucson police pummeled the community members with tear gas, shot rubber bullets into the group, and made more arrests.

In an unrelated event two days later, a man looked through the dark, barred window of a nondescript deportation bus. He had a slight smile on his face, and his hands were placed together as if praying. The man is slightly bowing to the activists who had stopped the bus in its tracks on the frontage road to Interstate 10 in Tucson. Through the window you could see chains cascading from his shackled wrists, chains wrapped around his waist. He was one of seventy such shackled people, in two such buses, that were headed to Operation Streamline proceedings. He was most likely captured in the desert and detained in Border Patrol custody. He had probably spent the night in a cold, overcrowded cell. Maybe he had a blanket, maybe he didn't. Maybe he ate a sandwich, but maybe all he had was a couple of crackers. The bus was en route to Tuscon's federal courthouse, where proceedings would take place to formally expel him from the country, perhaps banish him for life.

But on this day the buses did not make it to the federal courthouse where five activists had locked themselves to the front gate. The buses didn't make it any farther than the frontage road, approximately half a mile away from the courthouse. The act of civil disobedience was carefully planned and orchestrated by numerous local and national organizations, including the migrant justice organization Puente from Phoenix and the National Day Laborer Organizing Network, which fuels the campaign "Not One More Deportation." Nearly two dozen activists locked themselves to the tires of the buses. For a startling and almost magical moment in Tucson, between those stopping the buses and those who had locked themselves to the courthouse entrance gate, the deportation machine began to sputter and stall. A dramatic six-hour scene followed. The Border Patrol and police erected a law enforcement tent city, as cars and trucks zoomed by on the highway above.

Inside the deportation bus, the man's slight bow, slight smile, and hands in a gesture of prayer seemed an acknowledgement of the act of solidarity going on outside. The act of civil disobedience brought down a flurry of felony charges to the activists and at the same time loudly affirmed that cross-border relationships cannot be stopped, not by bars, nor by the armed guards who roam the area in camouflage tactical vests. For the first time ever, Operation Streamline proceedings were cancelled.

The original Iroquois law, we recall, urges consideration of the welfare of the whole people, and to bear in mind "the coming generations, even those whose faces are yet beneath the surface of the ground—the unborn."[22] The Iroquois are asking us to look not only into the eyes of our fellow human beings, but into the eyes of future human beings. They say it is appropriate to evaluate decisions made today in light of their impact on children seven generations, or 140 years, in the future.

There is ample evidence that the spirit of the Iroquois law is not dead. In July 2013, nine young people, none U.S. citizens, some who were in Mexico and some who crossed the border to Mexico to join their compañeros, put on graduation robes, went to the port of entry in Nogales, Arizona, and demanded that they be reunited with their families. In September, another thirty-four did the same thing, in Laredo, Texas, all risking incarceration, all risking their legal status to be in the United States. Different youth organizations have even been infiltrating immigration detention centers in an attempt to organize people fighting their deportation cases from inside. All of these youth had grown up in the United States but had been brought to the country by their parents when they were very young. The media message about these kids was that their parents were "irresponsible," to quote Arizona Governor Jan Brewer.

One of these youth, Dario Andrade, contested Brewer's notion and insisted that his parents are "the dreamers." He said, "Our parents are the ones who had the dream of coming over and providing a better life, getting a better job, just being there for their kids. They had to leave their families, their siblings, their parents, their friends; they had to leave it all to come to an unknown country where they don't speak the language. They can't really work. They can't get a driver's license. They can't get health care. They can't really do anything. Yet they had the guts to just make that decision and come over. And they work every day for their kids."[23] Indeed, it was their parents' looking forward "seven spans" that was an intimate, loving, and powerful action for their children.

Resistance to our becoming a Border Patrol Nation goes well beyond the immigration rights movement. It is the ACLU fighting CBP confiscation of electronic devices in courts, and fighting Border Patrol abuse at the state level, particularly in Arizona. It is nonprofit civilian groups, such as the women's organization Code Pink, organizing in the streets and in front of the AUVSI drone lobby conference, and bursting with creative efforts to alert our society to the consequences of living in a war-driven surveillance state. It is legal assistance organizations going into detention centers day in and day out to help people fight deportation. Resistance is the spontaneous emergence of movements like Occupy that scream out against the collusion of corporate and state power and openly call for a society where community and democracy are the real sources of power, decision-making, and security. It is the rallies in support of Private Chelsea Manning and Edward Snowden that stand with the whistle-blowers' conscience and dedication to a vision for the United States that is based on openness, accountability, and diplomacy, not secrecy, surveillance, and coercion.

Resistance is international. It is at the heart of any of the countless grassroots organizations and movements throughout Mexico, Central America, and the Caribbean actively engaging and creating a new world in which people have the right to migrate but the ability and community resources to stay.

The project of Border Patrol Nation is to gate people into a world of clear and enforceable divisions. These are not only divisions between citizens and foreigners, insiders and outsiders, but also between the haves (and all the "interests" they need to protect) and the have-nots. It is a division between the global North and the global South. In this brightly divided world, the more apparent crime is that of the individual straggling street walker, not the profit-obsessed system that abandons entire communities of children, youth, men, and women to grow up and live their lives in collapsing, contaminated, foreclosed ruins. The criminal is the person looking for a job without papers, not the "free trade agreements" that traditional communities call a "death sentence," forcing small farmers, factory workers, and small business owners to work for slave wages, emigrate, or organize rebellion. Never in the history of the world have there been so many hundreds of millions of people forced to leave their homes because they cannot endure the miserable poverty imposed by "free trade" and globalization.

The Border Patrol Nation convinces the country to comply with the expensive notion that we need to be protected from these dangerous outsiders coming for our safety. The country complies by handing over liberty, privacy, and free speech, so that those in authority can maintain constant surveillance, monitoring people's movements, emails, texts, phone calls, purchases, social networks, and associations in order to eliminate suspected threats before they fully develop. In short, almost everyone outside the upper echelons of political and monied power needs to be closely monitored.

This is the crux of the situation: according to today's Homeland Security regime all but the elite and all-powerful few should be monitored as a potential threat. "Americans have long understood that the rich get good lawyers and get off, while the poor suck eggs and do time," writes Matt Taibbi in the February 2013 issue of *Rolling Stone*. What we are seeing today, he continues, "is something different. This is the government admitting to being afraid to prosecute the very powerful—something it never did even in the heydays of Al Capone or Pablo Escobar, something it didn't do even with Richard Nixon. And when you admit that some people are too important to prosecute, it's just a few short steps to the obvious corollary—that everybody else is unimportant enough to jail. An arrestable class and an unarrestable class. We always suspected it, now it's admitted. So what do we do?"[24]

The very things we are supposed to fear from a foreign attack—not only the home invasions, physical abuse, detainments, interrogations, and confiscation of personal belongings already part and parcel of Border Patrol tactics, but also the eerie loss of free speech, the loss of what one can and can't study, and thus the loss of what one can and can't think—are already happening. Take the more than 7,000 people arrested and sent to jail for protesting at Occupy events. Take the 34,000 people incarcerated at any given moment in our profit-driven immigration detention system. Take the case of former Border Patrol agent Bryan Gonzalez, who dared to speak what he thought about his Mexican heritage and drug legalization.

Perhaps it is the words of Tucson-based attorney and activist of Isabel Garcia that best sum up the situation we see in our collapsing communities, towns, and cities in places like Niagara Falls and Nogales: "We all want security, we want a home, good housing. We want quality health care, we want good education, we want good roads, we want a healthy community. This is not giving us security at all. While we are firing teachers left and right, and closing schools everywhere . . . and we are hiring more and more Border Patrol agents."

As Garcia's words make clear, there are many people—families, communities, congregations, organizations, and networks—who are not willing to comply. There are, in fact, large numbers of people who are unconvinced and unwilling to trade in or in any way diminish their liberties, privacy, and civic power. In the nonviolent tradition of abolitionism and the civil rights movement, people of conscience on all sides of our borders are organizing together against the surveillance regime of walls, drones, mobile checkpoints, deportation, and the criminalization of people based on their residency status.

Those pushing against this world are the ones in the vision of Peacemaker. They are creating the foundation of a new future in which it will be possible to reach across to our Canadian, Mexican, and Haitian neighbors. They are proclaiming that the Border Patrol Nation that we are permitting to be installed, imposed, and exported is not inevitable. There is indeed a way to live securely that is much preferable and much more sustainable on all levels of community, from the local to the international. The Iroquois law says, "When a member of a [foreign] nation comes to the territory of the Five Nations and seeks refuge and permanent residence, the Lords of the Nation to which he comes shall extend hospitality and make him a member of the nation." Perhaps it is in this way, willing to look in to one another's other's eyes with care and respect, that we can one day achieve a place that is truly secure.

A double rainbow arcs over the border wall one mile east of downtown No-gales during the 2013 monsoon season. Photo by Murphy Woodhouse.

Acknowledgments

First of all, it would be a lie to say that I wrote this book alone. There are so many people who helped me in so many ways. There were so many conversations, so many people who took the time to read my manuscript and give me feedback, so many who let me into their homes or shared their lives, even at great risk. There are many whom I can't name here. And there are many who helped me as I scraped together pennies to do research trips throughout the Southwest borderlands, Detroit, Niagara Falls, Buffalo, Sodus, South Carolina, Puerto Rico, and the Dominican Republic.

The following is a hopelessly inadequate list, as there are countless people who have inspired me, whom I have learned from, whose work I've engaged with, with whom I've had conversations, or whose stories I have learned about but who will not appear in the list. I do hope, though, that many have already been acknowledged in the pages of the book.

I want to thank too the hundreds of people over a span of many years with whom I have met before they crossed, without papers, into the United States. I also thank my international friends who have showed me hospitality in their homes. I can only hope that they are given similar welcome in my country.

My partial list:

Joseph Nevins—your encouragement, insight, and wisdom are present throughout the book. I am grateful for the fact that you have been involved since the beginning stages, and for your friendship.

Greg Ruggiero—your enthusiasm is contagious, your poetic vision relentless, your editing awesome.

Rita and Don Gallagher—I love the camper! Your generosity and hospitality were amazing in Lewiston (Niagara Falls–Buffalo area).

Kelly Fay Rodriguez, José LaLuz, Braulio Torres, Jose "Lole" Rodríguez Báez, and Wilfredo Ramírez—thanks so much for your helping me organize everything in the beautiful Isla de Encanto.

Daniel Stein—thanks for your research and accompaniment; always remember the Stryker in New Mexico.

Mark Miller—thanks for your research; you know I love you, my brother.

West Cosgrove—thanks so much for letting me crash so many times at the Casa Puente.

City Lights Books—Greg, Stacey, Elaine, Robert, Jolene, it is such a pleasure to work with all of you. City Lights to me is hallowed ground.

Mario Sosa, Caroline Bettinger-López, Kelly Fay Rodríguez, Marianela Carvajal Díaz, Joselina Fay Rodríguez, Father Regino Martínez Bretón (and Solidaridad Fronteriza in Dajabón)—my work in the Dominican Republic could not have happened without your help and hospitality.

Tony Macias and David Hill—thanks so much for the shelter, wheels, food, and great company in South Carolina.

Laurie Melrood and Blake Gentry: How long did I stay in your guest room? How long did you let me use the Swedish tank? So grateful to you and for the beautiful friendship I have with you.

Geoffrey Boyce, Jimmy Johnson, Jonathan Contreras, Wade Schreiber, and Lena Masri (from CAIR-Michigan)—you are the reason my trip to Detroit was so fruitful. The conversations with you were so insightful.

John "Lory" Ghertner and Peter Mares—thanks so much for introducing me and accompanying me in Sodus. And so eloquently articulating its beauty and its horror.

Timothy Dunn, Monica Varsanyi, David Cates, Mizue Aizeki, Guadalupe Castillo, Joseph Nevins, John "Lory" Ghertner, Mathew Coleman, Lauren Dasse, Geoffrey Boyce, Tim Vanderpool—thanks so much for your careful readings and insightful feedback on parts (or all) of the manuscript. It is much better because of all of you.

Louise Misztal—thanks for your awesome cartography. Randall Serraglio and Louise, thank you for letting me crash in your house.

Lynda Cruz—thanks so much for your help with contacts in Tucson and Douglas. Patricia Hohl and Jonathon Shacat—thanks for helping me with connections in Bisbee and Naco.

David Garcia—thanks for being my guide and answering my thousands of questions on the Tohono O'odham Nation.

Gustavo Lozano—thank you my great friend for all your help and inspiration in Nogales.

Colin Deeds—thanks for the insightful meetings at Caffe Luce.

Bryan Gonzalez—thank you for sharing your incredible story. And Vicki Gaubeca from the New Mexico ACLU for helping connect me with Bryan and for all the knowledge you generously shared.

Elizabeth Bell—thanks for your careful eye and excellent edits.

Murphy Woodhouse—thanks for your beautiful photographs.

Lauren's family—especially Peggy, Dennis, Wes, Gahbah, Tom, and Shannon—thanks for all your support from the beginning to the end.

Tommy Bassett, Cafe Justo, and Frontera de Cristo—thanks for the hospitality, conversations, and insight in Douglas and Agua Prieta.

Thank you to all those who I can't thank by name, because you have asked me not to. You are the fuel that fires this book. Among you are undocumented people, U.S. citizens who have been hurt by border enforcement, and U.S. Border Patrol agents who have graciously shared your stories but wish to be anonymous.

Finally, all of the following have helped in very important ways. Names are not listed in any particular order: Matt Cleary, Michael Ratner, Sharon Hostetler (and the organization Witness for Peace), Kenneth Kennon (and the organization BorderLinks), Mike Fox (and everybody at NACLA), Pablo Morales, Tom Engelhardt (and TomDispatch), Heather Craigie, Nancy Mattina (and all the folks at Prescott College), Susan Yeich, Betsy Bolding, Kenneth Madsen, Vicki Gaubeca, Margi Ault Duell, Emily Breines, Christopher Krezmien, Betty Marin, Dereka Rushbrooke, Megan McDonough, Hector Suarez, Abby Graseck, Nancy Hiemstra, Jenna Loyd, Elaine Brower, Andrew S. Toomajian, Jake Ratner, Roxana Mesias, Arline, Harold Garrett-Goodyear, Kat Sinclair, Ben Beachy, Jeff Orlowski, Rachel Anderson, Liz O'Shaughnessy, Riley Merline, Brook Bernini, Jonathan Harris, Adam Shoop, Deva Abela,

Moravia de la O, Luis Amaury Báez, Randall Serraglio, Katie Hudak, Alexis Ball, Beth Poteet, Katie Sharar, Barry Stoner, Andrew C. Mills, Paul Magno, Robert M. Saper, Leon Fink, E. Ian Robinson, Susan DuBois, Dave Mitchell, Marina Adler, Alissa Escarce, Leslie Salgado, Carl Conn, Jane Stein, Josh Haney, Karen Green, William Dean, Richard Boren, Angie Black, Lorri Dobias, Alex Hartnett, Elisa Espiritu, Tshilo Galup, Harriet Heywood, Mary B. Gregory, Maura Gregory, Isaac, Kim Lettrich, Megan, Ralph Curcuru, Tim Doherty, Ann Rogers, Michael Stein, Sally Jones (and all the folks at the Unitarian Church of Staten Island), Jeffrey G. Hemmett, Mary Rogers, Sara Meza Romero, Ray Smith, Eric Williams, Sebastian Sanchez, Elena, Bob Jenkins, Mary Jo Jenkins, Barbara Corbett, Helen Miller, and Steve Miller.

Reina, for being my writing buddy.

Mom, for always encouraging me to read, write, and think critically about things. And for your constant support.

Dad, for teaching me to appreciate and love the natural world around me.

Lauren Dasse, you are beautiful and know I couldn't have done this without you.

Endnotes

CHAPTER ONE: THE SUPER PATROL

1. Roberto Lovato, "Building the Homeland Security State," *NACLA Report on the Americas*, November/December 2008. Accessed September 9, 2013: https://nacla.org/sites/default/files/A04106017_1.pdf

2. Natinoal Geographic Channel, *Border Wars*, "Super Sunday." Accessed September 9, 2013: http://channel.nationalgeographic.com/channel/border-wars/videos/super-sunday

3. Ibid.

4. Tom Engelhardt, "Hold Onto Your Underwear: This Is Not a National Emergency," *TomDispatch*, February 14, 2010. Accessed December 2, 2013: http://www.tomdispatch.com/blog/175206/tom_engelhardt_fear_inc

5. FLIR, "Career Opportunities at FLIR." Accessed November 25, 2013: www.flir.com/cs/apac/en/view/?id=41477

6. Jay Hermacinski, "Big Time Security in Place for Big Game," WISHTV.com, February 1, 2012. Accessed October 10, 2013: www.wishtv.com/super-bowl-xlvi/big-time-security-in-place-for-big-game

7. "CBP Border Patrol Graduates 1000th Class," customsborderprotect. Accessed September 11, 2013: www.youtube.com/watch?v=XDtdoTQcQeg

8. Peggy Noonan, "Rudy's Duty," *Wall Street Journal*, June 14, 2002. Accessed September 9, 2013: http://online.wsj.com/article/SB122418750653241949.htmlhttp://online.wsj.com/article/SB122418750653241949.html

9. "CBP Border Patrol Graduates 1000th Class," customsborderprotect. Accessed December 3, 2013: http://www.youtube.com/watch?v=XDtdoTQcQeg

10. Ibid.

11. Jay Mayfield, "A Powerful Presence," *Front Line U.S. Customs and Border Protection* 5, no. 1, 10–17.

12. Ibid.

13. "Forget Arizona, Obama Sends Border Patrol to Afghanistan," *Fox Nation*, January 4, 2011. Accessed December 4, 2013: http://nation.foxnews.com/border-security/2011/01/04/forget-arizona-obama-sends-border-patrol-afghanistan

14. "CBP Border Patrol Graduates 1000th Class," customsborderprotect. Accessed December 3, 2013: http://www.youtube.com/watch?v=XDtdoTQcQeg

15. NPR, "Ike's Warning of Military Expansion, 50 Years Later," National Public Radio, January 17, 2011. Accessed September 10, 2013: http://m.npr.org/news/Politics/132942244

16. President Dwight D. Eisenhower's Farewell Address (1961). Accessed September 10, 2012: www.usnews.com/usnews/documents/doctranscripts/document_90_transcript.htm

17. Joseph Nevins, *Operation Gatekeeper and Beyond: The War on "Illegals" and the Remaking of the U.S.-Mexico Boundary* (Routledge, 2010), 188.

18. Ibid., 19.

19. Tom Barry, "Is There a Border Security Industrial Complex?," Border Lines: TransBorder Project, Center for International Policy, August, 7, 2009.

Accessed September 10, 2013: http://borderlinesblog.blogspot.com/2009/08/is-there-border-security-industrial.html

20. Mickey McCarter, "Sunset for SBInet," *Homeland Security Today*, February 2011, 34.

21. Joe Wolverton II, "Border Patrol Loaning Predator Drones to Military, State, and Local Police," *The New American*, October 3, 2013. Accessed October 10, 2013: www.thenewamerican.com/usnews/constitution/item/16669-border-patrol-loaning-predator-to-military-state-and-local-police

22. Ryan Gallagher, "U.S. Border Agency Has Considered Weaponizing Domestic Drones to 'Immobilize' People," *Slate*, July 3, 2013. Accessed October 10, 2013: www.slate.com/blogs/future_tense/2013/07/03/documents_show_customs_and_border_protection_considered_weaponized_domestic.html

23. "Border Security Bill Specifies Treasure Trove of Investments in Technology," *Homeland Security Today*, June 24, 2013. Accessed October 10, 2013: www.hstoday.us/single-article/border-security-bill-specifies-treasure-trove-of-investments-in-technology/550c981a675f05f32ee225eb500b874b.html

24. Alexander Bolton, "Leahy: Border Security Measure Reads 'Like a Christmas Wish List for Halliburton,' " *The Hill*, June 22, 2013. Accessed October 10, 2013: http://thehill.com/homenews/senate/307205-leahy-border-security-measure-reads-like-a-christmas-wish-list-for-halliburton#ixzz2gh9OCaBQ

25. "Leahy Urges Bipartisan Compromise for Comprehensive Immigration Reform," press release, June 24, 2013. Accessed October 10, 2013: www.leahy.senate.gov/press/leahy-urges-bipartisan-compromise-for-comprehensive-immigration-reform

26. "CBP Assists Super Bowl XLIV Security Operation," February 9, 2010. Accessed September 10, 2013: www.cbp.gov/xp/cgov/newsroom/highlights/2010/super_bowl_assist.xml

PART I: HEARTS, MINDS, AND BODIES

1. Henry Giroux, "Violence, USA: The Warfare State and the Brutalizing of Everyday Life," *Truthout*, May 2, 2012. Accessed October 11, 2013: http://truth-out.org/opinion/item/8859-violence-usa-the-warfare-state-and-the-brutalizing-of-everyday-life

CHAPTER TWO: THE COMPLEX-BUILDERS

1. Felix Chavez, presentation at "Border Management Conference & Technology Expo," October 16, 2012.

2. Josiah Heyman, "Constructing a Virtual Wall: Race and Citizenship in U.S.–Mexico Border Policing," *Journal of the Southwest* 50, no. 3, Autumn 2008, 305–334.

3. Mickey McCarter, "Information Technology Border Security Technology: Roadmap for a Long, Hard Road," *Homeland Security Today*, August 20, 2012. Accessed September 10, 2013: www.hstoday.us/focused-topics/information-technology/single-article-page/border-security-technology-roadmap-for-a-long-hard-road/36173a591fed9b7f04fb557646eaa50c.html

4. Visiongain, "Global Border Security Market 2013-2023: UAVs, UGVs and Perimeter Surveillance Systems," August 1, 2013. Accessed September

10, 2013: www.visiongain.com/Report/959/Global-Border-Security-Market-2013-2023-UAVs-UGVs-and-Perimeter-Surveillance-Systems

5. Homeland Security Research, "U.S. Homeland Security & Public Safety Market—2013-2020," September 2012. Accessed September 10, 2013: www.homelandsecurityresearch.com/2012/09/u-s-homeland-security-public-safety-market-2013-2020/

6. Jonathan Easley, "Study Predicts 70K Jobs from Drones," *The Hill*, March 12, 2013. Accessed September 10, 2013: http://thehill.com/blogs/transportation-report/aviation/287649-study-predicts-70k-jobs-from-drones

7. Homeland Security Research, "Intelligent Video Surveillance, ISR & Video Analytics: Technologies & Global Market – 2013–2020." Accessed December 3, 2013: http://www.homelandsecurityresearch.com/2013/07/intelligent-video-surveillance-isr-video-analytics-technologies-global-market-2013-2020/

8. Homeland Security Research, "Non-Lethal Weapons: Technologies & Global Market – 2012–2020." Accessed December 3, 2013: http://www.homelandsecurityresearch.com/2011/10/non-lethal-weapons-technologies-global-market-2012-2020/

9. Homeland Security Research, "People Screening Technologies & Global Markets – 2012–2016." Accessed December 3, 2013: http://www.homelandsecurityresearch.com/2011/11/people-screening-technologies-global-markets-2012-2016/

10. Eric Lipton, "As Wars End, a Rush to Grab Dollars Spent on the Border," *New York Times*, June 6, 2013. Accessed October 10, 2013: www.nytimes.com/2013/06/07/us/us-military-firms-eye-border-security-contracts.html?pagewanted=all

11. Brian Bennett, "Radar Shows U.S. Border Security Gaps," *Los Angeles Times*, April 3, 2013. Accessed October 10, 2013: http://articles.latimes.com/2013/apr/03/nation/la-na-border-radar-20130404

12. BORDERS National Center for Border Security and Immigration, "Capabilities." Accessed September 11, 2013: www.borders.arizona.edu/cms/content/capabilities

13. "Could MVAs Be the Future of Securing the Border?," KVOA News 4 Tucson, February 25, 2011. Accessed September 10, 2013: www.kvoa.com/news/could-mvas-be-the-future-of-securing-the-border-/#!prettyPhoto/0/

14. Bruce Wright, interview with author, February 24, 2012.

15. Linda Valdez, "How the Border Can Help Grow Arizona's Economy," *Arizona Republic*, February 26, 2011. Accessed September 10, 2013: www.azcentral.com/arizonarepublic/viewpoints/articles/20110227arizona-economy-valdez.html

16. *Homeland Security News Wire*, "Border-Security Crisis Boosts Tucson's Economy," December 8, 2010. Accessed September 11, 2013: www.homelandsecuritynewswire.com/border-security-crisis-boosts-tucsons-economy

CHAPTER THREE: DOING NICE THINGS FOR CHILDREN

1. Timothy Dunn, *Blockading the Border and Human Rights: The El Paso Opera-*

tion that Remade Immigration Enforcement, (University of Texas Press, 2009), 52–53.

2. Joseph Nevins, *Operation Gatekeeper and Beyond: The War On "Illegals" and the Remaking of the U.S. - Mexico Boundary* (Routledge, 2010), 182.

3. Dunn, *Blockading the Border and Human Rights*, 54.

4. Jennifer Steinhauer, "Scouts Train to Fight Terrorists, and More," *New York Times*, May 13, 2009. Accessed October 1, 2013: www.nytimes.com/2009/05/14/us/14explorers.html?_r=0

5. CBP, "Brownsville Hosts First Joint CBP Explorer Academy," June 27, 2012. Accessed September 11, 2013: www.cbp.gov/xp/cgov/PrintMe.xml?xml=$/content/newsroom/press_releases/2012/june/15-30/06272012_4.ctt&location=/newsroom/news_releases/local/2012_news_releases/june_2012/06272012_4.xml

6. Jennifer Steinhauer, "Scouts Train to Fight Terrorists, and More," *New York Times*, May 13, 2009. Accessed October 1, 2013: www.nytimes.com/2009/05/14/us/14explorers.html?_r=0

7. Ibid.

8. Paul Babeu, "Babeu: Build Fence, Deploy Soldiers for Double Border Barrier," InMaricopa.com, August 8, 2011. Accessed October 10, 2013: www.inmaricopa.com/Article/2011/08/08/border-fence-sheriff-paul-babeu-illegal-drugs-immigration

9. Talila Nesher, "Border Police Train Israeli Teens to Detain Illegal Palestinian Workers," *Haaretz*, January 2, 2012. Accessed October 10, 2013: www.haaretz.com/news/national/border-police-train-israeli-teens-to-detain-illegal-palestinian-workers-1.405091

10. Karina Lopez, "Red Ribbon Fever Hits Sunflower Elementary School," *Imperial Valley Press*, October 26, 2012. Accessed September 13, 2013: http://articles.ivpressonline.com/2012-10-26/fever-hits_34754455

11. Gloria Bigger-Cantu, "'Shop with a Cop' Helps Local School Children," *Kingsville Record and Bishop News*, December 18, 2011. Accessed September 16, 2013: www.kingsvillerecord.com/news/2011-12-18/Front_Page/Shop_with_a_Cop_helps_local_school_children.html?print=1

12. Kelly Lytle Hernandez, *Migra! A History of the U.S. Border Patrol* (University of California Press, 2010), 206.

13. Jennifer Steinhauer, "Scouts Train to Fight Terrorists, and More," *New York Times*, May 13, 2009. Accessed October 1, 2013: www.nytimes.com/2009/05/14/us/14explorers.html?_r=0

14. Martin Alan Greenberg, "A Short History of Junior Police," *The Police Chief*, April 2008. Accessed September 11, 2013: www.policechiefmagazine.org/magazine/index.cfm?fuseaction=display_arch&article_id=1463&issue_id=42008

15. Lytle-Hernandez, *Migra!*, 207.

16. Martin Alan Greenberg, "A Short History of Junior Police," *The Police Chief*, April 2008. Accessed September 11, 2013: www.policechiefmagazine.org/magazine/index.cfm?fuseaction=display_arch&article_id=1463&issue_id=42008

17. Ibid.
18. Karl-Erik Stromsta, "Girls Gone Border Patrol," *LA Weekly*, July 26, 2006. Accessed September 11, 2013: www.laweekly.com/2006-07-27/news/girls-gone-border-patrol/full/
19. Susan Kinzie and Sari Horwitz, "Colleges' Hottest New Major: Terror," *Washington Post*, April 30, 2005. Accessed September 11, 2013: www.washing-tonpost.com/wp-dyn/content/article/2005/04/29/AR2005042901344.html
20. National Center for Border Security and Immigration UTEP, "Organized Research Center Profile." Accessed September 11, 2013: http://orspprofile.utep.edu/profilesystem/editprofile.php?pid=1962
21. Susan Kinzie and Sari Horwitz, "Colleges' Hottest New Major: Terror," *Washington Post*, April 30, 2005. Accessed October 2, 2013: www.washington-post.com/wp-dyn/content/article/2005/04/29/AR2005042901344.html.
22. "Homeland Security Degrees and Careers." CriminalJusticePrograms.com. Accessed September 11, 2013: www.criminaljusticeprograms.com/spe-cialty/homeland-security-degrees/

CHAPTER FOUR: "EXACTLY THE WAY WE THINK"

1. Image Media Services, "Philosophy." Accessed September 11, 2013: http://imagemediaservices.com/philosophy.html
2. Dannielle Blumenthal, "Breaking the Mold," *Frontline*, Fall/Winter 2008, 11.
3. U.S. Border Patrol recruitment commercial. Accessed September 11, 2013: www.youtube.com/watch?v=IQGgBFZbXVY
4. Blumenthall, "Breaking the Mold," *Frontline*.
5. Robert Lee Maril, *The Fence: Human Smuggling, Terrorists, and Public Safety along the U.S.-Mexico*, Texas Tech University Press (March 2011), 26.
6. Blumenthall, "Breaking the Mold," *Frontline*.
7. NASCAR Nationwide, "Robinson Signs Wallace." Accessed September 11, 2013: www.motorracingnetwork.com/Race-Series/NASCAR-Nationwide/News/Articles/2008/03/Robinson-Signs-Wallace.aspx
8. Maril, *The Fence*, 34.
9. Josiah McC. Heyman, "U.S. Immigration Officers of Mexican Ancestry as Mexican Americans, Citizens, and Immigration Police," *Current Anthropology* 43, no. 3 (June 2002), 479–507.

CHAPTER FIVE: UNFINISHED BUSINESS IN INDIAN COUNTRY

1. Fernanda Santos, "In Desert Outposts, Border Agents Keep Watch," *New York Times*, January 24, 2013. Accessed September 16, 2013: www.nytimes.com/2013/01/25/us/at-remote-outposts-border-agents-sift-for-clues.html?pagewanted=all
2. Written Testimony of the Honorable Ned Norris Jr., Chairman, Tohono O'odham Nation, to the Subcommittee on Fisheries Wildlife and Oceans and Subcommittee on National Parks, Forests, and Public Lands of the House Committee on Natural Resources, Joint Oversight Hearing, "Walls and Waivers: Expedited Construction of the Southern Border Wall and Collateral Impacts to Communities and the Environment," April 28, 2008.

Accessed September 16, 2013: www.tiamatpublications.com/docs/testimony_norris.pdf

3. "Border Security: Partnership Agreements and Enhanced Oversight Could Strengthen Coordination of Efforts on Indian Reservations," Government Accountability Office, April 2013, 5. Accessed September 16, 2013: www.gao.gov/assets/660/653590.pdf

4. Ibid.

5. "OCCUPATION and LOCKDOWN of Tucson Border Patrol HQ. 5/21/10," YouTube. Accessed September 16, 2013: http://youtube/6lKGFy2KR7o

6. "Indian Reservations Grapple with Drug Trafficking," National Public Radio, July 15, 2010. Accessed September 16, 2013: www.npr.org/templates/story/story.php?storyId=128539859

7. Ibid.

8. Ned Norris Jr., Written Testimony to the Subcommitee on Fisheries Wildlife and Oceans, etc, April 28, 2008 Joint Oversight Hearing: "Walls and Waivers: Expedited Construction of the Souther Border Wall and Collateral Impacts to Communities and Environment." Accessed December 3, 2013: www.tiamatpublications.com/docs/testimony_norris.pdf

9. Kenneth Dean Madsen, "A Nation Across Nations: The Tohono O'odham and the U.S.-Mexico Border," PhD diss.,Arizona State University, August 2005, 142. http://www.newark.osu.edu/facultystaff/personal/kmadsen/Documents/Madsen2005_diss-TON-border.pdf

10. J. D. Hendricks, *Resistance and Collaboration: O'odham Responses to U.S. Invasion*, Tiamat Publications #5 (2004). Accessed September 16, 2013: http://tiamatpublications.com/docs/Collaboration_and_Resistance.pdf

11. Karl Jacoby, *Shadows at Dawn: An Apache Massacre and the Violence of History*, (Penguin Press, 2008), 36.

12. Hendricks, "Resistance and Collaboration." Accessed December 3, 2013: http://tiamatpublications.com/docs/Collaboration_and_Resistance.pdf

13. Ibid.

14. John Gibler, *Mexico Unconquered: Chronicles of Power and Revolt* (City Lights Books, 2009), 6.

15. Jacoby, *Shadows at Dawn*, 37.

16. *In Hostile Terrain: Human Rights Violations in Immigration Enforcement in the U.S. Southwest*, Amnesty International USA, 2012, 32. Accessed September 16, 2013: www.amnestyusa.org/sites/default/files/ai_inhostileterrain_final031412.pdf

17. These numbers were informally told to me by agents; Border Patrol doesn't officially publish the numbers of agents assigned to each particular station.

18. "Final Environmental Assessment for the Proposed Construction, Alteration, and Maintenance for U.S. Customs and Border Protection Ajo Housing Development Project," U.S. General Services Administration, April 2011, 4. Accessed September 16, 2013: www.gsa.gov/graphics/pbs/nepa_environmental_assessment.pdf

19. This quotation is from the printed edition of the 2011 legislative hearing transcript.

20. "Indian Reservations Grapple with Drug Trafficking," National Public Radio. Accessed December 3, 2013: www.npr.org/templates/story/story.php?storyId=128539859

21. Ibid.

22. Madsen, *A Nation across Nations*, 156.

23. Ibid.

24. Navideh Forghani, "Tohono O'odham Nation Fighting New Drug Business Trend," ABC 15, May 7, 2012. Accessed September 16, 2013: www.abc15.com/dpp/news/state/tohono-oodham-nation-fighting-new-drug-business-trend#ixzz2f5DBndDJ

25. Madsen, *A Nation across Nations*, 142.

26. This quote comes from the printed edition of the 2011 legislative hearing transcript.

27. *In Hostile Terrain*, (Amnesty International USA 2012), 30.

28. "Harassment Allegations against Border Patrol in Tohono O'Odham Nation," KVOA News 4 Tucson, July 18, 2012. Accessed September 16, 2013: www.kvoa.com/news/harassment-allegations-against-border-patrol-in-tohono-o-odham-nation/#_

29. Ibid.

30. Guadalupe Castillo and Margo Cowan, *It Is Not Our Fault: The Case for Amending Present Nationality Law to Make All Members of the Tohono O'odham Nation United States Citizens, Now and Forever* (Tohono O'odham Nation, Executive Branch, 2001), 33.

31. Ibid.

32. Margaret Regan, *The Death of Josseline: Immigration Stories from the Arizona Borderlands*, (Beacon Press, 2010), 139.

33. Ibid.; Castillo and Cowan, *It's Not Our Fault.*

34. "Fact Sheet: ICE Shadow Wolves," ICE, June 2007. Accessed September 16, 2013: www.ice.gov/news/library/factsheets/shadow-wolves.htm

35. Nick Allen, "On Patrol with the Shadow Wolves, the Best Hunters of Humans in the World," *The Telegraph*, December 26, 2011. Accessed September 16, 2013: www.telegraph.co.uk/news/worldnews/northamerica/usa/8978006/On-patrol-with-the-Shadow-Wolves-the-best-hunters-of-humans-in-the-world.html

36. "Border Warriors: Ground Zero," National Geographic Channel, August 20, 2012. Accessed September 16, 2013: http://channel.nationalgeographic.com/channel/videos/border-warriors-ground-zero/

37. Brian Bennett, "Indian 'Shadow Wolves' Stalk Smugglers on Arizona Reservation," *Los Angeles Times*, November 21, 2011. Accessed September 16, 2013: http://articles.latimes.com/2011/nov/21/nation/la-na-adv-shadow-wolves-20111122

38. Ibid.

39. Ibid.

40. Jeff Hendricks, "An Interview with Ofelia Rivas of 'O'odham Voice

Against the Wall,' " *CASA*, March 2010. Accessed September 16, 2013: www.casacollective.org/node/75061

41. Ibid.

42. Brady McCombs, "O'odham Leader Vows No Border Fence," *Arizona Daily Star*, August 19, 2007. Accessed September 16, 2013: http://azstarnet.com/news/local/border/o-odham-leader-vows-no-border-fence/article_42e728a3-4314-5efb-a500-8d3c4b6a4b4b.html

43. Erik Eckholm, "In Drug War, Tribe Feels Invaded by Both Sides," *New York Times*, January 24, 2010. Accessed September 16, 2013: www.nytimes.com/2010/01/25/us/25border.html?pagewanted=all&_r=0

44. Rob Capriccioso, "Chertoff: Tohono O'odham Chairman Got It Wrong," *Indian Country Today*, July 11, 2008. Accessed September 16, 2013: http://indiancountrytodaymedianetwork.com/ictarchives/2008/07/11/chertoff-tohono-oodham-chairman-got-it-wrong-2-93232

45. Ned Norris Jr., Written Testimony to the Subcommitee on Fisheries Wildlife and Oceans, etc.

46. "State of Arizona Tribal Liason Year-End Report," Arizona Department of Homeland Security, July 1, 2011 – June 30, 2012. Accessed September 16, 2013: http://azcia.gov/Documents/TCP/2012/AR_FFY12_AZDOHS.pdf

47. "Border Patrol Reaches out to Arizona's Tohono O'odham Nation," cbp.gov, August 2, 2013. Accessed December 3, 2013: http://www.cbp.gov/xp/cgov/newsroom/news_releases/local/2013_nr/aug13/08022013_10.xml

48. "Border Patrol Attends Tohono O'odham College Event," cbp.gov, August 20, 2012. Accessed September 16, 2013: www.cbp.gov/xp/cgov/PrintMe.xml?xml=$/content/newsroom/press_releases/2012/august/15-31/08202012_4.ctt&location=/newsroom/news_releases/local/2012_news_releases/aug_2012/08202012_4.xml

CHAPTER SIX: THE NOT-SO-SOFT UNDERBELLY OF THE NORTH

1. "Legacy of 9/11: The World's Longest Undefended Border is Now Defended," *Globe and Mail*, September 11, 2011. Accessed September 11, 2013: www.theglobeandmail.com/commentary/editorials/legacy-of-911-the-worlds-longest-undefended-border-is-now-defended/article593884

2. Geoffrey Boyce, "Arizona Everywhere: Immigration Policing and the United States' Expanding Borderlands," Alliance for Global Justice, June 7, 2013. http://afgj.org/arizona-everywhere-immigration-policing-and-the-united-states-expanding-borderlands

3. "Editorial: The Soft Underbelly Up North," *Washington Times*, January 29, 2009. Accessed September 11, 2013: www.washingtontimes.com/news/2009/jan/29/the-soft-underbelly-up-north/#ixzz2dnSjdinX

4. U.S. Government Accountability Office, "Border Security: Enhanced DHS Oversight and Assessment of Interagency Coordination Is Needed for the Northern Border," December 2010. Accessed September 12, 2013: www.gao.gov/new.items/d1197.pdf

5. Edwin Mora, "Canadian Border Bigger Terror Threat than Mexican Border, Says Border Patrol Chief," cnsnews.com, May 18, 2011. Accessed Septem-

ber 12, 2013: http://cnsnews.com/news/article/canadian-border-bigger-terror-threat-mexican-border-says-border-patrol-chief#sthash.jgYG5GSg.dpuf

6. Peter Andreas, "The Mexicanization of the U.S.-Canada Border," *International Journal*, Spring 2005, 449–462.

7. Erika Lee, *At America's Gates: Chinese Immigration during the Exclusion Era, 1882–1943*, University of North Carolina Press (2003), 153.

8. Ibid., 6.

9. Wendy Koch, "U.S. Urged to Apologize for 1930s Deportations," *USA Today*, April 5, 2006. Accessed October 10, 2013: http://usatoday30.usatoday.com/news/nation/2006-04-04-1930s-deportees-cover_x.htm

10. Margaret Kimberley, "Freedom Rider: Tar Sands Hell in Detroit," *Black Agenda Report*, August 7, 2013. Accessed October 14, 2013: www.blackagendareport.com/content/freedom-rider-tar-sands-hell-detroit

11. Chad Selweski, "New Homeland Security Center Opens at Selfridge," *Macomb Daily News*, April 11, 2012. Accessed October 10, 2013: www.macombdaily.com/article/MD/20110324/NEWS/303249970

12. American Civil Liberties Union, "Are You Living in a Constitution Free Zone?," December 15, 2006. Accessed September 12, 2013: https://www.aclu.org/national-security_technology-and-liberty/are-you-living-constitution-free-zone

13. Legal Information Institute, "8 CFR 287.1 – Definitions." Accessed September 12, 2013: www.law.cornell.edu/cfr/text/8/287.1

14. Statement of Senator Patrick Leahy (D-VT), Homeland Security Subcommittee Hearing on the DHS Fiscal Year 2009 Budget, March 4, 2008.

15. Border Patrol Free, "What Is the Border Patrol Doing on Washington's Olympic Peninsula?" Accessed September 12, 2013: www.bpfree.org/thestory.html

16. Families for Freedom, New York Civil Liberties Union, New York University Law Immigration Rights Clinic, "Justice Derailed: What Raids on Trains and Buses Reveal about Border Patrol's Interior Enforcement Practices," November 2011. Accessed September 12, 2013: www.nyclu.org/files/publications/NYCLU_justicederailedweb_0.pdf

17. Families for Freedom, New York University Law Immigration Rights Clinic, "Uncovering USBP: Bonus Programs for United States Border Patrol Agents and the Arrest of Lawfully Present Individuals," January 2013. Accessed September 12, 2013:
http://familiesforfreedom.org/sites/default/files/resources/Uncovering%20USBP-FFF%20Report%202013.pdf

18. Families for Freedom, New York Civil Liberties Union, New York University Law Immigration Rights Clinic, "Justice Derailed: What Raids on Trains and Buses Reveal about Border Patrol's Interior Enforcement Practices," November 2011. Accessed September 12, 2013: www.nyclu.org/files/publications/NYCLU_justicederailedweb_0.pdf

CHAPTER SEVEN: AMERICA'S BACKYARD

1. "Dajabón: entre pobreza y contrabando," *Diario Libre*, May 27, 2008. Accessed September 12, 2013: www.diariolibre.com/noticias/2007/05/28/

i137044_dajaban-entre-pobreza-contrabando.html

2. "MINUSTAH: United Nations Stabilization Mission in Haiti." Accessed September 12, 2013: www.un.org/en/peacekeeping/missions/minustah/

3. Mark Memmott, "Remembering to Never Forget: Dominican Republic's 'Parsley Massacre,' " National Public Radio, October 1, 2012. Accessed September 12, 2013: www.npr.org/blogs/thetwo-way/2012/10/01/162092252/remembering-to-never-forget-dominican-republics-parsley-massacre

4. David Howard, "Dominican Republic Spurns Haitian Migrants: Rejection of African Heritage Fuels Anti-Haitian Views," *NACLA Report on the Americas*, Sept./Oct. 2001, 24–28.

5. Ibid.

6. Junot Diaz, *The Brief Wondrous Life of Oscar Wao* (Penguin, 2008), 2.

7. Edwidge Danticat, *Farming of the Bones*, (Soho Press, 1998), 193.

8. Ibid.

9. James Anderson and Liam O'Dowd, "Borders, Border Regions and Territoriality: Contradictory Meanings, Changing Significance," *Regional Studies*, April 1999, 593–604.

10. Ibid.

11. *Dominican Today*, "US Team Reveals Weaknesses at the Dominican-Haiti Border," August 7, 2006. Accessed September 12, 2013: www.dominicantoday.com/dr/local/2006/8/7/16173/US-team-reveals-weaknesses-at-the-Dominican-Haiti-border

12. Justin Clarke, "Investigación en relación al Cuerpo Especializado Fronterizo de la RD," Columbia Law School and Solidaridad Fronteriza, internal report. Summer 2009.

13. Ibid.

14. "What to do? A Global Strategy," *The 9/11 Commission Report*, W. W. Norton (2004), 362.

15. Juan Gonzalez, *Harvest of Empire: A History of Latinos in America*, Revised Edition, Penguin Books (New York: 2011), 54.

16. Lyndon Baines Johnson, "Report on the Situation in the Dominican Republic," Miller Center, University of Virginia, May 2, 1965. Accessed September 12, 2013: http://millercenter.org/president/speeches/detail/4033

17. Ibid.

18. Ibid.

19. Noam Chomsky and Edward Herman, *The Washington Connection and Third World Fascism: The Political Economy of Human Rights* (South End Press, 1979), 242–251.

20. Ibid.

21. Gonzalez, *Harvest of Empire*, xvii–xviii.

22. Ibid.

23. Michael Flynn, "Where's the U.S. Border? Portraits of an Elastic Frontier," LASA 2006 paper, January 9, 2005. Accessed September 12, 2013: www.globaldetentionproject.org/fileadmin/publications/Flynn_LASA.pdf#page=1&zoom=auto,0,800

24. Ibid.

25. James C. McKinley Jr., "Homeless Haitians Told Not to Flee to U.S.," *New York Times,* January 18, 2010. Accessed September 12, 2013: www.nytimes.com/2010/01/19/us/19refugee.html?_r=0

26. Mike M. Ahlers and Mike Mount, "Radio Station in the Sky Warns Haitians Not to Attempt Boat Voyage," CNN, January 19, 2010. Accessed September 12, 2013: www.cnn.com/2010/WORLD/americas/01/19/haiti.broadcast.warning/index.html

27. Elysa Delcorto, "Mass Exodus Fears: Haitians Seeking Refuge in U.S. Will Be Returned," naplesnews.com, January 18, 2010. Accessed September 12, 2013: www.naplesnews.com/news/2010/jan/18/mass-exodus-fears-haitians-seeking-refuge-us-will-/?print=1

28. William J. Clinton, "Alien Smuggling," Presidential Decision Directive-9, June 18, 1993.

29. U.S. Department of State, Bureau of Public Affairs Factsheet, "The Central America Regional Security Initiative: A Shared Partnership," August 16, 2012. Accessed September 12, 2013: www.state.gov/p/wha/rls/fs/2012/183455.htm

30. Customs and Border Protection Today, "CBP Attachés: Extending the Zone of Security," May 2004. Accessed September 12, 2013: www.cbp.gov/xp/CustomsToday/2004/May/other/cbpAttaches.xml

31. Ibid.

32. Cbp.gov, Office of International Affairs, Assistant Commissioner, Charles E. Stallworth. Accessed September 12, 2013: www.cbp.gov/xp/cgov/about/organization/assist_comm_off/international_affairs.xml

33. Michael S. Schmidt, "U.S. Security Expands Presence at Foreign Airports," *New York Times,* June 13, 2012. Accessed December 3, 2013: http://www.nytimes.com/2012/06/14/world/europe/us-security-has-beachhead-at-foreign-airports.html?_r=0

34. Dave Gibson, "DHS Official: Our Southern Border Is Now with Guatemala," examiner.com, September 22, 2012. Accessed September 12, 2013: www.examiner.com/article/dhs-official-our-southern-border-is-now-with-guatemala

35. Kevin Edmonds, "Empty Promises and Empty Bellies: Bill Clinton's Doubletalk on Haitian Agriculture," nacla.org, May 17, 2010. http://nacla.org/news/empty-promises-and-empty-bellies-bill-clinton%E2%80%99s-doubletalk-haitian-agriculture

PART III: THE WAR WITHIN

1. According to documented reports compiled by OccupyArrests.com, 7,765 arrests took place in 122 U.S. cities in the two-year period from September 2011 to September 2013. Accessed October 15, 2013: http://stpeteforpeace.org/occupyarrests.sources.html

CHAPTER EIGHT: FEEDING THE MONSTER

1. Mathew Coleman, "Immigration geopolitics beyond the Mexico–US Border," *Antipode* 39, no. 1, (February 2007), 54.

2. Daniel Kanstroom, "Deportation Nation," *New York Times,* August 30,

2012. Accessed September 16, 2013: www.nytimes.com/2012/08/31/opinion/deportation-nation.html?pagewanted=all&_r=0

3. "Meet the Marshals," Crime and Investigation Network. Accessed September 16, 2013: www.crimeandinvestigation.co.uk/shows/manhunters/meet-the-marshals.html

4. "Sneaking Back In," *Manhunters: episode, TV Guide*, December 23, 2008. Accessed September 16, 2013: www.tvguide.com/tvshows/manhunters-fugitive-task-force-2008/episode-6-season-1/sneaking-back-in/296185

5. Ibid.

6. Ibid.

7. Bess Chiu, Lynly Egyes, Peter L. Markowitz, and Jaya Vasandani, "Constitution on Ice: A Report on Immigration Home Raid Operations," Cardozo Immigration Justice Clinic, 2009. Accessed September 15, 2013: http://cw.routledge.com/textbooks/9780415996945/human-rights/cardozo.pdf

8. Ibid.

9. Ibid.

10. "Sneaking Back In," *Manhunters episode*. Accessed December 3, 2013: www.tvguide.com/tvshows/manhunters-fugitive-task-force-2008/episode-6-season-1/sneaking-back-in/296185

11. Jacqueline Stevens, "America's Secret ICE Castles," *The Nation*, January 4, 2010. Accessed September 16, 2013: www.thenation.com/article/americas-secret-ice-castles?page=0,0#axzz2f1mpI2y2

12. Elise Foley, "Secure Communities Costs Los Angeles County More than $26 Million a Year: Report," *Huffington Post*, August 23, 2012. Accessed September 16, 2013: www.huffingtonpost.com/2012/08/23/secure-communities-los-angeles_n_1824740.html

13. Ted Robbins, "Little-Known Immigration Mandate Keeps Detention Beds Full," National Public Radio, November 19, 2013. Accessed December 3, 2013: http://www.npr.org/2013/11/19/245968601/little-known-immigration-mandate-keeps-detention-beds-full

14. Yana Kunichoff, " 'Voluntary' Work Program Run in Private Detention Centers Pays Detained Immigrants $1 a Day," *Truthout*, July 27, 2012. Accessed October 10, 2013: http://truth-out.org/news/item/10548-voluntary-work-program-run-in-private-detention-centers-pays-detained-immigrants-1-a-day

15. Nina Bernstein, "City of Immigrants Fills Jail Cells with Its Own," *New York Times*, December 26, 2008. Accessed September 16, 2013: www.nytimes.com/2008/12/27/us/27detain.html?pagewanted=all&_r=0

16. Ibid.

17. "2012–2016 Border Patrol Strategic Plan, Mission: Protect America," U.S. Customs and Border Protection, U.S. Border Patrol. Accessed September 16, 2013: http://nemo.cbp.gov/obp/bp_strategic_plan.pdf

18. Elliot Spagat, "Border Patrol to Toughen Policy on Illegal Immigrants," *Arizona Republic*, January 17, 2012. Accessed September 16, 2013: www.azcentral.com/news/articles/2012/01/17/20120117border-patrol-toughen-policy-illegal-immigrants.html#ixzz2f24LnuNR

19. Suleika Acosta, "Tucson Border Patrol Gets Tougher on Illegal Immigrants," *Tucson News Now*, KOLD/KMSB, January 14, 2008. Accessed September 16, 2013: www.tucsonnewsnow.com/Global/story.asp?S=7622765
20. Ibid.
21. "2012–2106 Border Patrol Strategic Plan," U.S. Border Patrol.
22. "Testimony of Michael J. Fisher, Chief, United States Border Patrol, U.S. Customs and Border Protection, Department of Homeland Security Before House Committee on Homeland Security, Subcommittee on Border and Maritime Security on "Securing our Borders – Operational Control and the Path Forward," February 15, 2011. Accessed September 16, 2013: www.dhs. gov/news/2011/02/15/us-customs-and-border-protection-border-patrol-chief-michael-fishers-testimony
23. Ibid.
24. "Shattered Families: The Perilous Intersection between Immigration Enforcement and the Child Welfare System," Applied Research Center, November 2011. Accessed September 15, 2013: http://arc.org/shatteredfamilies
25. Chris Kirkham, "Private Prisons Profit from Immigration Crackdown, Federal and Local Law Enforcement Partnerships," *Huffington Post*, June 7, 2012. Accessed September 16, 2013: www.huffingtonpost.com/2012/06/07/private-prisons-immigration-federal-law-enforcement_n_1569219.html
26. Michelle Alexander, "The New Jim Crow: Mass Incarceration and Institutional Racism," presentations from the General Assembly, Unitarian Universalist Association of Congregations, June 20–24, 2012. Accessed October 10, 2013: www.uua.org/multiculturalism/ga/200393.shtml

CHAPTER NINE: THE BORDER POLICE STATE

1. Douglas S. Massey, "Racial Formation in Theory and Practice: The Case of Mexicans in the United States," *Race and Social Problems* 1, no. 1 (March 1, 2009). Accessed October 10, 2013: www.ncbi.nlm.nih.gov/pmc/articles/PMC2931357
2. Nancy A. Wonders, "Chapter 4: Global Flows, Semi-Permeable Borders and New Channels of Inequality: Border Crossers and Border Performativity," *Borders, Mobility and Technologies of Control*, Springer (2006), 66.
3. Noelle Phillips, "Border Patrol Possible for S.C. under Bill," *Myrtle Beach Online*, March 11, 2011. Accessed September 12, 2013: www.myrtle-beachonline.com/2011/03/11/2031738_border-patrol-possible-for-sc.html#storylink=cpy
4. Joseph Nevins, "Waging Anti-Immigrant Lawfare—From Alabama to Washington, D.C.," nacla.org, June 15, 2011. Accessed September 12, 2013: https://nacla.org/blog/2011/6/15/waging-anti-immigrant-lawfare%E2%80%94-alabama-washington-dc
5. Ibid.
6. Guillermina Gina Núñez and Josiah McC. Heyman, "Entrapment Processes and Immigrant Communities in a Time of Heightened Border Vigilance," *Human Organization* 66, no. 4, (2007), 356.
7. Andrew Becker, "Local Cops Ready for War With Homeland Security-

Funded Military Weapons," *Daily Beast*, December 21, 2011. www.thedailybeast.com/articles/2011/12/20/local-cops-ready-for-war-with-homeland-security-funded-military-weapons.html

8. Mark Krikorian, "Downsizing Illegal Immigration: A Strategy of Attrition through Enforcement," Center for Immigration Studies, May 2005. Accessed September 12, 2013: www.cis.org/ReducingIllegalImmigration-Attrition-Enforcement

9. Center for Immigration Studies, "About the Center for Immigration Studies." http://www.cis.org/About

10. Krikorian, "Downsizing Illegal Immigration."

11. Page Ivey, "Jake Knotts' 'Raghead' Remark: Nikki Haley, Obama Called Indian Slur by South Carolina State Senator," *Huffington Post*, June 4, 2010. Accessed September 12, 2013: www.huffingtonpost.com/2010/06/04/jake-knotts-raghead-remar_n_600238.html

12. John Hudson, "Nikki Haley Act 3: " 'Raghead'-Gate," *The Atlantic Wire*, June 4, 2010. Accessed September 12, 2013: www.theatlanticwire.com/politics/2010/06/nikki-haley-act-3-raghead-gate/19591

13. Kimberly Wise, "SC Immigration Unit Measures Successes, Challenges," Associated Press, May 12, 2013. Accessed September 12, 2013: www.wltx.com/news/article/236415/2/SC-Immigration-Unit-Measures-Successes-Challenges-

14. Stephen Largen, "New S.C. immigration enforcement unit making arrests," (Charleston, SC) *Post and Courier*, October 25, 2012. Accessed September 12, 2013: www.postandcourier.com/article/20121025/PC16/121029522

15. Ashley Byrd, "DPS Director: 'There Was No Roadmap to Follow' for Immigration Team," South Carolina Radio Network, October 25, 2012. Accessed September 12, 2013: www.southcarolinaradionetwork.com/2012/10/25/dps-directorthere-was-no-roadmap-to-follow-for-immigration-team

16. Ibid.

17. Ibid.

18. "South Carolina Immigration Unit May Not Ask about Status," Fox News Latino, August 14, 2012. Accessed September 12, 2013: http://latino.foxnews.com/latino/news/2012/08/14/south-carolina-immigration-unit-may-not-ask-about-status/#ixzz2eXQlO25o

19. "Secret Immigration Enforcement Memo Exposed," ACLU, September 7, 2005. Accessed September 12, 2013: https://www.aclu.org/immigrants-rights/secret-immigration-enforcement-memo-exposed

20. Monica Varsanyi, *Taking Local Control: Immigration Policy Activism in U.S. Cities and States* (Stanford University Press, 2010), 11.

21. Sonia Nazario, "The Heartache of an Immigrant Family," *New York Times*, October 14, 2013. Accessed November 13, 2013: http://www.nytimes.com/2013/10/15/opinion/the-heartache-of-an-immigrant-family.html?_r=0

22. Meghan G. McDowell and Nancy A. Wonders, "Keeping Migrants in Their Place: Technologies of Control and Racialized Public Space in Arizona," *Social Justice* 36, no. 2 (June 22, 2009) 54–72.

23. Ibid.

24. Jefferson Morley, "The Man behind Romney's 'Self-Deportation' Plan," *Salon*, February 22, 2012. Accessed September 13, 2013: www.salon.com/2012/02/22/the_man_behind_romneys_self_deportation_dreams

25. Ibid.

26. McDowell and Wonders, "Keeping Migrants in Their Place," 54–72.

CHAPTER TEN: U.S. CITIZENS IN NAME ONLY

1. "Instances of Harassment of Muslims at the US-Canada Border & at Airports," Council on American Islamic Relations-Michigan, 2011.

2. "Brief Overview of the World War II Enemy Alien Control Program." National Archives. Accessed September 14, 2013: www.archives.gov/research/immigration/enemy-aliens-overview.html

3. George Takei, "We Japanese Americans Must Not Forget Our Wartime Internment," *The Guardian*, April 27, 2012. Accessed September 14, 2013: www.theguardian.com/commentisfree/2012/apr/27/we-japanese-americans-wartime-internment

4. Mattea Kramer and Chris Hellman, " 'Homeland Security': The Trillion-Dollar Concept That No One Can Define," *TomDispatch*, February 28, 2013. Accessed September 14, 2013: www.tomdispatch.com/post/175655

5. Dana Priest and William Arkin, *Top Secret America: The Rise of the New American Security State* (Little, Brown, 2011).

6. "Lawsuit: Mentally Ill US Citizen Wrongly Deported," Associated Press, October 14, 2010. Accessed September 14, 2013: www.rawstory.com/rs/2010/10/14/lawsuit-mentally-ill-citizen-wrongly-deported/

7. *Mark Daniel Lyttle v. The United States of America*. Accessed September 14, 2013: https://www.aclu.org/files/assets/2010-10-13-MarkLyttleComplaint-NorthCarolina.pdf

8. Ted Robbins, "In the Rush to Deport, Expelling U.S. Citizens," National Public Radio, October 24, 2011. Accessed September 14, 2013: www.npr.org/2011/10/24/141500145/in-the-rush-to-deport-expelling-u-s-citizens

9. Alex Perez and BJ Lutz, "American Citizen Faced Deportation," NBC Chicago, June 30, 2011. Accessed September 14, 2013: www.nbcchicago.com/news/local/eduardo-caraballo-puerto-rico-deportation-94795779.html

10. Paul McEnroe, "U.S. Citizenship No Defense against Deportation Threat," *Minnesota Star Tribune*, November 27, 2011. Accessed September 14, 2013: www.startribune.com/local/north/134541773.html

11. Robbins, "In the Rush to Deport."

12. *Abidor v. Napolitano* Complaint. Accessed September 14, 2013: https://www.aclu.org/free-speech-technology-and-liberty/abidor-v-napolitano-complaint

13. Ibid.

14. Ibid.

15. Glenn Greenwald, "U.S. Filmmaker Repeatedly Detained at Border," *Salon*, April 8, 2012. Accessed September 14, 2013: www.salon.com/2012/04/08/u_s_filmmaker_repeatedly_detained_at_border

16. Ibid.

17. Xeni Jardin, "Wikileaks Volunteer Detained and Searched (Again) by US Agents," *boing boing*, January 12, 2011. Accessed September 14, 2013: http://boingboing.net/2011/01/12/wikileaks-volunteer-1.html?utm_source=feedburner&utm_medium=feed&utm_campaign=Feed%3A+boingboing%2FiBag+%28Boing+Boing%29

18. John A. Hawkinson, "David House Sues US after Search of Laptop," *The Tech*, April 6, 2012. Accessed September 14, 2013: http://tech.mit.edu/V132/N16/house.html

19. Kevin Gosztola, "Documents: Why Homeland Security Agents Seized Manning Support Network Co-Founder's Electronic Devices," *Dissenter Firedoglake*, September 10, 2013. Accessed September 14, 2013: http://dissenter.firedoglake.com/2013/09/10/why-homeland-security-agents-seized-manning-support-network-co-founders-electronic-devices

20. "Detained in the U.S.: Filmmaker Laura Poitras Held, Questioned Some 40 Times at U.S. Airports," *Democracy Now!*, April 20, 2012. Accessed September 14, 2013: www.democracynow.org/2012/4/20/detained_in_the_us_filmmaker_laura

21. Ibid.

22. Peter Maass, "How Laura Poitras Helped Snowden Spill His Secrets," *New York Times*, August 13, 2013. Accessed September 14, 2013: www.nytimes.com/2013/08/18/magazine/laura-poitras-snowden.html?pagewanted=all

23. Stephan Salisbury, "Surveillance, America's Pastime," *TomDispatch*, October 3, 2010. Accessed September 14, 2013: www.tomdispatch.com/archive/175303

24. David Kravets, "DHS Watchdog OKs 'Suspicionless' Seizure of Electronic Devices along Border," *Wired*, February 8, 2013. Accessed September 14, 2013: www.wired.com/threatlevel/2013/02/electronics-border-seizures/

25. Ibid.

26. James Bamford, "The NSA Is Building the Country's Biggest Spy Center (Watch What You Say)," *Wired*, March 15, 2012. Accessed September 14, 2013: www.wired.com/threatlevel/2012/03/ff_nsadatacenter/all

27. Tom Engelhardt, "Data Mining You: How the Intelligence Community Is Creating a New American World," *TomDispatch*, April 3, 2012. Accessed September 14, 2013: www.tomdispatch.com/blog/175524/tomgram%3A_engelhardt,_the_intelligence_bureaucracy_that_ate_our_world

28. "Exclusive: National Security Agency Whistleblower William Binney on Growing State Surveillance," *Democracy Now!*, April 20, 2012. Accessed September 14, 2013: www.democracynow.org/2012/4/20/exclusive_national_security_agency_whistleblower_william

29. Barton Gellman and Ashkan Soltani, "NSA Collects Millions of E-mail Address Books Globally," *Washington Post*, October 14, 2013. Accessed October 21, 2013: www.washingtonpost.com/world/national-security/nsa-collects-millions-of-e-mail-address-books-globally/2013/10/14/8e58b5be-34f9-11e3-80c6-7e6dd8d22d8f_story.html?hpid=z3

30. Somini Sengupta, "Privacy Fears Grow as Cities Increase Surveillance," *New York Times*, October 13, 2013. Accessed October 21, 2013: www.nytimes.

com/2013/10/14/technology/privacy-fears-as-surveillance-grows-in-cities.htm
l?pagewanted=1&adxnnlx=1381949035-JIdcj1Vv4WE/Xa0uN06eyw

31. Josiah McC. Heyman, "United States Surveillance over Mexican Lives at the Border: Snapshots of an Emerging Regime," *Human Organization* 58, no. 4 (1999), 431.

32. Josiah McC. Heyman, "Why Interdiction? Immigration Control at the United States-Mexican border," *Regional Studies* 33, no. 7 (October 1999) 628.

33. Ibid.

34. Joseph Nevins, *Operation Gatekeeper and Beyond: The War on "Illegals" and the Remaking of the U.S.-Mexico Boundary* (Routledge, 2010), 126.

35. Heyman, "United States Surveillance over Mexican Lives at the Border," 431.

CHAPTER ELEVEN: RE-IMAGINING THE NIAGARA FRONTIER

1.   Ginger Strand, *Inventing Niagara: Beauty, Power, and Lies* (Simon and Schuster, 2010), 195.

2.   Ibid.

3.   Mark Hughes, "Decline and Falls: An American City in Crisis," *The Telegraph*, December 26, 2012. Accessed September 15, 2013: http://www.telegraph.co.uk/news/worldnews/northamerica/usa/9765945/Decline-and-falls-an-American-city-in-crisis.html

4.   Mark Scheer, "Niagara Falls Housing Authority Deals with Federal Cuts," *Niagara Gazette*, February 14, 2012. Accessed November 25, 2013: http://niagara-gazette.com/local/x960121118/Niagara-Falls-Housing-Authority-deals-with-federal-cuts

5.   Rick Pfeiffer, "Street Walker Crackdown," *Niagara Gazette*, June 20, 2012. Accessed September 15, 2013: http://niagara-gazette.com/local/x1326972485/Street-walker-crackdown

6.   Ibid.

7.   Ibid.

8.   Ibid.

9.   Thomas Prohaska, "Layoffs, Tax Hike Proposed in Falls Mayor's 'Disaster Budget,'" *Buffalo Evening News*, November 1, 2012. Accessed September 15, 2013: http://www.buffalonews.com/apps/pbcs.dll/article?AID=/20121101/CITYANDREGION/121109905/1010

10. Meg Rossman, "Falls Budget Calls for Tax Increase, Layoffs," YNN Buffalo, November 1, 2012. Accessed September 15, 2013: http://buffalo.ynn.com/content/news/609514/falls-budget-calls-for-tax-increase—layoffs/

11. Norma Higgs, "Meeting Members of the 'Long Green Line'," *Niagara Gazette*, July 9, 2012. Accessed September 15, 2013: http://niagara-gazette.com/normahiggs/x1058726901/HIGGS-Meeting-members-of-the-long-green-line

12. Norma Higgs, "A Trip to the Falls Border Patrol Station," *Niagara Gazette*, July 16, 2012. Accessed September 15, 2013: http://niagara-gazette.com/normahiggs/x748660947/HIGGS-A-trip-to-the-Falls-Border-Patrol-station

13. Ibid.

14. Ibid.

15. Rick Pfeiffer, "Local Border Patrol Agents Train to Confront a Gunman Whose Goal is 'Mass Murder,' " *Niagara Gazette*, August 14, 2012. Accessed September 15, 2013: http://niagara-gazette.com/local/x994535150/Local-Border-Patrol-agents-train-to-confront-a-gunman-whose-goal-is-mass-murder

16. Ibid.

17. Rick Pfeiffer, "Bloods: Law Enforcement Army Hits Falls Street Gang," *Niagara Gazette*, March 15, 2009. Accessed September 15, 2013: http://niagara-gazette.com/local/x681338582/BLOODS-Law-enforcement-army-hits-Falls-street-gang/print

18. Ibid.

19. Mark Scheer, "Border Patrol to the Rescue for Falls Air Base?" *Niagara Gazette*, February 16, 2012. Accessed September 15, 2013: http://niagara-gazette.com/local/x960122697/Border-Patrol-to-the-rescue-for-Falls-air-base/print

20. Paul A. W. Wallace, *White Roots of Peace: The Iroquois Book of Life* (Clear Light Publishers, 1994).

21. Murphy Woodhouse, "Interview: Waging the Fight for Migrant Justice from under a Border Patrol Truck," *Truthout*, March 12, 2013. Accessed September 15, 2013: http://truth-out.org/news/item/14982-an-ordinary-arrest-an-extraordinary-act-of-civil-disobedience-and-the-fight-for-migrant-justice-worldwide

22. "The Constitution of the Iroquois Nations: The Great Binding Law," Gayanashagowa. http://www.indigenouspeople.net/iroqcon.htm

23. Alex Devoid, interview with Dario Andrade.

24. Matt Taibbi, "Gangster Bankers: Too Big to Jail," *Rolling Stone*, February 14, 2013. Accessed October 21, 2013: http://www.rollingstone.com/politics/news/gangster-bankers-too-big-to-jail-20130214?page=4

Index

Page numbers in *italic* refer to illustrations. "Passim" (literally "scattered") indicates intermittent discussion of a topic over a cluster of pages.

For the past fifteen years Todd Miller has researched, written about, and worked on immigration and border issues from both sides of the U.S.-Mexico divide for organizations such as BorderLinks, Witness for Peace, and NACLA. The bulk of this work was done in Tucson,

Arizona, and Oaxaca, Mexico, with stints in New York City sprinkled in. Between Tucson, where he is now based, and the Buffalo–Niagara Falls region of New York State where he grew up, he has spent the majority of his life close to U.S. international boundaries, South and North. His writings about the border have appeared in the *New York Times*, *TomDispatch*, *Mother Jones*, *The Nation*, *Al Jazeera English*, *Le Monde diplomatique*, *Salon*, and many others.